Head Hand Heart

DAVID GOODHART

Head Hand Heart

The Struggle for Dignity and Status in the 21st Century

ALLEN LANE
an imprint of
PENGUIN BOOKS

ALLEN LANE

UK | USA | Canada | Ireland | Australia
India | New Zealand | South Africa

Allen Lane is part of the Penguin Random House group of companies whose
addresses can be found at global.penguinrandomhouse.com

Penguin
Random House
UK

First published 2020
001

Copyright © David Goodhart, 2020

The moral right of the author has been asserted

Set in 10.5/14 pt Sabon LT Std
Typeset by Integra Software Services Pvt. Ltd, Pondicherry
Printed in Great Britain by Clays Ltd, Elcograf S.p.A.

A CIP catalogue record for this book is available from the British Library

ISBN: 978-0-241-39157-0

To my children, in the hope that they might finally read something I have written

Contents

PART THREE
Hand and Heart

PART FOUR
The Future

Preface

I wrote most of this book before the Covid-19 crisis struck. Yet the crisis and its likely consequences have a direct bearing on its main theme: the lop-sided distribution of status that has become such a feature of rich societies in recent decades. For one thing, it has made the unthinkable thinkable. If we can close down society and economic life for months and collectively underwrite at least some of the cost, then it becomes a bit easier to imagine that we might adjust the status balance in our educationally stratified, post-industrial societies by a few degrees.

Most of us have wanted things to return to normal as swiftly as possible, but these coming years will also surely prove a hinge moment for politics in those rich countries in Europe and North America that have been overwhelmed by the crisis. There are several ways in which the crisis will enable, in the language of this book, Hand (manual work/basic jobs) and Heart (care work) to claim back some of the prestige and reward they have lost to Head (cognitive work) in recent decades.

At the most macro level a new version of globalization is now possible, summed up in one of the wittier slogans of the crisis: workers of the world unite, you have nothing to lose but your supply chains. Full-scale deglobalization is highly undesirable and is not going to happen; we have learned the lessons of 1930s protectionism. But some restraints on what economist Dani Rodrik has called 'hyper-globalization' – the globalization that has favoured large corporations, financial markets and mobile skilled professionals – can be put in place.

The crisis has been the hour of the nation-state and national social contracts, at least in Europe, though in the United States it is the relative weakness of the central state that has been exposed. National democracies are likely to claim a greater say in the next phase of globalization. There will be some reshoring and shortening of those long, vulnerable supply chains. Lowest-cost globalization which regrets the closure of the manufacturing plant but sees it as a price worth paying for cheaper goods from Amazon will no longer win the argument so easily. Most of us are producers as well as consumers, and we might be prepared to pay a few pounds more for a smartphone produced closer to home.

Some of this sentiment was strengthening before the crisis. World trade fell slightly in 2019 partly as a result of the argument between the United States and China about what constitutes fair trade arrangements. The existing model of helter-skelter globalization has been producing too many losers, not least the global environment.

Western society has been dominated in the past two generations by *centrifugal* forces that have spread global openness and individual freedom but weakened collective bonds and enabled Head work to claim undue reward while Hand and Heart work has diminished in dignity and pay. The knowledge economy has placed cognitive meritocracy at the centre of the status hierarchy, and the cognitively blessed have thrived, but many others feel they have lost place and meaning.

Recent political trends, surely reinforced by the pandemic, suggest we are moving into a more *centripetal* phase, in which the nation-state will be consolidated and economic and cultural openness will be a little more constrained. This phase will place more stress on localism, social stability and solidarity, and it will be more sceptical of the claims of the cognitive class and more sensitive to the humiliations built into modern, achievement societies, including for ethnic minorities.

As I was writing the book in 2019, I would not have dared to imagine those public appreciations of the Hand and Heart workers that became such a dominant image of the early weeks of the crisis. People were applauding not just those working in health services but also those who maintain the hidden wiring of our everyday lives – the supermarket shelf-stackers, the bus drivers and delivery people, those who maintain the food and drug supply chains and remove household waste. In a brief inversion of the status hierarchy, many of the truly key workers turned out to be people who did not go to college, maybe those less adept at manipulating information. Not all are Hand workers in a literal sense, nor the factory workers of old, but all do essential jobs, and in the UK at the height of the crisis it was males in those frontline jobs, especially older ethnic minority males, who were twice as likely to die from Covid-19 as the wider working population.

The pause for reflection that the lockdown imposed on normally hectic, achievement-orientated societies, and individuals, may leave the deepest traces of all. Many of us, perhaps especially the fortunate, better-educated people who could work from home, were forced to reconsider what we value most deeply. As we looked up from our busy, mobile existences, we often met a neighbour properly for the first time and actually felt rooted in a physical community. And then, stepping out from our front doors, we smiled and nodded at strangers even while politely giving them a wide berth.

This new sense of rootedness and connection along with the heightened awareness of our mortality can spill over into a mawkish sentimentality and a 'safetyism' that eschews all risk and refuses all trade-offs. Think of all those people who didn't want lockdown to end. At the other end of the spectrum, many people have desperately wanted to reclaim their old freedoms, including the freedom to treat our fellow citizens with normal indifference. Some predict not so much a gentler, more caring society emerging from the crisis but a wilder and angrier one, a new roaring twenties. Perhaps the Black Lives Matter eruption was a premonition of that.

But the care economy has been at the centre of the crisis, and that in itself is likely to prompt some re-evaluation of mainstream economic and political thought. Just as old attitudes to large-scale government debt, and even printing money, have had to be revised even by conservative-minded politicians, so we may be pushed to reconsider our attitudes to productivity and even the very idea of the economic sphere.

Rich western societies already spend a large part of GDP on care, health and welfare; this share is likely to increase another step in the wake of the crisis. And we will need to more openly acknowledge that what we want in many parts of the care economy, from ICUs to elderly care homes, is *lower* productivity, not higher. We want fewer

beds per nurse, not more. This is true in large parts of the Heart economy, in health and in education. And if we are to upwardly revalue
the public care economy, and fund better the Cinderella parts such
as elderly care, then what about the work done in the private care
economy of the home looking after the young and the old? Should
that not also be valued more too and not just seen as a shadow world
of lost opportunity?

That raises big questions about the gender division of labour and
how to revalue domesticity without undoing the freedoms that women
have achieved in recent decades. Our enforced confinement in the
home caused much family tension, couple separation and even vio-
lence. But it was also a reminder to many people of the primary value
of family and the hard work of nurture and education that takes place
within its walls. If Britain's health service is, as the Prime Minister,
Boris Johnson, declared, 'powered by love', then how much more so
the care delivered in the private realm of the family.

This is how I see the crisis as strengthening the Hand and Heart
and readjusting the status balance somewhat with Head. To put it in
political language, I see the crisis, particularly in Europe, as reinforcing an unusual coalition – a conservative preference for the local, the
national, and the family, along with a social democratic preference for
higher social spending and modest collectivism, combined too with
a renewed concern for the environment. But that is what I thought
before the virus struck too, as you can see from reading this book, so
I have to plead guilty to Covid confirmation bias – the tendency to see
your own assumptions about how the world should evolve confirmed
by the pandemic.

There are two main counter arguments to these claims. The first is
that, contrary to Head being reined in by the crisis, the Head experts –
whether highly educated medics or vaccine scientists or epidemiologists – have proved their vital importance and therefore dispatched
the populist disdain for expertise. The second points out that the
institutions that have become even more central to our existence during the crisis – the big tech digital platforms – are the epitome of the
disembodied world of data-manipulation that tends to reinforce a
Head worldview.

Both points have validity, but I don't think they carry enough weight to dislodge my Covid-19 rebalancing thesis. Moreover, the first claim misunderstands the complaint against experts. Only a rather small number of people (though more in the US than Europe) in what one might loosely call the populist movement have ever been against the 'hard' scientific, technical or medical experts. Their argument was, and is, against economists, social scientists and highly educated people in general, passing off their often liberal presumptions about, for example, European integration or immigration as neutral truth. And while the digital platforms have indeed proved their worth in the crisis, they have often done so not by reinforcing the 'belong anywhere' message we have associated with them in the past but rather by making it easier for real local communities to support each other via Facebook or WhatsApp groups. Indeed, so successful have they been that they have truly established themselves as utilities comparable to water and electricity, and they will thus surely come to be subject to some of the same degree of regulation as the traditional utilities. But that is another story.

In the meantime, I think there are some grounds for optimism emerging from the crisis. In our open, fractious societies, divisions and disagreements have noisily continued – not least in the reaction to the killing of George Floyd in Minneapolis – yet, below the surface, there has also been a greater sense of common destiny than usual, at least in most of Europe if not the US. Arguments between liberals and conservatives, and left and right, will continue, yet I think there is a decent chance that one legacy of the crisis will be to acknowledge a wider range of human aptitudes in our allocation of reward and prestige – which will help us to achieve the better balance between Head, Hand and Heart that this book is advocating. The bleak alternative is that the scars left by the epidemic will exacerbate our pre-crisis divisions and resentments.

PART ONE

Our Problem

I

Peak Head

We need to apply ourselves to something we do not yet quite
know how to do: to eradicate contempt for those who are
disfavoured by the ethic of effortful competition.

Kwame Anthony Appiah

What has gone wrong in rich, western democracies? Political polarization. Economic stagnation. A weaker sense of common interest.
Disappointed expectations among the university-educated mass elite.
A rising tide of depression and loneliness. A crisis of meaning. Even
before the Covid-19 crisis struck there was a mood of despondency
in our politics – a sense that losers were outnumbering winners in
nations buffeted by invisible global forces, that the public realm was
being slowly poisoned by social media, and that mainstream politics was failing to accommodate a widespread yearning for stability,
belonging and purpose in mainly Godless western countries. But
there's an overarching explanation for many of these discontents that
is hiding in plain sight. In recent decades in the interests of efficiency,
fairness and progress western democracies have established systems
of competition in which the most able succeed and too many of the
rest feel like failures.

And who are the most able? People with higher levels of cognitive
ability, or at least those *certified* as such by the education system.
One form of human aptitude – cognitive-analytical ability, the talent
that helps people to pass exams and then handle information efficiently in their professional lives – has become *the gold standard of
human esteem*. And those with a generous helping of this aptitude
have formed a new kind of expanded cognitive class – a mass elite

– who now shape society, and do so broadly in their own interests. To put it more bluntly: smart people have become too powerful.

How is this different from the past? Seventy years ago, just after the Second World War, when we lived in somewhat less complex societies, the people who ran government and business were generally brighter and more ambitious than the average – as they still are today. What's different is that, back then, skills and qualities other than cognitive-analytical intelligence were held in higher regard. Education had not yet emerged as the main marker of social stratification. In the 1970s most people in rich societies left school with no qualifications at all and as recently as the 1990s many professional people lacked university degrees.

In the language of political cliché, the 'brightest and the best' today trump the 'decent and hardworking'. Qualities such as character, integrity, experience, common sense, courage and willingness to toil are by no means irrelevant, but they command relatively less respect. And when such virtues count for less it can contribute to what social conservative critics call a 'moral deregulation' in which simply being a good person is not valued, and it becomes harder to feel satisfaction and self-respect living an ordinary, decent life, especially in the bottom part of the income spectrum.

Without us really noticing it, something fundamental has got out of kilter. As I write at the end of April 2020, it is too early to tell whether the Covid-19 crisis will contribute to a better balance between aptitudes based on Head, Hand and Heart. But we need one. The three aptitudes overlap to differing degrees, but the modern knowledge economy has produced ever rising returns for 'Head' workers – who are highly qualified academically – and reduced the relative pay and status of much manual ('Hand') work. At the same time, many aspects of caring ('Heart') work, traditionally done mainly by women in the gift economy of the family, continue to be undervalued even as care work has become an increasingly critical part of the public economy and was so widely applauded (literally) at the height of the crisis. An economic and social system in rich countries that once had a place for a range of aptitudes and abilities – in the skilled and semi-skilled jobs of the industrial era, on the land, in the military, in the church, in the private realm of the family – now favours the cognitive classes and the educationally successful.

4

The diminishing sway of those older structures and ways of life is a necessary condition of freer, more open societies, especially for women. But what many of those institutions also provided were forms of unconditional recognition, based simply on being you, and a role and a purpose for the many people, both men and women, whose strengths lie elsewhere than in the cognitive-analytical. Just doing your duty and making a contribution brought a degree of respect.

Moreover, whereas until recently different social classes and groups and regions had their own separate leaders and hierarchies and measures of prestige, today in most developed countries there is something more like *a single, common elite* that has passed through the same funnel of higher education and then into the top quartile of professional and managerial occupations. (At the very top these national elites merge into a semi-global one that studies at the same universities, works at the same corporations and institutions and consumes the same media.)

For most of human history, cognitive-analytical ability was scattered more or less randomly through society, with only a tiny minority attending university, religious seminaries or similar elite academies. But in recent decades in rich countries, a huge sorting process has taken place, in which most of the young exam-passers are swept up and sent in unprecedented numbers into higher education. This has triggered a significant decline in the status of much non-graduate employment and also made promotion from below much harder for those without the passport of a university degree.

This does not mean, however, that we now live in a true meritocracy. Family income and the educational background of your parents still correlates strongly with educational and career success, and indeed with performance in IQ-type tests. The children of two-parent professional families are far more likely to be brought up by parents who are well connected, understand what is required for children of even middling academic ability to enter good universities and obtain higher-status professional jobs and have the wherewithal to invest heavily in them.

The evidence also suggests that most rich societies are at least somewhat open and that many of the cognitively able from lower social classes can, and do, rise via higher education (helping, thereby, to legitimize the status quo).

The end result may be the emergence of a partially hereditary meritocracy, especially in the US. (Though a few seem to get there by playing the system.)* Many people, particularly members of the cognitive class themselves, might protest that progress has always been driven forward by the cognitively blessed and that modern, technologically advanced societies simply need more clever people – especially in software and computer science – than ever before. Moreover, they might add, the so-called Flynn Effect (named after the New Zealand academic James Flynn) shows that *everyone* is getting brighter, that average IQ levels have been rising throughout the twentieth century as a result of both improved general nutrition and living conditions and human minds adapting to a more demanding cognitive environment.[1] They argue that as long as the social biases mentioned above are ironed out, through greater spending on education and a sustained effort to give people of all backgrounds a fair chance at joining the cognitive class, all will be well.

This book disagrees. In the tradition of Michael Young's dystopian satire on rule by the cognitive elite *The Rise of the Meritocracy*, Daniel Bell's *The Coming of Post-Industrial Society* and Charles Murray's *Coming Apart* – a socialist, a centrist and a conservative – it argues that today's 'achievement society' has replaced one system of domination by another.

It is true that the knowledge created by human reason continues to drive forward civilization, and in our data-based economies this is not about to decline in importance. The Covid-19 crisis has underlined the vital significance of cognitive virtues such as medical expertise, pharmaceutical innovation and the mathematical modelling of epidemiologists. (Though it has revealed too our dependence on those performing vital non-cognitive Hand and Heart functions.) It is also true that the opening up of the cognitive class through the expansion of higher education has broadened the base of privilege. IQ + effort – in Michael Young's formula for describing what is required to excel in the meritocracy – is undoubtedly a better selection criterion

---

* This was placed in the spotlight in early 2019, when overt corruption, including getting other people to sit an applicant's exams, was uncovered by the US Department of Justice to get undeserving candidates into top colleges including Yale and Stanford.

than nepotism or patronage. A cognitive class that puts innate talent to good use in invention and innovation is obviously preferable to a hereditary one, and certainly produces more prosperity. So a meritocratic society has a lot to be said for it: by putting human ability to work, it creates a dynamic and wealthy society that appears to be fair, or at least fairer than the alternatives, and creates opportunities for some people born into disadvantage.

But inclusions often require new exclusions, in this case of those who do not have the good fortune or aptitude to acquire a university degree – which is still a majority of adults in most rich countries. And people no more *earn* their upbringing or innate intelligence than they earn being born into a rich family.

Further, although IQ-type tests and exams measure raw cognitive ability, they do not capture things like social intelligence and imagination that we today associate with a rounded, capable person. Intelligence is a complex, fuzzy and often highly context-dependent phenomenon, as I will unpack in Chapter 3, but in the UK, US and France, though less so in parts of continental Europe, it is the most abstract forms of reasoning that have historically attracted the most prestige.

Michael Young argued sixty years ago, in his critique of meritocracy, that people blessed with advanced cognitive skills can feel *less* obligation to those of below-average intelligence than the rich felt traditionally to the poor. Meritocracy sharply divides winners from losers in the education system, while giving losers less psychological protection from their low status.

There will, of course, always be hierarchies of competence. But it is important to distinguish between meritocratic *selection systems* for highly skilled jobs and a meritocratic *society*. The former is necessary and desirable: you obviously want capable nuclear scientists running your nuclear programme. But the latter is not the hallmark of a good society and is potentially a source of mass resentment.

There are two challenges to this critique. The first is this: can you have meritocratic selection *without* a meritocratic society? I believe you can because there is not a single scale of human worth. A broader valuation of human qualities and aptitudes than those promoted by a cognitive meritocracy is an achievable goal. Human flourishing is compatible with a wide range of abilities and aptitudes.

The second challenge, often expressed by people who have clambered up into the elite from ordinary or disadvantaged homes, runs like this: I agree meritocracy is not perfect, but can we have a proper one first before you start attacking it? Do you really want to go back to a dominant class selected on the basis of inherited property and status?

No, of course, I do not want to turn the clock back, I want an elite as open as possible and as much social fluidity as a fair society requires. And in principle it ought to be possible to have plenty of upward (and downward) mobility based on cognitive selection while also respecting and rewarding those who have other skills and aptitudes. But in practice this is hard to achieve. Not everyone can be above average. And if high mobility is the main mark of the good society, as both centre-left and centre-right politicians have often argued in recent years, then we are in trouble, because mobility inevitably slows when 'smart produces smart'. What then?

How close we are to that point and how much mobility we can expect in a fair society is contested, as I will show in Chapter 3. It depends on how much family, class and environmental factors can tilt the system in favour of the only moderately able and how much ability is heritable. Given that both of those factors are clearly of some significance, and assuming we continue to live in relatively free societies that allow families to pass on advantage, the meritocracy either will be partial at best or will ossify into a hereditary system. In practice meritocracy tends towards oligarchy.

One of the most difficult balancing acts of open, modern societies is also seldom articulated: namely, how to constrain our partial cognitive meritocracies in a way that prevents disproportionate levels of status, prestige and remuneration flowing to high-cognitive-ability jobs without at the same time disincentivizing the cleverest and most ambitious. To some extent intelligence should be its own reward, but the contribution some of the most talented people make requires some special recognition.

The pleasure of mastering a task and performing it as well as you are able is available to people of all abilities. It is properly the case that more complex and difficult tasks, such as designing a building or helping to invent a new Covid-19 vaccine, will receive, and deserve to receive, more esteem and reward than delivering parcels or cleaning offices.

But it is also the case that a significant proportion of jobs that require quite high levels of academic qualification are demonstrably less useful and productive than many low-qualification jobs. Can we really argue that the work of a junior account manager in a City PR firm is more useful than that of a bus driver or an adult care worker? Moreover, many jobs in law, finance and other highly remunerated professions are often zero-sum: one individual or corporation wins and another loses. Public welfare has not been enhanced.

A successful society must balance the tension between the *inequality of esteem* that arises from relatively open competition for highly rewarded jobs and the ethos of *equality of esteem* that flows from democratic citizenship. It is a tension that pits economic inequality against political equality. That means a democratic society that wants to avoid a powerful undercurrent of resentment must sufficiently value and reward a broad range of achievement embracing both cognitive and non-cognitive aptitudes and must provide meaning and respect for people who cannot – or do not want to – achieve in the examination room and professional career market. After all, half the population must always by definition be in the bottom half of the cognitive ability spectrum, or indeed any spectrum you care to choose.

In recent years, we have failed to get the balance right. Indeed, it may be the case that industrial societies, for all their failings, were better at distributing status and self-respect, especially for men, than the post-industrial societies we have become.

For many people on the left, this is mainly a problem of income and wealth inequality that can be solved by more redistribution and greater investment in education. Yet despite noisy claims to the contrary, income inequality has not, in fact, been rising sharply in many of the countries, including Brexit Britain, where there has been the biggest push-back against the cognitive class status quo.[2] If income inequality was the driving force behind political alienation and national populism, how come it is also thriving in the most equal societies on the planet in Scandinavia?

It is true that slow or non-existent wage growth is harder to bear when a small minority, most notably bankers, seem insulated from austerity. And thanks to the rise and rise in house values in certain parts of rich countries there is a lottery aspect to wealth distribution – in the UK one in five baby boomers is worth £1 million or more[3] – while younger people struggle to get on the housing ladder.

But this misses an even bigger – though less tangible and measurable – story about esteem and how valued people feel in the social order. Angus Deaton, the Nobel prize-winning economist, who has pioneered the work on 'deaths of despair' in the US (suicides and deaths from drug and alcohol abuse), says he is struck by how *little* material deprivation has to do with such deaths. Recent happiness research, similarly, finds income to be of little significance in levels of well-being.

I call myself a social democrat and would like to live in a fairer and more equal society. But I think a big part of our problem lies in the undervaluing of everything that is not cognitively complex. If we attached more value, both in terms of prestige and income, to the carers and the skilled trades, income would naturally spread more evenly across society and economic growth would be more consistent and stable.

Western rationalist philosophy, from Plato to Descartes, reinforced by Christianity, has tended to privilege the mind as the source of immutable truth and understanding and looked down upon the body as the source of irrational appetite and moral inconstancy. Embodied, emotional labour such as nursing and care for the young and old has suffered lower prestige as a result, along with the fact that they are overwhelmingly female occupations.

And all too often, cognitive ability and meritocratic achievement is confused with moral worth. The Latin root of meritocracy – *meritum* – means worthy of praise. It creeps into the language of everyday life. Newspapers are far more likely to highlight the accidental death of a promising 22-year-old medical student than a 22-year-old who works as a hairdresser. And how often when you hear someone describing positively a new friend or work colleague will they say before anything else 'Oh, he/she is so smart'? What they usually mean is quick and entertaining. How often do you hear people described as generous or wise?

There's also a clear trend in modern politics to place a special value on cognitive skills. High cognitive or analytical ability and success in the knowledge economy correlate strongly with support for the modern liberal virtues of individual autonomy, mobility and hostility to tradition – the opposite of parochialism. Creative and intellectually gifted people tend to have an interest in the free flow of ideas across borders and boundaries. They may also have an interest in the relatively free flow of people across borders providing them with multinational career options. These habits of mind dominate in the expanded higher education sector of modern societies, making it hard for highly educated people to understand small-c conservatives.

ANYWHERES AND SOMEWHERES

This was one of the themes of my last book, *The Road to Somewhere*, in which I described the value divides in British society revealed starkly by the Brexit vote. On the one hand is the group I describe as the 'Anywheres'. They make up about 25 to 30 per cent of the population; are well educated (mainly with at least an undergraduate degree); often live far from their parents; tend to favour openness and autonomy; and are comfortable with social fluidity and novelty. On the other hand is a larger group of people I call the 'Somewheres'. They comprise about half of the population; are less well educated; more rooted; and value security and familiarity. They place a much greater emphasis on group attachments (local and national) than the Anywheres. (There is also an Inbetweener group who share the two worldviews almost equally.)

Anywheres are generally comfortable with social change because they have 'achieved identities', a sense of themselves derived from educational and career achievements, which allows them to fit in pretty much, well, *anywhere*. Whereas Somewheres tend to have 'ascribed identities', rooted more in place or group, which means that they are more easily discomforted by rapid change to those places and groups.

The Anywhere/Somewhere divide is very loose and fuzzy and full of overlaps and inconsistencies, and, however useful it might be for explaining big social trends, most individual lives are too idiosyncratic to fit neatly within the divide. Nor does the divide map neatly onto the high/low cognitive ability divide. There are Anywheres of below-average cognitive ability and Somewheres of very high cognitive ability. In any case, as we shall see, there is some disagreement about what cognitive ability actually is and whether it is well captured in IQ tests or exams. Most of us know highly able people who have been poor at passing exams, and people with impressive academic credentials who appear quite dim.

Both the Anywhere and Somewhere worldviews are decent and legitimate, but the values and priorities of Anywheres have come to dominate modern politics and all mainstream political parties. And the Anywhere answer to everything from social mobility to improved productivity has been the same: more academic higher education, in the quintessentially Anywhere institution of the modern university.

The Anywhere/Somewhere divide has certainly been exacerbated by the narrow focus on cognitive ability of recent decades. Yet, as David Lucas, the children's author and illustrator, has persuasively argued, society needs the cognitive skills of the knowledge economy but also needs the craft skills of artisans, technicians and the skilled trades, the imagination of artists and the emotional intelligence of those in caring jobs.[4] He observes that the chronic undervaluing of Hand and Heart skills has unbalanced our societies and alienated millions of people. It also lurks beneath the surface of many contemporary crises, from mental health to recruitment problems in nursing and adult care.

Of course, bright people from whatever background should travel as far as their talents will take them and for many of the very brightest young people attending an elite research university is the most appropriate way to nurture their abilities. There are also many other people, some smart and creative, whose intelligence manifests itself in a non-academic way who are not suited to higher education and would do better going straight into jobs. But today's American, British and indeed European 'dreams' have become too narrowly defined as going to university and into a professional job. This isn't surprising when in the US 93 per cent of House members and 99 per cent of Senators hold at least bachelor's degrees, compared to a national US average of 32 per cent, and more than 90 per cent of British MPs are graduates, up from less than half in the 1970s.

Politicians of all stripes make the same point. In his celebrated speech about inequality at Osawatomie, Kansas, President Obama said that 'a higher education is the surest route to the middle class'. Left Democrats like Bernie Sanders and Elizabeth Warren go even further and demand 'college for all'.

Not everyone can be a winner, however you design the game. In some fields such as law, medicine, technology, and some corners of business, 'winner takes all' markets have provided exceptional rewards to exceptional people – people like Mark Zuckerberg, Jeff Bezos, Elon Musk – who have both high cognitive skills and practical knowledge of something that gives them a big first mover advantage in new digital markets. Below them is a wider group of highly educated, and highly credentialized, people from top universities who have the intelligence and personality attributes to propel them into the top layer of jobs. Another level down is what one might call the rank and file of the cognitive class, the mass elite. These are people who have, in recent years, been directed into the expanded higher education sector by parents, teachers, financial incentives and, too often, by the lack of other post-school options (at least in the UK and US). In the UK there are now more graduates than non-graduates among the under-thirties. Many have earned valuable qualifications and launched successful professional careers; too many others find themselves with degrees of little value in jobs with only school leaver cognitive requirements (and student debts to pay off).

Moreover, it is not clear that people in these last two groups are necessarily cleverer than the average citizen – after all, the majority of people achieve average or above-average scores on IQ-type tests. Their entry into the cognitive class is just as much attributable to background, social convention and the character traits – self-discipline, application and so on – that make academic success possible. Nevertheless, they often acquire expectations of professional status that, especially in the case of the mass elite group, are not satisfied by the relatively routine jobs they often go into.

Studying Sanskrit or *Middlemarch* at university can be a personally enriching experience, but, looked at through another lens, many university degrees, especially in the humanities, are not so much about what you know but a signal to employers that you have certain attributes. And from the point of view of the graduate your degree level is something that fixes you in a hierarchy above, or below, your peers.

Making many occupations like nursing and policing graduate-only is not necessarily wrong, but there is an element of 'if you can't beat 'em, join 'em' about it: if an undergraduate degree has become the only route to respect and prestige for an occupation then why should nurses and police officers be denied it? But as the sociologist of education Randall Collins has pointed out, this can lead to a cycle of credential inflation that 'could go on endlessly, until janitors need PhDs and babysitters are required to hold advanced degrees in child care'.

In the UK there has been some attempt in recent years to offer better options to the half of school leavers who do not go on to university, with a training levy on bigger employers to promote apprenticeships. But in the UK, unlike in many continental European countries, it is almost impossible to compete with the prestige of the university route, and the lack of a well-trodden, properly funded, sub-university, vocational/ technical route has left the economy starved of essential workers. In 2017 42 per cent of UK employers said they were struggling to fill vacancies for skilled trades jobs.[5] It is a similar story in the US.

Meanwhile Heart jobs in social care for the elderly, early years education and child care continue to be undervalued (and often underpaid). Most nursery workers earn around £17,000 a year, and a child-minder, even in London, is paid about £6 an hour per child.

Today's women's equality movement has focused primarily on breaking glass ceilings and competing equally with men in the world of professional careers. It has been more ambivalent about trying to raise the status of caring and nurturing roles, which are traditionally identified as female. Women now have many more opportunities than in the 1950s or 1960s, and fewer are volunteering for caring roles. Not many men are picking up the slack. Hence, in part, the crisis in social care and in nurse recruitment.

Of course, as noted, Head, Hand and Heart are always interacting. The Heart and Head are combined in the modern graduate nurse, who has become a quasi-doctor. And many skilled trade Hand roles, like a plumber or car mechanic or IT support worker, require cognitive diagnostic skills that are not that different to the problem-solving abilities of a medical consultant. The distribution of cognitive status can sometimes seem quite arbitrary.

BELONG ANYWHERE

Yet Head abstraction and detachment increasingly dominate our culture. The ethos of the digital giants like Google and Facebook is self-consciously unrooted and global. It is best summed up in Airbnb's oxymoronic slogan: 'Belong Anywhere'. Advances in technology reduce opportunities for craft, and the need for human contact or attachment to specific places, though tech company platforms can also be good at enabling local communities to come together more easily. By contrast, it is the undervalued *embodied* skills of Hand and Heart that promote belonging and attachment. (The reduction in face-to-face contact during the Covid-19 crisis made us more dependent on digital attachment. But in the medium term this crisis will surely weaken the 'Belong Anywhere' worldview.)

Across the developed world, the one quality-of-life indicator that is said to be *declining* is mental health. Mental well-being depends on a sense of meaning and purpose, and a feeling that we are part of something larger than ourselves, useful to and needed by others (as confirmed by happiness research). It is our attachments that give us meaning and purpose. The most powerful route to meaning is through love, mutual dependence and serving others. In other words, the realm of the Heart.

This can apply to the Hand too. Productive work with your Hand and Head on a farm or in a bicycle repair workshop produces the pleasure of being immanent, in this place and time, the awareness of being much more than a disembodied intellect, a brain in a jar. The American philosopher Matthew Crawford wrote a book – *The Case for Working with Your Hands* – which is partly about the *intellectual* satisfaction of Hand work.

Yet, especially in the Anglo-Saxon countries, achievement, success, even happiness, have increasingly become associated with physical mobility and disconnection from presence and place, custom and practice. (This is reflected in political philosophy by what Patrick Deneen has called the 'false anthropology' of social contract theory, which imagines an impossible pre-social, isolated 'individual from nowhere' contracting into society.)[6]

And the fact is that joining the world of cognitive achievers often does require geographical mobility, especially in the UK, where this is reinforced by residential universities. In a speech in 2017, Justine Greening, the UK's former Secretary of State for Education, said: 'All the years I spent growing up in Rotherham, I was aiming for something better . . . a better job, owning my own home, an interesting career, a life that I found really challenging . . . I knew there was something better out there.'[7]

The longing to spread your wings and seek fame and fortune in the big city is a common enough impulse across all times and in all places. Yet the unselfconscious way in which a (then) British cabinet minister doubts whether it is possible for an able, ambitious person to live a fulfilled life in a town of 120,000 people (which is a thirty-minute commute from Sheffield, a city of more than half a million) reveals something flawed about modern Britain. Many towns like Rotherham lose 20 to 30 per cent of their brightest eighteen-year-olds every year to university. Many of them never return, exacerbating the country's geographical divisions.

The American writer Michael Lind has described this as Hubs versus Heartlands: the former are home to most of the professional class and are where high-end business and professional services are located, the latter are where you find most goods production and mass services. The Hubs are socially liberal, home to most ethnic minorities and astonishingly unequal: the gap between richest and poorest in New York City is comparable to Swaziland.[8] The Heartlands are particularly neglected in Britain thanks to an over-mighty capital city. (The so-called 'red wall' of traditionally Labour seats that turned Tory in the 2019 UK election were Heartland seats, the Hubs remained mainly Labour.) But there are similar patterns in parts of the ex-industrial US, France (where the Gilets Jaunes movement was a cry for recognition by the French Heartland) and Germany, especially eastern Germany.

Peter Lampl, of the UK's social mobility charity the Sutton Trust, says that 'it is those who are most mobile who are most likely to find success' and wants to encourage more people from lower socio-economic groups to enjoy the 'migration premium'.[9] But not everyone wants or needs to uproot themselves. Even if they did, there are limits on how many people can rise up into the cognitive class. Yet all of us need to feel we have a valued place in society, from where we can participate and contribute, even if we are not mobile high achievers.

As Joan Williams pointed out in her book *White Working Class: Overcoming Class Cluelessness in America*: 'For many perfectly able working class people their dream is not to join the upper middle class with its different culture but to stay true to their own values in their own communities, just with more money.' And physical mobility has in fact been declining quite sharply in the US in recent decades. Michael Lind, in his book *The New Class War*, says that 57 per cent of Americans have never lived outside their home state and 37 per cent have never lived anywhere but their home town. And according to an Upshot analysis published in the *New York Times* in 2015 the typical American adult lives only 18 miles from his or her mother. The number of people crossing a county boundary for work has halved since the 1950s and now stands at just 4 per cent of the working population.[10]

This brings us to the central challenge for democratic politics in all rich countries. How to achieve an open society, and elite, while continuing to value relatively stable, meaningful, communities? How can ambitious people follow their desires and leave without making those who stay feel that they have been left behind and diminished? How can the stayers have the same opportunity to live successful and fulfilled lives, in their own way, as the leavers?

The technology of connection that makes it easier for leavers to stay in touch may also make it easier for stayers to feel they do not need to leave to be part of what matters. But the Anywhere-dominated political class has not been addressing this dilemma and for a quarter of a century has ruled too much in its own interests: promoting mobility, pushing for the most open possible economy and society and hugely expanding generalist, academic higher education.

The ethos of service and duty that used to underpin so many professions often seems to have been replaced with a claim to moral leadership by the better-educated. And the political focus on social mobility, on moving up and out, often sounds like a form of cognitive class narcissism – 'you too can be like us' – combined with a belief that ordinary lives are less valuable.

Meanwhile, the political class has felt able to ignore some of the basic political intuitions of the Somewheres: the importance of stable neighbourhoods and well-managed national borders; the idea of national social contracts, and placing the rights of national citizens ahead of universal rights; the evolution but not abolition of the gender division of labour. And they have failed to grasp the need for narrative and recognition among those who cannot thrive in a professionalized Head-based economy. Ideas like the dignity of labour and working for the common good of the nation, the enterprise or the public now seem positively quaint. And while for many professional people work is a central source of meaning and identity, for around half the population in both the UK and US a job is just a way of earning a living, with people finding meaning in other aspects of their lives.

Highly educated Anywheres, because they are often more articulate and better trained in assessing information, flatter themselves with the belief that their values flow from reason and evidence. In fact, as with Somewheres, their priorities and intuitions usually come first, and invariably facts are found that fit with them – so-called motivated reasoning. They are also just as subject to 'group-think' as Somewheres, as British Conservative politician Michael Gove was pointing out in his famous comment about experts. And, after all, experts have not covered themselves in glory in the past twenty years: the failure to predict how Iraqis might respond to invasion; the failure to see the financial crisis of 2007/8, or the Brexit vote and the election of Donald Trump. Perhaps, too, the failure to properly prepare for Covid-19, which had, after all, been very widely predicted. Very few of us, even populists, are hostile to scientific or medical experts (apart from anti-vaccine people), and the status of such experts is likely to rise in the aftermath of the crisis. But many people will remain sceptical about political and economic and social-scientific experts passing off their often politically driven views as objective truth.

The Head, Hand and Heart triumvirate have slipped more out of kilter in the US and UK than in most of continental Europe, which retains stronger communitarian traditions and respect for 'practical and vocational intelligence' and people doing basic jobs. It is also in the UK and US where in the twentieth century there has been most reliance on IQ-type tests – the eleven-plus in the UK and SAT tests in the US – which claim to reveal *innate talents* rather than test how hard people have worked and how much they know. And it is no surprise that it's in the Anglo-Saxon countries, with Brexit and Trump, that we have seen the biggest backlash against cognitive class hegemony, despite – or perhaps because of – such a large proportion of graduates.

THE END OF PEAK HEAD

Later in this book I will trace what has happened to each of the three broad streams of human aptitude – Head, Hand and Heart – in the past seventy years. I will also sketch out some of the heated debates about the nature of cognitive ability, how it is distributed and whether it is properly measured in IQ tests (see Chapter 3).

The book will trace my own journey too, from a leftish journalist who saw politics mainly through the prism of economic motivations (and for whom data was key) to my growing sense, in the last decade or so, of people's need for meaning and recognition, and the power of emotion and storytelling, in our politics and daily lives. As the Israeli historian Yuval Noah Harari has put it, in the modern world we exchanged meaning for power. But too many people feel they have lost meaning without acquiring power.

Questions of value underpin all these arguments. What is human worth? What is cultural value? As Jonathan Sacks, the UK's former Chief Rabbi, has complained, without God we have increasingly adopted a utilitarian and economic definition of human worth, and questions of meaning and value have been relegated to the private sphere.

One of the reasons why the language and methods of cognitive assessment have swept all before it in recent years is because they appear to be fair and easy to measure. Indeed, one of the reasons for the academic drift in education is that it is easier to mark and measure *written* tests than tests of manual skill or speaking ability. This means that people with reasonable ability in writing skills and a university degree are often preferred even in forms of employment, such as a manager in a department store, suitable to someone with high social intelligence or so-called domain-specific skills derived from long experience of doing one thing.

Is a better balance between Head, Hand and Heart achievable? Yes. Human norms and values lie behind the market signals of supply and demand, and they can change with surprising speed, as we may witness in the light of the Covid-19 crisis. In most European countries at least 40 per cent of the economy is under direct or indirect public control (a bit less in the US), and the corporate sector is sensitive to shifts in public attitudes and values. Consider the way in which environmental or gender equality concerns have impacted the business plans of big corporations in recent decades.

One of the forces currently driving change is political pressure from voters who don't share the interests of the cognitive classes. And there are other trends that suggest the Head will soon face a more even contest with Hand and Heart.

A dystopian trend was suggested by American journalist Nicholas Carr, in his book *The Shallows*, in which he argued that we are all being made dumber by the internet.[11] Carr argued that sustained exposure to the internet is reordering our synapses in ways that make us crave novelty and struggle to focus. This may bring improvements in some fields, but overall it means significant losses in linguistic facility, memory and concentration.

But there are some other more positive trends and forces that will, I believe, strengthen Hand and Heart. One such force is the simple fact that, while Hand and Heart may have been economically diminished relative to Head in recent decades, they remain vital human impulses. Consider the modern focus on cooking. Coverage on television and in newspapers is enormously greater than thirty years ago, which is surely a reflection of the continuing desire for meaningful Hand experiences on the part of many people who no longer use their hands at work except on a keyboard. The same might be said for programmes on gardening, renovating houses and repairing things.

Consider too what people do when they retire. It invariably involves something embodied and rooted, a sporting or 'making' hobby of some kind. Similarly, consider the centrality of sport and acting/singing celebrity in our public culture. Although these activities often require significant cognitive ability, they are rooted in Hand and Heart, closer to craft or artisanal skills than essay writing/analytical ability. And still a way out of the working class for men is the skilled physicality of becoming a sportsman, and for women it is beauty, the working-class schoolgirl spotted by the modelling agency (or entering the world of stylists, high-end hairdressers, Instagram style influencers, and so on). In fact, human leisure, recreation and ritual is almost all Hand- and Heart-based, though with significant aspects of Head too. Artisanal skills are also being rediscovered in some corners of the economy, especially in food and drink production, often by affluent young professionals.

Indeed, a shift away from Head and towards Hand and Heart seems to be programmed into many of the biggest social and economic trends: in the knowledge economy's declining appetite for all but the most able knowledge workers, the growing concern for place and environmental protection, including more labour-intensive organic farming, and the inevitable expansion of care functions of various kinds in an ageing society. These trends are likely to be reinforced by the Covid-19 crisis, which revealed that most of the 'key workers' who support our daily lives were Hand and Heart workers, mainly people without university degrees.

There is one very big fact that modern politics will need to confront in the next decade. Political parties of both centre-left and centre-right have taken as axiomatic that modern society will see a continuing expansion of secure, middle-class, professional, graduate jobs. Both education and social mobility policy are based on this assumption. Yet it is almost certainly wrong. The knowledge economy does not need an ever-growing supply of knowledge workers (see Chapter 9). It still needs a top layer of the cognitively most able and original, but much of the work required of middle-ranking professionals is already substantially routinized, a kind of digital Taylorism.

The American economist Paul Krugman spotted this back in 1996. Writing for the *New York Times* but imagining himself looking back from 100 years in the future, he saw that manipulating information was going to lose its value: 'The prophets of the "information economy" seem to have forgotten basic economics. A world awash in information will be a world in which information per se has very little market value. And in general when the economy becomes extremely good at doing something, that activity becomes less rather than more important.'[12] (Luciano Floridi points out that before the internet the value of information was contained in aggregating the answers. Now the answers are free online, the value lies in convening the questions.)[13]

According to the British academics Phil Brown and Hugh Lauder the proportion of jobs in big corporations requiring a significant application of cognitive skill and judgement is in sharp decline – with as few as 10 to 15 per cent of staff with 'permission to think'. And it is precisely the more routinized aspects of professional work in the law, accountancy, medicine, public administration and so on that will in the near future be vulnerable to both Artificial Intelligence and to being exported to low-wage economies. It is much easier for an algorithm to replace a mid-level accountant than a refuse collector or a child-carer.

This suggests that the rapid expansion of the traditional university sector over the past thirty years will stop. Already in the UK nearly one-third of graduates are working in non-graduate jobs five years after graduating, and the graduate pay premium over those who don't go to university is dwindling to almost nothing for young men from non-elite universities. The disappointment of a substantial section of young people who felt that they had been promised entry, via higher education, into a secure, high-status world of professional accomplishment is one of the factors behind Labour's shift to the left in the UK and the Democrats' shift to the left in the US. It may also have been a factor behind the Black Lives Matter protests, at least in the UK.

The neglect of higher Hand skills, especially in the UK and the US, will have to be reversed. Britain in the last two decades has overproduced general bachelor's degrees and basic apprenticeships and neglected the technical skills that are still required to make the world function smoothly. This has partly been obscured by free movement of people from the EU, which has helped to plug the gap. Similar trends are observable in the US, though less so in continental Europe, especially the Germanic countries, where employer-based vocational training remains strongly embedded. Even in Germany, however, there has been a sharp rise in university participation in the past decade.

Automation has cut mainly blue-collar jobs, but Artificial Intelligence is now coming for the more routinized end of professional jobs.

The disruption experienced by relatively well-educated professionals could lead to a new sympathy for people performing Hand and Heart work, partly because many former accountants and lawyers will find themselves doing those jobs. The educated people who voted against populism will be far more sympathetic to reallocating status when automation has abolished their jobs, predicts Richard Baldwin in *The Globotics Upheaval*.

At the same time, the pay, conditions and training of Hand and Heart jobs are likely to improve because of the simple operation of supply and demand. And most of these face-to-face service, care and everyday jobs, from car mechanic to parcel deliverer and nursery nurse, cannot be exported or done by a robot. Low-skill work is not, as widely predicted by economists, disappearing. In Gordon Brown's penultimate budget speech as Chancellor of the Exchequer in 2006 he predicted there would be just 600,000 low-skill jobs in the UK by 2020. Depending on how one defines low skill, there are likely to be at least 8 million low-skill jobs in the British economy next year.

Indeed, one of the explanations for the slowdown in productivity growth in rich economies in recent years, associated with the theory of economist William Baumol, is that workers no longer needed in the more automated sectors end up in low-productivity jobs. Or, as *The Economist* put it: 'Technological progress pushes employment into the sectors most resistant to productivity growth. Eventually, nearly everyone may have jobs that are valued for their inefficiency: as concert musicians, or artisanal cheese makers, or members of the household staff of the very rich.'[14] And, indeed, as medical or nursing staff in an intensive care unit.

People will always be needed to clean offices, work in supermarkets and cafés, deliver things, work in fields and fix your car and computer. Digital platforms such as Amazon may be reducing jobs in shops but they are creating them in warehouses and delivery firms. Some of these functions will be automated and some can be done by immigrants, allowing rich country workers to move up the employment chain. But given the unpopularity of large-scale immigration, especially in Europe, it makes more sense to try to make these jobs more attractive to national citizens. There is an unavoidable element of drudgery to some of these roles, but if they are decently paid, and people feel respected and useful (as many supermarket staff did at the height of the Covid-19 crisis) and fairly managed, they can provide sociable, purposive activity without necessarily providing meaning and identity in the way that professional jobs can – but people find meaning in other areas of life: family, sport, hobbies and so on.

The final relevant trend that will surely raise the status of Heart work is linked to two irreversible social facts: the increased numbers of older people, who will need significant levels of care in their final years (2020 was the first year in human history when there were more people over sixty-five than under five), and the more prominent place of women in the public realm. The #MeToo movement, which exposed the predatory behaviour of men in the entertainment industry, politics and elsewhere, didn't happen thirty years ago because there were simply too few women in positions of authority in the media and politics.

One of the most important questions in developed countries over the next generation is whether women's greater political weight will be wielded to increase the limited market power of women now doing most Heart jobs. The women doing these jobs, many working part-time or as agency staff, usually have strong obligations to those they care for so cannot easily apply pressure on those who employ them. Strikes by care home workers are rare. Professional women have successfully gender-desegregated the upper end of the labour market in areas such as medicine and law, but the middle and bottom end of the labour market remains highly gender-segregated. Will the greater power of highly educated professional women in due course mean a £15-an-hour minimum wage in adult social care? Or are such professionals too detached from the interests of the kind of women who might be employed part-time in a care home?

The Anywhere, liberal professional worldview is very public realm focused and tends to look down on domesticity. Yet it is hard to imagine an upward revaluation of care work in the public economy without valuing it more in the home too (whether done by women or men). Britain and America are outliers among rich countries in their laissez-faire approach to support for families with children and both experience high levels of family breakdown, one big factor behind the increase in deaths of despair in the US. Valuing care more in the private realm, whether of young children or elderly parents, raises the question of who does the caring. Many women feel, quite reasonably, that they already perform the burdensome 'double shift' at work and home and want men to bear a fairer share of domestic care. This does seem to be happening, albeit rather slowly, but survey evidence in the UK also shows that most women with children would like to spend more time at home caring for pre-school children if they could afford to, working either part-time or not at all.[15] And yet family and gender policy, especially in the US and UK, focuses on making it easy for both parents *to spend as little time as possible in the family.*

Every day in rich countries there are more hours spent caring, in its many forms, than in any other activity. And caring work is some of the most emotionally and physically draining labour of all. Yet, as the writer Madeleine Bunting, author of *Labours of Love*, argues, the ethos of care does not sit easily with the ethos of an individualistic, achievement society. Care, especially in the private realm, is about duty to others, and its results are sometimes nebulous and hard to measure (see Chapter 8). There is some potential for the use of smart technologies in elderly care, with more remote monitoring and so on (and this could draw more men into the sector). But most caring jobs cannot easily be automated or performed by machines. Even in ageing Japan, with its antipathy to mass immigration, Filipino carers are preferred to robots and are gradually being welcomed in larger numbers.

The rise and rise of cognitive-analytical ability – Head work – as a measure of economic and social success, combined with the hegemony of cognitive class political interests, led to the great unbalancing of western politics even prior to the Covid-19 crisis. The disaffection of large minorities, even majorities, in many countries, is linked intimately to the declining status and self-respect attached to work associated with the Hand and the Heart.

The new discipline of happiness research generally finds that more equal societies are happier than less equal ones, yet leading researchers such as John F. Helliwell do not find the cause in income equality itself, rather in the mutual respect and equality of status that tends to go along with it.

Status is a slippery concept, it is both highly subjective – how we feel about ourselves and where we think we stand in the eyes of others

– and quite objective – people in higher professional jobs (a surgeon, a barrister) and celebrities of most kinds are almost universally recognized as having more of it. And status usually follows the money (with some exceptions such as vicars or artists), though they can be more or less closely aligned at different times. The substantial element of subjectivity in the concept of status makes it hard to measure the decline that I believe has been suffered by many people in post-industrial societies, though I have grappled with it in Chapter 7.

Income inequality is easier to measure, and many people, especially on the left, find it more comfortable to focus on because it points the finger of blame at the rich and big business. But the preferences of the cognitive class – especially the 'creative class' end in the arts and universities – for openness, autonomy and change are also a source of discomfort and conflict.

There is a broad agreement in developed societies about the importance of individual freedom and social justice, though fierce disagreement about the exact contours of both. There is much less consensus about cultural-psychological issues – the security, status, respect and identity themes – which shape how people feel about themselves in daily life. For example, some people on the left would challenge whether it is legitimate for someone to feel discomforted by disruption to familiarity – a neighbourhood rapidly changed by immigration, say. It is these psychological issues that cause so many people to feel unmoored from a proper sense of meaning and belonging, the people who tell pollsters that the past was better than the present. A renewed respect for aptitudes connected to Hand and Heart as well as Head – a 'triumvirate' rather than a cognitive meritocracy – is at least part of the answer to their discomfort.

Let's aim for a society as open and mobile as possible but not restrict our political ambition to designing a better ladder up. Instead, our politics should place more emphasis on a wider spread of respect, dignity and regard, and on offering a valued place to people who play by the rules but do not excel cognitively. We need, in other words, to treat people democratically. It is an adjustment our democracies are now demanding.

2

The Rise of the Cognitive Class

Recruits should be segregated at entry into a hierarchy of grades, ranging from clerical officers who conduct routine tasks, through to those who provide policy advice to ministers ... Promotion should be on merit, not preferment, patronage, purchase, or length of service.

Conclusions of the Northcote-Trevelyan Report into civil service reform in Britain 1853

In the rich, liberal societies of Europe and North America many of the things that we value have become significantly less self-evident. We are free to value radically different things from our fellow citizens, even from our close relatives (especially across generations). In the UK an institution like the BBC increasingly struggles to speak for, and to, the whole country. (In the US, a common, trusted national media voice no longer exists.) But there are still plenty of assumptions that most people hold in common and that are reinforced in the public and political conversation forming the collective 'common sense' of a society – albeit one that is constantly, imperceptibly, shifting.

This is sometimes hard to be precise about until an unexpected event reveals something that has been evolving below the surface. I am writing this in the early stages of the Covid-19 crisis, so it is too early tell what, if anything, that will reveal, but the reaction to the death of Princess Diana displayed a Britain that was far more emotional and far less wedded to the stiff upper lip than most people (including most British people) expected. The Brexit and Trump protest votes in 2016 were another crystallizing moment, revealing not so much a shift in values as a value *divide* based around different attitudes and intuitions, arising in part from different experiences of education and the processes of cognitive selection. About 75 per cent of people with minimal educational qualifications voted for Brexit and about the same proportion with degrees or more voted to remain.[1] Similar divides were reflected in the Trump vote.

It is the central claim of this book that the protest vote was in part an understandable reaction to a profound status shift that has been gathering pace for over fifty years, one that has bestowed an increasing amount of recognition on cognitive-related aptitudes and jobs – what I call the Head – and quietly sucked it away from most others, above all those related to the Hand and the Heart. This has been happening in most rich societies, as the pyramid-shaped industrial society, with its large number of people doing basic manual jobs or working full-time in the home, has given way to a more light-bulb-shaped post-industrial society and a more knowledge-based economy.

Until quite recently almost everyone worked in order to support their family. Work was a means to an end found in the domestic realm. But increasingly in the latter part of the twentieth century work, especially higher-status professional work, came to be a source of esteem and self-worth and self-expression – an end in itself. This has coincided with rising concern for gender equality that has focused on enabling women to compete more equally with men in the public sphere of work and the professions. Perhaps inevitably this has contributed to a devaluing of the private realm and the traditional caring functions for the young and elderly, mainly carried out by women. The proportion of families where one parent stays at home full-time when children are young is one-quarter in the UK and only slightly higher in the US.[2] (The unexpected and prolonged refamiliarization with the private realm as a result of the Covid-19 lockdown came as an unwelcome shock to many people.)

The education system, and the years people spend in school, have grown significantly in recent decades, and a quasi-meritocratic education system, above all in the modern university, has become the main distributor of status and position. It is true that some of the richest and most powerful modern businesspeople such as Bill Gates dropped out of higher education, but the ethos of these 'cognitive entrepreneurs' is certainly not hostile to the increased status of 'nerdy' cognitive aptitudes, quite the opposite. The digital giants such as Google, Facebook and Amazon recruit their senior people overwhelmingly from elite universities. Indeed, universities are increasingly complaining that they are losing their best researchers, especially in AI, to big tech.

POST-INDUSTRIAL DISENCHANTMENT

This cognitive shift is a surprisingly recent thing in developed societies, and not enough thought has been given to its implications. It is hard to speak with any confidence about the mentalities, or levels of contentment, of people in earlier eras. But it may be that industrial society, especially in its most recent phase in the second half of the twentieth century, including democratic equality and welfare states, was better at distributing self-respect and status than today's cognitively stratified post-industrial society, especially for men. We are richer and freer but often more adrift and resentful.

The movement from the country to the town in Britain in the early nineteenth century was often traumatic and involved, at least for a period, an increase in suffering and reduced longevity. But life quite soon become significantly better in the town than it had been in the countryside. Indeed, 1845, the year that Friedrich Engels published his description of industrial misery, *The Condition of the Working Class in England*, was just about the point when things started to improve.

Improved public hygiene, the spread of literacy and the arrival of cheap food from Australia and the Americas were just three ways in which the lives of most people were transformed for the better in the second half of the nineteenth century. This was not just about incomes and living conditions: new forms of meaning and self-respect soon established themselves too. The urban identity itself quickly came to be seen as superior to the rural one; indeed, the term 'peasant' was soon adopted as a term of abuse, and there was no discernible movement back from the town to the country. Moreover, new forms of skilled and semi-skilled work in the factories and workshops conferred status and respect on both men and women. Urbanization was associated with education and betterment, as opposed to what Marx called the idiocy of rural life – it is no surprise that when, in Britain, the franchise was extended to the ordinary man (at this stage not the ordinary woman) it was the urban householder who was entrusted with the vote almost two decades before his rural cousin.

For all of the external upheaval in the early decades of industrialization, people's inner life and moral universes often remained surprisingly unchanged. There was significant continuity in traditional understandings of the world and in gender roles and family structure. Christianity remained the central organizing belief system for most people, although it took new forms in the expanding urban centres in low church Methodism and similar radical forms of Protestantism. Women worked outside the home in larger numbers, but family life appears to have been strengthened, not weakened, with the movement into towns, as rates of illegitimacy fell throughout the nineteenth century, at least in Britain.[3] In the UK and the US the multi-generational extended family remained the most common form well into the twentieth century. In 1850 75 per cent of Americans older than sixty-five lived with relatives; by 1990 only 18 per cent did.[4]

It is in the nature of class-stratified societies for status, meaning your place in the pecking order of social respect, to be a powerful *given* that few people can escape. This restricts human opportunity but also gives people an explanation for their position in the hierarchy that has little bearing on their abilities or intelligence. In the relatively immobile class society of the nineteenth and much of the twentieth centuries if you failed to rise from the working class into more genteel society it was no reflection on your own aptitudes, it was just the way things were.

Immobility can also consolidate a sense of group solidarity and make a project of *collective* advance – such as trade unionism or socialism – seem more relevant than individual aspiration. Trapped in steerage together, the passengers will probably develop a sense of common interest. Given a ladder to the upper decks, people are more likely to elbow each other out of the way.

And this is partly what has happened in our post-industrial societies. The main distributor of status and income is *individual* educational achievement and the ethos, if not the reality, of the society is open and meritocratic. Those who do not enter into the cognitive class by taking A levels at school (or graduating from high school in the US, taking the Baccalauréat in France or the Abitur in Germany) and going into higher education have in the main more restricted opportunities and lower social status than those who do. And this lower status is partly the result of their own cognitive limitations, or at least is widely perceived to be so by society and by many of the individuals themselves.

Some people have the resilience to avoid feelings of failure and may achieve a degree of success despite being in society's slow lane, but many others internalize a feeling of low self-respect which creates a pervasive sense of anxiety and uselessness.

There are several compounding problems that contribute to post-industrial disenchantment. Post-industrial society has eroded the compensating belief systems provided by religion, which recognizes you for your moral character, not your ability, and (in theory) sees everyone as equally valued in the eyes of God. It has done the same to the traditional roles in the private realm – such as male breadwinner or nurturing mother and home-maker – which constrained opportunity, especially for women, but also conferred meaning and purpose. The institutions that have historically accepted you as a member unconditionally – family, church, nation – are all weakened in a freer, more mobile and more individualistic society. Achieved identities based on educational and career success have eclipsed ascribed identities based on attachment to place and group. (Of course, those are not always good roles: the serfs of pre-modern Europe or the *Dalit* – 'Untouchables' – in India.) Post-industrial society elevates the values and priorities of the highly educated to a more dominant position, and those views tend to be secular, individualistic, anti-tradition and anti-authority. Post-industrial modernity is often fluid and disorientating – more wealth, but less meaning, as Yuval Noah Harari says – and is easier for some people to adapt to than others.

There is another problem, which I mentioned earlier. We now have, since the arrival of mass higher education, a *single* route into a *single* dominant cognitive class. And although the graduate cognitive class is now much bigger, more open and more democratic than it was fifty years ago, it passes through a narrower funnel: go to a good university and then into a professional middle-class career. Until quite recently there were many more and varied routes to a degree of achievement and respect. There were many short ladders up, some of which led to taller ones. There was a working-class elite, for example, in the trade unions, friendly societies and parties of the left, different regional elites in provincial cities and, at a workplace level, meaningful progression from below was possible without higher educational qualifications.

It looks increasingly likely in today's economy that the cognitive class, at least in occupational terms, is going to stop growing – undermining the central promise of developed societies that everyone can, and should, become a middle-class professional. We will continue to need a thin layer of highly talented people who write the relevant software and provide the top professionals in everything from law to medicine, engineering, design, and finance, but the next round of AI is going to cut a swathe through the middle ranks of professional life and potentially create an even bigger status gulf between the most able and the rest.

Moreover, the frame of comparison that people use to evaluate their lives has become much wider. People used to compare themselves in terms of wealth or talents of various kinds to people in their own village. Even after urbanization people in a stratified class society would mainly compare themselves to people a few rungs above or below them on the ladder. For many the shop steward, the supervisor or lay preacher was a figure of respect and an achievable model for emulation. With mass media, television and radio, and now social media, it is harder for people to avoid comparing themselves unfavourably with the brightest, most beautiful and most talented in the world, which is thought to be one of the causes of rising mental stress.

People seek meaning in their lives and a sense of being useful to others as well as material comfort, freedom and justice. It is not desirable or possible to go back to a past when social horizons and life chances were far more limited, but a recognition of some of the merits of earlier eras might help us perceive more clearly the biases and failings of today's post-industrial achievement society.

The idea of being a successful or unsuccessful person is a comparatively recent one in historical terms, outside of the elites, and even now most people do not think of their lives in these terms, and yet in more fluid, individualistic, competitive and transparent societies it is increasingly hard to protect oneself from such status judgements. And the sorting house for higher-status opportunity has increasingly become higher education, with a university degree serving as the passport to recognition. Theoretical or abstract reasoning, as opposed to merely empirical knowledge of facts or practical intelligence, is the aptitude that increasingly determines life chances. Practical knowing 'how' has traditionally been seen as distinct from, and inferior to, abstract knowing 'that', in the distinction made famous by the philosopher Gilbert Ryle, especially in England.

Our societies depend now not only on relatively high levels of general education, especially in literacy and maths, but also on a significant number of specialist cadres in scientific, technological, legal, as well as generalist analytical and administrative, fields. And the proportion of Head jobs has grown disproportionately relative to Hand and Heart jobs in the course of the twentieth century.

Head work and professional jobs are not exactly synonymous, and as we will see later many apparently professional jobs involve relatively little cognitive ability or independent judgement. Nonetheless, 'professional' status does act as a rough proxy for Head, so it is worth looking at how the numbers of professional jobs have expanded in the last 200 years.

In Britain in 1841 it is estimated that just 2.5 per cent of adults were in higher or lower professions, rising to 4.3 per cent in 1911. The proportion for France in 1911 is roughly the same as Britain and for the US it is slightly higher at 6.2 per cent. By 2018 those numbers had risen to over 30 per cent in Britain, 36 per cent in the US, 38 per cent in France and 41 per cent in Germany.[5]

The world has become more complex and abstract, and it makes sense that those with the greatest facility for hypothetical reasoning and symbolic thinking should dominate many of the most important and prestigious positions. But politics, and the wider culture, is sending the signal that this cognitive revolution has gone too far for the countervailing democratic ethos of equal human worth and self-respect to bear – we have reached 'peak Head'.

Rather reassuringly, about 70 per cent of us are in the middle range of the cognitive ability spectrum as measured by IQ tests. Yet, as already noted, half the population will always, by definition, be in the bottom half of that spectrum, and a system that rewards too generously the top 10 to 15 per cent of the most cognitively blessed will run up against a mass democratic resentment.

Before considering the cognitively blessed more closely we need to pause to consider some history and some definitions. The next section of this chapter examines the historical emergence of the cognitive class, in Britain and the US in particular, and its methods of selection. The following chapter then considers the arguments about what cognitive ability actually is, how it is measured, how innate it is, and what this means for meritocracy and social mobility. The following three chapters will then look at the consolidation of cognitive domination in recent decades in the worlds of education, the economy and politics.

PROFESSIONS AND UNIVERSITIES

Social selection processes based on intelligence, rather than manual skill or physical strength or beauty, have existed from the beginning of human society itself. Counsellors to the powerful were not generally chosen for their looks or their athletic prowess. In Christian Europe advisers, such as Cardinal Wolsey the son of an Ipswich butcher, usually emerged from ecclesiastical selection systems. In China the Han dynasty more than 2,000 years ago introduced competitive exams, testing knowledge of Confucian principles of government, to determine entry to the higher bureaucracy.

Some professions that require a relatively high degree of abstract reasoning such as physician, lawyer, priest, teacher, architect and diplomat have long histories stretching back into the mists of time. In early modern Europe most of these roles were still connected to the church, and most people seeking advancement in them took holy orders too. But gradually the professions secularized, and in the twelfth century the clergy were prohibited from practising law and medicine in England. This was an important step. Law was the first organized secular profession with judges appointed by the crown and the Inns of Court established in the fourteenth century. The Royal College of Physicians was established in England in 1518, but training and selection by examination was not institutionalized in medicine or law until the nineteenth century. In the meantime both professions – and indeed most skilled occupations – adopted a system of pupillage, with students of medicine or law becoming the pupil of an established practitioner.[6]

The Enlightenment in the eighteenth century carved out a bigger role for human reason in the most developed societies of Europe. It helped to challenge and weaken traditional religious belief and opened the intellectual space for modern science and technology to thrive. Knowledge was no longer derived from ancient texts but could be *created*. Yet, 200 years later, in the year that I was born, 1956, cognitive selection via education still played only a minor role in the lives of most people in rich countries. It was still possible then to walk straight into an apprenticeship or a decently paying job without any exams or other qualifications to one's name. And the more able and ambitious could rise up the ranks by supplementing basic education with qualifications gained at night school or other part-time study. Late entry into professional jobs – accountant, lawyer, engineer – was commonplace. British banks used to recruit mainly from school leavers well into the 1980s. According to the 1991 UK census fewer than half of people in professional, managerial and technical positions held university degrees.[7]

How different the world looks today with the onward march of cognitive selection for all school children, a university degree an increasing necessity for almost all jobs in the top 40 per cent of the occupational hierarchy and around one-third of all jobs in Europe and North America loosely categorized as 'professional'.

In Britain this story of educational selection, even of meritocracy itself, is often seen to have properly begun with the publication of the Northcote-Trevelyan Report on civil service reform in 1853. The Northcote-Trevelyan Report, following an earlier initiative from Thomas Babington Macaulay at the East India Company, recommended the principle of competitive exams for entry into an expanded civil service replacing earlier systems of nomination, patronage and even purchase of positions. It began to be widely accepted that expertise and ability should replace patronage and nepotism; the well-trained professional should replace the gentleman amateur especially after the failures of the Crimean War (1854) and the Indian mutiny (1857), both of which were seen at the time as illustrating the limits of the amateur, aristocratic ethos. The report, which now seems like common sense, was greeted with some hostility, including from Queen Victoria herself. And at the time its most important consequence was not so much in entrenching meritocratic selection but in enabling the creation of a politically neutral senior civil service.

The principle of entry into elite jobs by competitive exam or educational qualification rather than nepotism became more common in Britain, America and continental Europe, in the second half of the nineteenth century and start of the twentieth. The industrial revolution created a demand for technical and scientific institutions and places of learning across Europe and North America, and the second industrial revolution of the 1880s, followed by the two world wars of the first part of the twentieth century, reinforced the expansion of a scientific-technical class increasingly drawn from non-elite backgrounds.

In most countries touched by industrial take-off the universities, initially, had little to do with the training of the new scientific and technical class, and this was especially true of England, where Oxford (established in 1096) and Cambridge (established 1209) remained the *only* universities well into the nineteenth century.

Most of the innovations associated with the first industrial revolution in Britain – from the formation of the Royal Society in 1660 to the key inventions such as James Hargreaves' spinning jenny (1764) or James Watt's steam engine (1775) – had nothing to do with England's fossilized 'Oxbridge duopoly'. Learned societies like the Lunar Society of Birmingham were far more intellectually significant. And although the philosopher John Locke graduated from Oxford in the mid-seventeenth century, having studied medicine, natural philosophy and philosophy, the Enlightenment too had only a limited impact on the two institutions, which remained dominated by the Anglican church and the teaching of theology and the classics (with some mathematics and natural sciences), until the latter part of the nineteenth century. Both Newton in the seventeenth century and Darwin in the nineteenth century attended Cambridge, but it left little intellectual mark on either of them. In the mid-eighteenth century, Adam Smith found Oxford intellectually stifling compared with Glasgow.

There were no formal entrance examinations for Oxford or Cambridge colleges until the mid-nineteenth century, but from the early nineteenth century you had to pass an exam in order to receive a degree. In the case of Oxford you had to show a knowledge of the Gospels in Greek, the Thirty-Nine Articles and Joseph Butler's *Analogy of Religion*. The development of the vocational professions (apart from clergymen and civil servants) and their training and examination systems happened largely independently of the two universities.

The first half of the nineteenth century in Britain saw the establishment of the Royal College of Surgeons, the Institution of Civil Engineers, the forerunner of the Law Society, the Royal Institute of British Architects, the Pharmaceutical Society of Great Britain, the Institution of Mechanical Engineers. The 1858 Medical Act established a national register of doctors, the qualification for which was a university degree or equivalent. And the 1860s and 1870s saw more such bodies established: the Royal Institution of Chartered Surveyors, the Institution of Electrical Engineers, the Royal Institute of Chemistry, the Institute of Chartered Accountants.[8]

These bodies were responsible for professional standards and ethics and in most cases for entry into the profession via public examination. By the 1880s exams had to be passed to become a barrister, solicitor, doctor, surgeon, clergyman, pharmacist, merchant navy officer, mining engineer, architect, chartered accountant and many more such professions. Competitive exams were also conducted for admission into the Home and Indian Civil Service and for a commission into the armed services.[9]

The story was broadly similar in the US, with local professional associations established in the first half of the nineteenth century and national ones in the second half of the century. Curiously, despite America's justified reputation in the nineteenth century for a rough and ready social equality and a weaker class structure than Europe, it was not until 1883 that civil servants were hired on the basis of exam results.

The American openness and opportunity that so appealed to French observer Alexis de Toqueville writing in 1835 – 'The first thing that strikes one in the United States is the innumerable crowd of those striving to escape from their original social position ... Every American is eaten up with a longing to rise' – was not especially connected to educational achievement. Benjamin Franklin began his career as an ordinary apprentice.

Nevertheless, the US did pioneer free elementary education in the middle of the nineteenth century, several decades before most European countries, and then free secondary education (normally to the age of sixteen) at the start of the twentieth century, with nearly half of the population graduating from high school by 1940. In 1944, as Britain's Education Act was catching up with America's mass secondary education system, America was pulling ahead again, with President Roosevelt signing the GI Bill, which ushered in mass *higher* education.

By the latter part of the nineteenth century and early twentieth century, academic selection and educational qualifications had become part of everyday life in much of Europe and North America, at least among the elites.

The respective roles of professional associations, universities and the state in certifying membership of the cognitive class played out differently in different countries. Similarly with the different degrees of prestige attached to the academic and the technical.

In Britain and America, with their shared common law heritage, the formation of professional organizations was largely a bottom-up story; in Germany and France it was more top-down, with the state and universities playing a bigger role. In France this was via the elite universities, the so-called Grandes Écoles, established by Napoleon and in Germany via civil service licensing. There was also more stress in those countries on technical and industrial disciplines inspired by the national goal of catching up with the first industrial pioneer over the Channel in England.

In England, as we have seen, most of the important developments were happening outside higher education, which remained subject to the stranglehold of Oxford and Cambridge. The numbers attending the two universities remained tiny, with the proportion of young people remaining roughly constant between the end of the English Civil War and the end of the First World War. Oxford and Cambridge used their political influence to stifle the creation of any rival institutions until the early nineteenth century. Mathematics was introduced at

Cambridge in the eighteenth century, but Oxbridge remained for most students a sort of upper-class finishing school. Instead of a network of local universities and colleges, as in most of the rest of Europe and the US, England had just two socially prestigious *national* seats of learning that students travelled to from across the country and then boarded at.

There is an amusing account of the amateurishness of the cognitive selection process in England in the 1860s by Sir George Kekewich, who had resisted his family's desire for him to become a clergyman and was reading for the Bar: 'So I was driven, as hundreds of other unemployed products of the Universities have been, to the legal profession, which appeared to be the only one, except the Church, for which I was not absolutely unfit.'[10] He had wanted to go into business, but business had decided that 'a knowledge of Greek, Latin, ancient history, and philosophy were not the best of foundations for a commercial life.' But before he could complete his legal studies he was offered the job of Examiner in the Education Department, an institution 'of the very existence of which I was previously unaware'. It seems that by 1868 the Northcote-Trevelyan reforms had made little headway, as Kekewich reports that the civil service was 'crowded by the dependents and friends, and friends of friends, of the Ministers in whose hands the patronage lay'.

Yet despite the irrelevance of Oxford and Cambridge in relation to the industrial revolution, the Enlightenment and the development of the professions, their social and political prestige – almost all British prime ministers were educated at one or the other in the eighteenth and nineteenth centuries – allowed them to establish themselves in the latter part of the nineteenth century, as they did finally modernize, at the centre of academic and educational life.

By the 1870s Oxford and Cambridge had succumbed, like other national institutions, to the reforming zeal of the Victorian upper-class moralists. They also became more affordable for the business and professional classes, though an Oxbridge education still cost around £200 a year, more than the annual income of a manual worker. The curriculum too began to modernize, especially at Cambridge, which became a key centre of scientific research after the foundation of the Cavendish laboratories in 1874. The great economist Alfred Marshall started teaching economics at Cambridge in 1884, although there was not an official economics course there until 1903.*

This modernization was also in response to the challenge to Oxbridge dominance from London. University College London was established by radical liberals, followers of Jeremy Bentham, in 1829 as a rational, secular, non-residential, meritocratic alternative to conservative, Anglican, residential, privileged Oxbridge. Influenced by both German and Scottish higher education models, UCL, and later King's, required both entrance exams and graduation exams. In 1858 London University external degrees were created so anyone in the country could get a high-level qualification and in 1878 it admitted women to full degrees.

Following this breakthrough, the end of the nineteenth century and start of the twentieth century saw the establishment of several new 'red-brick' universities serving the industrial cities of Manchester, Liverpool, Leeds, Sheffield and Birmingham. (The more traditional, clerical, and residential, Durham, had been founded in 1834.)

The 1870 Education Act in Britain introduced free elementary schooling for the whole population for the first time, catching up with the US, and the rest of Europe did the same around the same time (though literacy was already quite high in Britain and America prior to universal basic education). Secondary schooling was patchy in Britain even after the 1902 Education Act established a national system, but both public schools for the wealthy and state-aided schools of various kinds started, around this time, to formalize syllabuses and exams in conjunction with the universities.

Significantly, this was a mainly top-down process, with the pinnacle of Oxbridge and the London universities essentially standardizing learning lower down the system to fit with their own academic ethos and requirements. A story that remains true to this day in England with the continuing domination of A levels in the school system,

---

* My American grandfather eagerly signed up for one of the new economics courses at Cambridge just before the First World War, only to be told that his proposed tutor at Trinity College was away for the year. Trinity suggested an alternative young economist at King's but warned that he was not 'sound'. His name was John Maynard Keynes. My grandfather decided to study law instead.

designed purely for the purpose of entry into university and academic study.

In 1873 the Oxford and Cambridge Schools Examination Board was established to administer the exams for public schools and the emerging state grammar schools. The Board even took over some of the exams for students at local mechanics institutes. The dominance of Oxford and Cambridge was also reinforced through their scholarships for grammar school pupils, mainly to study classics.

England's historic bias against technical and vocational (Hand) education was evident not only in the universities but in the secondary schools too, which established a curriculum based on the traditional public school academic model. Robert Morant, the permanent secretary at the education department at the start of the twentieth century, was an academic traditionalist who resisted attempts to introduce more vocational elements into secondary education. The 1889 Technical Instruction Act had already expressly stated that schools should not be involved in the instruction of any trade or industry. There was, however, a parallel technical British tradition that worried about the educational roots of lost industrial competitiveness, especially after the Paris International Exhibition of 1867 and the loss of the dye-stuffs industry, an industry invented in England but developed by superior German chemists into an international monopoly. This technical tradition, often associated with protectionist thinking, had some influence too. In the late nineteenth century several official commissions expressed admiration for German technical education, and this influenced the curriculum at the new red-brick universities. It also led to the creation of several new technical colleges, in some cases opened by local authorities, and the founding of Imperial College in London.[11]

The trade unions were often hostile to technical education, preferring the time-served apprenticeship system. But a tradition of working-class self-improvement and education as the route out of poverty was found in the Workers Education Association and the idea of university 'extension' colleges in the new industrial centres. Toynbee Hall was established in east London in 1884 to take the gospel of education to workers and artisans, and Ruskin college at Oxford was founded in 1899. But educational historian Robert Anderson points out that the ancient universities mainly failed to respond to the 'yearning after knowledge of self-educated artisans' as described in Thomas Hardy's tragedy *Jude the Obscure* (1895).[12]

The tension evident in most education systems between prioritizing raising the general educational level and competence of the population and selecting an academic elite was largely resolved in favour of the latter in late-nineteenth-century England. The English university system had established itself as socially exclusive, partly because it was overwhelmingly residential and therefore expensive, and national, as opposed to local, in character. And the pedagogical tradition was theoretical and general rather than vocational and specific – knowing 'that' rather than knowing 'how'.

American writer Matthew Crawford describes the distinction:

> It corresponds roughly to universal knowledge versus the kind that comes from individual experience. If you know *that* something is the case then this proposition can be stated from anywhere. In fact such knowledge aspires to a view from nowhere . . . Occupations based on universal, propositional knowledge are more prestigious, but they are also the kind that face competition from the whole world as book learning becomes more widely disseminated in the global economy.[13]

The higher education story in America and the rest of Europe was somewhat different from England. At the time of the Enlightenment at the end of the eighteenth and beginning of the nineteenth centuries the best universities in Europe were probably in Scotland (St Andrews and Glasgow had both been established in the fifteenth century, Edinburgh in the sixteenth), though Germany was catching up fast, as the different states and principalities competed with each other to create the most prestigious seats of learning.

After Prussia's defeat by Napoleon, Wilhelm von Humboldt, the Education Minister, proposed a new type of university – the prototype of the modern university – that not only taught a social elite but also undertook research. The University of Berlin was founded in 1810 on these principles.

Meanwhile, in France, the French Revolution simply abolished the existing system of universities, replacing them with the Grandes Écoles, specializing in different skills such as engineering, which continue to exist today, alongside the public university system, educating much of the French higher elite, most notoriously in the tiny École Nationale d'Administration (ENA) established in 1945.

America's Ivy League emerged in colonial times partly because of the stranglehold of Oxbridge in England; Harvard was established in 1636. The Test Acts, which restricted Oxford and Cambridge to members of the Church of England, meant that non-Anglicans often looked to America for higher education, and in 1790, after the War of Independence, there were already nineteen institutions called a college or university.

The US system in the nineteenth century was decentralized and market-driven. Local civic pride and religious diversity created the incentive for a rash of smaller colleges to spring up all over the country. As David Labaree puts it: 'Colleges were founded with an eye toward civic boosterism, intended to shore up a community's claim to be a major cultural and commercial centre rather than a sleepy farm town.'[14] The total number of colleges in 1880 was an extraordinary 811 (at a time when England had fewer than ten) but the average number of students per institution was just 130.

Some of America's great universities, such as Johns Hopkins, founded on the German research university template, were already up and running at the end of the nineteenth century, but most universities avoided Oxbridge-style elitism and were local, middle-class institutions, relatively easy to get into and extensions of the local community. The Morrill Acts of 1862 and 1890 established the US's public state universities by granting land to states, who used it to establish colleges. Most of the 'land-grant' public colleges subsidized tuition, which further opened up higher education. Like the red-bricks in England the land-grant colleges tended to pursue a more applied curriculum than the private liberal arts colleges.

Technical and vocational education in the US had its strong supporters but tended, as in England, to play second fiddle to academic education. In 1917 the Smith-Hughes Act gave a big boost to vocational education, including federal funding. But John Dewey, the American philosopher and educationalist, in a famous debate with 'social efficiency' advocate David Snedden, was hostile to narrow skills training in favour of nurturing the intellectual capacity and critical spirit of all citizens. A version of the Dewey spirit has broadly prevailed in the US.

In England, more than in continental Europe (or Scotland), the idea of the gentleman generalist scholar pursuing knowledge for its own sake, as described by Cardinal Newman in *The Idea of a University* or Matthew Arnold in *Culture and Anarchy*, trumped that of the vocational specialist. The generalist intellectual tradition was also reinforced by the demands of empire. Colonial administration required capable polymaths, 'training the whole man', as a training manual for the Colonial Service described it, something that Germany with only a small overseas empire did not have to concern itself with.

The US, too, had a bias towards the generalist. People should be selected for higher education 'not for their suitability for specific roles but for their general worth, as if they were an updated Puritan elect,' wrote Nicholas Lemann in his gripping account of the rise of the American meritocracy, *The Big Test*.[15]

But England lagged way behind both Germany and the US in sheer numbers going to university and in the numbers doing technical subjects. At the turn of the twentieth century England had six universities compared to Germany's thirty and America's several hundred. Oxford remained strongly attached to the classics: in 1900 136 of its 297 academic fellowships were still in classics.

In the US the shortage of labour meant more capital-intensive industry. At the end of the nineteenth and start of the twentieth centuries the US roared ahead in mass production and machine tools, and the engineer, and technical education, enjoyed high status for a few decades. By contrast, England had a surplus of workers arriving in the cities out of the depressed countryside, which helped to create a more labour-intensive economy that was less mechanized and with less prestige attaching to technical education.[16]

The US also benefitted not only from secondary education to age sixteen from the end of the nineteenth century and a tradition of excellence in engineering but also from its pioneering management and business schools.

England on the eve of the First World War had roughly 25,000 university students compared with 60,000 in Germany and 150,000 in the US. In 1910 there were 16,000 engineering students in German technical high schools and just 4,000 in British universities. There were 5,500 graduate chemists in Germany and just 1,500 in Britain.[17] (Though it is true that the German population was around 25 per cent larger than England's and the US's, at 75 million, almost twice as large.)

In England the domination of Oxbridge continued into the twentieth century: on the eve of the Second World War the total student population had risen to 50,000, but 20 per cent were accounted for by Oxford and Cambridge alone. The Oxbridge model of the residential, academic community, pursuing knowledge for its own sake, apart from obviously vocational courses like medicine, remained the national ideal.

The red-brick universities in England, such as the College of Science in Birmingham or Owens College in Manchester, were mainly non-residential, for local students, and sponsored by local industrialists. They taught practical subjects alien to Oxbridge, such as metallurgy and mining engineering. Sheffield specialized in steel, Leeds in textiles, Liverpool in shipping. Yet many of the teachers and administrators were themselves Oxbridge-educated, and there was never a concerted attempt to establish an alternative national ethos of higher education in the provincial universities.

Student numbers trebled in Europe between 1870 and 1914, but, with the exception of more open America, most students continued to be drawn from a tiny, almost all-male, social elite. In England what they were studying, especially at the most prestigious institutions, was equipping them at best for the most ancient of professions. At the beginning of the twentieth century you needed Latin and Greek (and sometimes Hebrew) to get into most universities apart from the red-bricks; Latin was dispensed with as part of the entry requirement for Oxford and Cambridge only in 1960.

The world and its wealth-producing machine do today make greater cognitive demands both on ordinary people and elites than in the nineteenth and early twentieth centuries. The British and American economies would not work with the literacy levels of 1800. But at a time when we seem to fear for our national future if more than half of school leavers do not go on to university it is worth noting that between 1800 and 1950 Britain gave birth to an industrial revolution, governed a far-flung empire, saw vast increases in per capita income, introduced democracy and a welfare state and mobilized successfully to fight and win two titanic military conflicts (dominated by techno-logical competition) all with only the most rudimentary education for the vast majority of the population and very basic systems for selecting the most able. The most common selection system was life itself and how people performed in their allotted roles. Failure could be costly, as Admiral Byng famously discovered when he failed to prevent the French taking Menorca in 1756 and was court martialled and executed by firing squad.

Much of the above list would also apply to the US, minus the empire but with the added task of fashioning a new society from scratch. But some Americans worried that their country's democratic and class-less character had curdled into something much less attractive at the start of the twentieth century. Frederick Jackson Turner, the historian of the American West, argued that what had made the US a country of opportunity was the availability of land on the western frontier. With the frontier no more and cities filling up with collectivist-minded immigrants, this dream was over, he argued. Moreover, America had also produced a distinct Great Gatsby-style upper class.[18]

Nicholas Lemann shows in *The Big Test* how this analysis motivated the men behind the Educational Testing Service and the introduction of the biggest IQ-style tests in the western world, the Scholastic Apti-tude Test (SAT), designed to create a new meritocratic leadership for American society as it became the most powerful country in the world.

Approaching the mid-point of the twentieth century some of the groundwork has thus been laid for the great leap forward of the cogni-tive class that was to come in the latter part of that century (as I will describe in Chapter 4).

It was no longer a matter of merely 'putting yourself down' for Harvard in the US or Oxford in England, you now had to pass a com-petitive exam to get into elite academic institutions. Yet the social base of such institutions remained extremely narrow. As Charles Murray puts it, prior to the Second World War 'Harvard was full of rich kids with a few really smart ones, 50 years later it was full of really smart kids with a few merely rich ones.'[19]

England was even narrower in its elite university intake in the first part of the twentieth century and also had a more radical status divide than Germany or France between generalist academic forms of knowledge and specific practical forms. Nonetheless, the exam principle was firmly established in the lives of the upper and middle classes. Professional associations now monitored entry into both the higher and lower professions with tests of cognitive competence of various kinds alongside straightforward know-how.

By the 1930s the proportion of the adult male population in broadly defined professional occupations remained below 10 per cent in all rich countries, and the cognitive class was too small to have significant political or cultural influence. The world was still largely ruled by tradition, religious belief and the 'practical men' who, according to John Maynard Keynes, writing in 1936, 'believe themselves to be exempt from any intellectual influences, but are usually slaves of some defunct economist'.

Keynes was a member of the loose grouping of English intellectuals and artists known as the Bloomsbury Group whose avant-garde ideas and ways of life – 'they lived in squares, painted in circles and loved in triangles' as Dorothy Parker is said to have put it – had almost no impact on British society in the 1930s. Today their ideas are commonplace, an apt metaphor, perhaps, for the rise and rise of the cognitive class through the latter part of the twentieth century.

But before considering that history we need to pause to consider in greater depth what we actually mean by cognitive aptitude.

3

Cognitive Ability and the Meritocracy Puzzle

> To equate IQ with human virtue or wisdom or character, or a
> host of other measures of a person's value is ridiculous . . . IQ
> is equivalent to chip speed, and superior chip speed enables
> things that inferior chip speed will not enable. But that is true
> of almost any human attribute.
>
> *Charles Murray*

Human intelligence and ingenuity are at the core of modern civilization and will remain so. But it is *un*intelligent both for individuals and
societies to attach too much prestige, and reward, to just one kind of
human aptitude.

Why? Human dignity is part of the answer. Intelligence, for the
first time in human history, has become central to social stratification, but this has happened in an era in which rich societies are both
more democratic than ever before and place a high value on equality.
Given that intelligence, like wealth, is distributed unevenly, how can
we ensure that those blessed with more modest levels of cognitive ability, or who prefer to develop other aptitudes, receive their fair share
of dignity and respect, without overly constraining human freedom
or discriminating against the intelligent?

We cannot redistribute intelligence in the way we can wealth but
we can regard both as, in part, products of chance and only properly
exercised in society. Polly Mackenzie, a British political commentator,
puts it neatly:

> There are endless debates about whether ability comes from our genes,
> or the environment in which we are raised. It doesn't matter. The one

thing those two factors share is that you have no control over them. My parents gave me my genes, and they gave me my childhood. It would be as wrong for me to claim credit for my talents as it would be to let them go to waste. Talent, or merit, is an obligation as much as a gift.[1]

Another big reason for wanting to reallocate some of the prestige and reward away from cognitive ability is more pragmatic. If too many of those in the middle range of intelligence are encouraged to nurture mainly their cognitive skills, as has been happening with the rapid expansion of higher education in many rich countries, then the other aptitudes and skills that society needs will be neglected.

Placing a special value on cognitive ability in economically unequal societies seems fair and neutral, in part because it appears easy to measure. But it turns out that it is not so easy to measure. Or rather the qualities we admire in a rounded, intelligent person will only partly relate to raw cognitive functioning – what intelligence researchers call *general intelligence* or *g* – that is measured in IQ-type tests.

A person is unlikely to do well in exams or rise in an organization – whether an inner-city gang or a multinational corporation – without a decent measure of general intelligence. But that is a necessary not a sufficient condition of what one might call general human *capability*, which also requires social intelligence, judgement, imagination and so on. These are qualities that are only partially captured by IQ-type tests or, indeed, exams more generally. We know, for example, that some people with very high cognitive functioning, and usually very high IQs, are 'on the spectrum' for autism and often lack social intelligence. Most of us have no idea of our own IQ or that of the people we work with and know well, but we do have a sense of some people being 'brighter' than others. But it is not obvious that the people we regard as the brightest people in our social circles would also be those with the highest IQs.

There's no universally accepted definition of intelligence, but the following one, from the American psychologist Linda Gottfredson, is popular:

> Intelligence is a very general mental capability that, among other things, involves the ability to reason, plan, solve problems, think abstractly, comprehend complex ideas, learn quickly and learn from

experience. It is not merely book learning, a narrow academic skill, or test-taking smarts. Rather, it reflects a broader and deeper comprehension of our surroundings – 'catching on', 'making sense' of things, or 'figuring out' what to do.[2]

This is a wide and somewhat vague definition, but it does point to something that varies between people, that allows people to function well in the real world and is concerned with mental abilities. But it also distinguishes, as I have done above, between a broader, more intangible notion of intelligence and quantifiable 'test-taking smarts', the computational ability to retrieve, sift and apply information.

General intelligence, g, is evidently a real thing, and I describe some of the history behind it and the arguments that swirl around it below. How much is innate? Can it really be measured without cultural bias? But we should, in any case, treat it with caution and regard it as our servant, not our master, in human selection systems. It is only *part* of the story of human capability, as almost all intelligence researchers would accept. For intelligence in the broader sense is not only dependent on obvious things like the quality of your education but also on the general context of your life. Some examples.

Ben, the twenty-four-year-old son of an acquaintance, comes from a very academic family in London – both his parents are successful professionals, and his three brothers all went to good universities. But he rebelled against the academic pressure and failed his A levels. He ended up doing an aerospace apprenticeship near Bristol, leaving home to live in a bedsit. It was a testing time. He learned a lot during his three-year apprenticeship and was keen to go on learning, but there seemed few opportunities to progress, and two years later he quit and decided to do an aerospace engineering degree at the University of the West of England in Bristol. In 2019, having failed his A levels only a few years earlier, he passed his foundation year exams with a first-class grade and now wants to train to be a pilot when he graduates.

Like the biblical parable of the sower, in which some seeds fall on stony or thorny ground and others on fertile ground, it is the context of our lives that so often decides whether intelligence, or some other aptitude, develops or shrivels. People of exceptional talent – Shakespeare,

Mozart, Einstein – have some innate quality, some seed of greatness inside them, but it still needs fertile soil in which to grow.

My friend David Lucas, the children's author and illustrator, describes the less happy experience of his own father. He was a bright working-class boy who got into grammar school at a time when new opportunities were opening up in the 1950s. But where he lived, in Middlesbrough, the only employer was heavy industry. He wasn't suited to that and managed to escape to art school in London in the 1970s, even though he was by then in his mid-thirties and had five kids in tow.

> Metrosexual, trendy, arty London was just a step too far for him. He did his best to try to find a place for himself. I remember him listening to jazz and buying modern furniture trying to reinvent himself, but he couldn't really do it. He soon withered away, he couldn't get work and used to say, 'It's not what you know, it's who you know.' He retreated into bitterness and disappointment. My dad had the same genetic make-up at sixty as at thirty. But at thirty he had a wife who loved him, he had kids who looked up to him, he had his mum and dad rooting for him. He was on the up. He had none of those things at sixty. Our audience is crucial to how well we perform.

IQ, or raw ability of various kinds, has to be seen in so many dimensions and across time: blossoming and fading. Or, frozen until the sun shines, and it can suddenly bloom. Or, in many cases, just never being given the right conditions to bloom at all.

I can, with some trepidation, also illustrate this point by reference to my own life. I think I count as a relevant case study in the fluidity and context-dependency of intelligence. As a child and adolescent I never felt clever and have a dim recollection of taking part in an IQ test at school and coming out just a smidgeon above average. I was easily intimidated by my more confident and articulate peers, though I had a good memory (which probably helped with the IQ test) and so performed well enough academically at school up to the age of sixteen. A rebellious streak then appeared, which contributed to a disastrous performance in my A levels (D, E and fail) despite being educated at one of the most prestigious private schools in the country

(Eton). I benefitted from a second chance at a London crammer and squeezed into a decent university.

Five years after my A level disaster I got a first-class degree in history and politics from York University thanks, in part, to absorption in student Marxism. I was motivated to become interested in ideas and intellectual matters by guilt about my upper-class background and a vague desire to make the world a better place. Marxism provided an insecure and immature young man with a protective shield of certainty, and a reason to have a view about almost everything.

After getting a job as a trainee journalist on the local newspaper in York in my mid-twenties, a certain restlessness and maybe insecurity drove me to seek a higher-status job on a national newspaper in my late twenties, moving politically from far left to centre left (and now somewhere around the centre, depending on the issue) along the way. That eventually gave me the confidence to think for myself for the first time in my life. Almost thirty-five years later, I write books and get invited to express my opinions on television and radio and at academic conferences. So what happened?

Was it the gradual emergence of some innate general intelligence or the delayed influence of my privileged background? Clearly my background has helped. Not least it gave me a second chance after failing my A levels, which many people don't have. Yet none of my six siblings has followed a similar path. My father was a Conservative politician of independent mind, though a notoriously poor public speaker, and not present enough in my youth to discuss politics, or anything else. My mother was a pre-equality housewife who was capable and quick-witted but lacked much formal education.

The magic ingredient for my intellectual evolution was confidence, or what Carol Dweck calls the acquisition of a 'growth mindset'.[3] The belief – which so many people lack – that my own thoughts and ideas mattered acted as a kind of elixir, causing more and more of them to pop into my head. Everyone comes alive if they feel someone is interested in what they have to say; it's a dynamic process between speaker and listener, performer and audience. We all know people who make us feel dumb, and our lasting friendships or romantic attachments are usually with people who make us feel smart and witty and admirable (at least initially!). Was my evolution a kind of delayed onset of that infamous Etonian confidence? Or a need to prove myself to my high-achieving father? Maybe that is part of it, but I think just as plausible is that it followed on from achieving something in my own right, at least partly independently of the privileges of my background and schooling.

That something was leading a team that set up a magazine, *Prospect*, and finding, for the first time in my late thirties, something I could do really well, namely commission and edit essays on current affairs and intellectual themes. Successfully editing *Prospect*, a monthly magazine of ideas in 1995, also gave me a degree of personal prestige that I had never before enjoyed.

I now feel, in my early sixties, more intellectually alert than ever despite the fact that my memory is in decline and many of my other mental functions are slower and less reliable. But to offset that decline I have the accumulation of knowledge, and the lessons I have drawn from experience, to guide my thinking. Other aptitudes too have taken time to reveal themselves. I've always enjoyed singing but never regarded myself as able to sing since being turned down for the choir at school. Confidence and encouragement from friends have helped put that tuneless failure behind me, and in recent years I've been an active member of several singing groups.

Thinking about my own life for the purposes of this book has reminded me not only how context-dependent intelligence can be but also of the significant role played by chance in deciding a life course. One reason for that rebellious streak emerging in my late teens was the result of my first brush with failure: I failed to get into my school's first eleven cricket team. (It was a weak response to a minor setback, but I was glad to read many years later that John Strachey, a minister in the postwar Labour government, became a leading communist in the 1930s after also failing to get into the Eton first eleven cricket team!) If I had been slightly better at cricket, my life might have taken a more conventional course into banking or law. Similarly, a few years later, while at York university, I stood on the far left ticket for a full-time student union job and lost by just six votes. If I had won that vote I would have become immersed in the self-important world of left-wing student politics and might have ended up as a Labour MP or a full-time politician of some kind.

CAN WE MEASURE INTELLIGENCE?

Can intelligence, narrow or broad, be more or less accurately measured through tests? Most of the academics and researchers working in the field of cognitive intelligence are convinced that general intelligence or *g* is a real and partly innate thing, a product of both biology and subsequent environmental influence with around 50 per cent of the differences in *g*, between people, accounted for by genes.[4] They also think it can be measured accurately.

The most radical critics dismiss the whole idea of innate intelligence. But the more mainstream sceptics argue that *g* is only one aspect of a broader notion of human capability and that IQ-type tests are too narrow, too much of a snapshot and too far removed from real life to properly capture something so complex and social context-dependent, as I have argued above. Moreover, tests are biased towards those whose parents have been able to invest in them in various ways.

Let me be clear. This book is in part an argument about *the limits of cognitive meritocracy*. Even if intelligence of the most socially functional kind were something that *was* measurable and even if the cognitive meritocracy was fairly selected, without class bias, that would not in itself legitimize allocating such a disproportionate share of society's collective gains to the cognitive elite. Nevertheless, highly intelligent people are also socially useful and we all benefit from their work as we have seen in the Covid-19 crisis. They are also good at certain tasks – organization, innovation, scientific research – that are essential to modern societies and economies. There is therefore a utilitarian argument for rewarding smart people sufficiently, so they will perform those socially useful tasks instead of loafing around or getting rich through socially predatory activities such as crime. Moreover, even in a society of the future which did spread reward and status more evenly across different human attributes selection systems would still be needed to make sure the most appropriate people are being selected for the right jobs. For these reasons it is important for non-experts to try to understand at least some of the arguments that intelligence researchers make about cognitive ability and its distribution, and indeed to understand something of the history of intelligence research itself.

So what is *g*? *g* describes what is common in cognitive performance across a range of IQ type measures. An analogy would be with sporting ability: at school there were some people who were good at sport and if they were good at football they also tended to be good at rugby and cricket. That would reflect a high level of sporting *g*. Similarly with musical ability. Intelligence researchers say that test scores for cognitive *g* are more or less stable across a lifetime – unlike, for example, the Myers-Briggs personality tests – and that IQ performance has strongly predictive powers in many areas of life including educational and career success. They point to the several cognitive domains underlying the tests such as verbal comprehension, perceptual organization, processing speed and working memory. And researchers typically claim that tests based on these domains are among the most accurate in all of psychology.

The critics, mainly outside the field of intelligence research, point to the narrowness of the activities measured by IQ and the potential circularity of the claims, arguing that IQ tests have evolved to measure a form of ability that is defined by the tests themselves. Many critics also question the degree of innateness of *g* and want to place much more emphasis on the plasticity of intelligence and the importance of social class and other environmental factors, including pure chance, in shaping it. They point, for example, to the likelihood that a family history of being read to and talked to when young (or not) is likely to have a significant impact on verbal abilities. Some research has also found that material incentives can significantly increase test scores.

James Flynn, the academic whose work has revealed the existence of significant global IQ gains over time, stresses the environmental influence on *g*, though he would not deny that some people have more efficient thought processes than others. Flynn also points to the importance of human sub-cultures, both ethnic and class, some of which encourage cognitive pursuits more than others, in helping to explain average differences between groups. Average group IQ differences is probably the most controversial subject in the whole of social science and uncomfortably connects intelligence research to an earlier era when it was closely linked to eugenics and so-called scientific racism.

The study of intelligence in the nineteenth and part of the twentieth centuries did, indeed, attract people with a certain cluster of beliefs. 'They thought of intelligence as being by far the single most important human trait, and therefore the one around which society should be organized; they believed it was genetically inherited; they believed that the world's darker-skinned races were inferior in intelligence to its lighter-skinned ones; and they were concerned that unintelligent people were reproducing at a more rapid rate than intelligent ones, which would eventually bring down the IQ of the entire human species,' as Nicholas Lemann sums it up in his book *The Big Test*.[5]

Several generations later intelligence research is, however, now a respectable branch of psychology, and psychometric tests based on IQ are widely used in business and large organizations to select candidates for jobs. And the early twentieth-century origins of modern cognitive tests in Europe were actually provoked by a benign concern for children with learning difficulties at the dawn of mass free education.

The Binet-Simon test was created in 1905, when French psychologists were asked to determine which children might need more assistance at school. American psychologist Lewis Terman at Stanford University then revised the Binet-Simon scale, creating the Stanford-Binet Intelligence Scales (1916). The concept of IQ (intelligence quotient) was introduced by William Stern and used in this test. It became the most popular test in the US in the earliest part of the twentieth century and began to provide a single useable number.

The concept of g itself – that aspect of intelligence that can be detected in what remains constant between different tests – was invented in 1904 by British psychologist and army officer Charles Spearman.

The first large-scale use of intelligence testing was by the US army in the First World War to screen out those considered intellectually inadequate. Like many tests it was criticized for class and racial bias, but the US military continued to use variations of it in the Second World War and Vietnam War. Robert Yerkes and Lewis Terman, the main figures behind the US army testing programme, also carried their methods into education, where they became the basis for the Scholastic Aptitude Test or SAT, which continues to be central to entry into selective higher education in the US.

Today *g* is most commonly measured using the Wechsler Adult Intelligence Scale. The first version of this was published in 1955 by the American psychologist David Wechsler. The results from a ninety-minute examination of comprehension, vocabulary and arithmetic are combined to derive a final IQ score. The Wechsler test was substantially revised in the late 1960s, by Wechsler in collaboration with Alan Kaufman, in response to complaints of cultural and ethnic bias, especially from African Americans. Critics pointed to the fact that some test questions were merely testing acquired knowledge (for example, who wrote *Romeo and Juliet*?), rather than raw ability, and that children with a good maths education were going to perform better than equally bright children without one.

The revised tests turned out to be good at predicting certain things like school achievement, but the question is how useful is this and what does it tell us about something as big and fuzzy as intelligence? If *g*, as revealed by IQ-type tests, is just a form of pattern recognition should it be afforded such a large space in educational and career selection processes?

And that influence is still significant. In Britain the eleven-plus is an IQ-type test, but since the abolition of most grammar schools, and selection at eleven, IQ tests are not used routinely in schools. Nevertheless most eleven-year-olds when they move to secondary school are given something close to an IQ test (a CATs test), which is then used to sort them into sets and predict their future exam outcomes.

In the US some school districts do routinely use IQ tests for academic selection (though schools in California are barred from using them for certain placement decisions involving black students for fear of racial bias). And the SAT test in the US is sometimes described as a 'cousin' of the IQ test. It was first used in 1926 by the College Board, the association of twelve elite northeastern universities, and with the surge in college enrolment with the GI Bill after the Second World War as many as 800,000 people were taking it a year in the early 1960s. The SAT is the subject of heavy and persistent criticism, particularly from progressive and African American educationalists in the US, but it is still widely used – more than 2 million students took a SAT test in 2018, the highest number ever.

Both Britain with the eleven-plus and the US with the SAT test have a history of testing, or trying to test, for underlying *innate* ability rather than what you have learned. In the US it is still the case that high-school students are sorted according to 'scholastic aptitude' as measured by the SAT, with the highest scorers going to the most selective colleges.

Exams of a more conventional kind as used in France, Germany, indeed most countries, still select for an elite but not by trying to excavate some innate quality 'analogous to taking a blood-sample,' as Nicholas Lemann puts it. France, like most countries, has an Education Ministry that controls the school curriculum and then tests students on their mastery of it.

Critics of the IQ/SAT test, such as Lemann, say that the message of a national achievement test should be that life is about how hard you work and how much you learn – that is, what you accomplish – rather than about innate ability or the manipulation of supposed measures of innate ability.

Nevertheless, as noted, many corporations and public bodies throughout the developed world do use psychometric tests, mostly based on IQ principles, when selecting candidates for senior jobs. About three-quarters of organizations in the US with more than 100 employees rely on aptitude and personality tests for external hiring and the number is expected to rise in the next few years.[6]

Most mainstream intelligence researchers do acknowledge that *g* is just one form of intelligence that does not predict reliably for creativity, imagination or what is sometimes called social intelligence. The American intelligence researcher Christopher Chabris argues that 'there are neural systems which evolved for relating to other people which are distinct from the neural systems for more abstract reasoning'.[7]

Then there are also the personality traits that contribute both to intelligence and to the broader notion of being an effective or successful person: energy, drive, conscientiousness, leadership qualities, the wisdom to draw the right lessons from one's experiences, or the ability to defer gratification. People who might excel in some of these latter qualities could have average IQs. One American psychologist, Angela Duckworth, who has written extensively about the concept of 'grit', even claims that it is often a better predictor of success than IQ.

In a notably intemperate critique of IQ in early 2019, Nassim Nicholas Taleb, the financial market trader turned essayist, complained that it selects for 'exam-takers and paper shufflers' and that creativity and leadership correlate poorly with IQ because both are big-picture skills not mechanical pattern-recognition aptitudes.[8] His 'skin in the game' idea also implies that intelligence is only triggered by real-world motivations and cannot easily be replicated in a test. But like many critics, Taleb expresses open contempt for the whole idea of IQ based partly on the historical controversies surrounding classification by race and class and a visceral revulsion at the idea of reducing human beings to a number.

Many of the other challenges to the standard psychometric analysis of intelligence – such as James Flynn's observations about rising IQ scores around the world, Howard Gardner's theory of multiple intelligences, Daniel Goleman's notion of emotional intelligence, Robert Sternberg's concepts of practical, analytical and creative intelligence or Carol Dweck's ideas about mindsets – are less iconoclastic than Taleb and focus more on widening the meaning of intelligence than on assaulting the idea of IQ.

The 'Flynn effect' accepts that IQ tests have some utility but stresses the influence of the environment on test scores both for individuals and whole populations. Those who stress the environmental influence on IQ differences over time or between people often point to improvements to nutrition or health or education. Flynn goes further and argues that modernity itself confers cognitive skills relating to abstraction, symbolic thinking and classification that our ancestors lacked.[9] He showed that across a number of rich countries average IQ was rising at the rate of about three points a decade in the twentieth century.[10] His original paper showed an increase of fourteen points over forty-six years (1932 to 1978) in the US.[11] There is some debate as to whether the Flynn effect has halted, or even been reversed, in recent decades but no conclusive evidence.

The defenders of the innateness and heritability of IQ do not in general deny the reality of the Flynn effect but they have a simple answer: IQ is like height. Average height has been increasing around the world in recent centuries partly due to improvements in nutrition, but that does not affect differences in height between individuals or the innateness, or high heritability, of height.

Another challenge to the standard psychometric model comes from Howard Gardner and his theory of multiple intelligences, which was briefly popular in education circles in the 1980s.[12] Gardner supports the commonsense observation that different people are often good at different intellectual skills – someone is good at maths but poor at English and vice-versa – which itself challenges the g assumption that performance on one cognitive task correlates with performance on others. The theory of multiple intelligences also fits comfortably with the egalitarian 'all must have prizes' culture of much of modern education.

But there are two problems with the Gardner theory (which, unlike Flynn's work, is generally dismissed by intelligence researchers). First, he provides no empirical evidence for the idea of multiple intelligences. Second, he proposes eight separate intelligences to replace the g of mainstream psychometric research, but these are his own inventions and have not arisen from close observation of human behaviour. The eight intelligences are: musical-rythmic; visual-spatial; verbal-linguistic; logical-mathematical; bodily-kinesthetic; interpersonal; intrapersonal; naturalistic.

Gardner's theory may have been widely repudiated, but the idea underlying it remains an intuitively attractive one, and the theory has inspired other attempts to loosen the grip of general intelligence such as Raymond Cattells's fluid and crystallized intelligence.

Indeed, the wider culture remains suspicious of the idea of the innateness of intelligence, preferring to attribute success to opportunity, luck or self-improvement. Malcolm Gladwell's book *Outliers* popularized the idea that 10,000 hours of practice was needed to become world class in any field. Intelligence levels can, indeed, depend on how much you actually use your brain. The American academic Melvin Kohn showed back in 1974, in a paper in the *American Sociological Review*, that dull, routine jobs really can make you dumber while cognitively complex work makes the people doing it smarter – the test scores of people doing these different kinds of jobs falling and rising, respectively, over time. He and collaborators replicated it in Japan in the 1980s and Poland in the 1990s.

This also helps to explain the increase in average IQ in Ireland between the 1970s, when it was still an overwhelmingly agricultural country with a lower average IQ than England, to a highly educated, mainly urbanized society with a higher average IQ than England today.

Mainstream intelligence researchers are not opposed to the commonsense idea that talents, and even IQ scores, can be improved with training – just as muscles can be built up by weightlifting – but would claim that those with high innate ability would reach master level more quickly than those of lower ability.

All behaviour is a mix of innate, inherited traits and the environment. Yet, to repeat, if the classic IQ tests and the exams that are based on them, like the SAT test in the US, are testing just one network in the brain and are too narrow to have much to say about creativity, imagination or empathy, then they are of limited use as a signalling device to employers or elite college admissions staff. And what about the impact of personality traits on test and exam performance? Some people do less well in exams because they lack self-control or perform less well under time pressure. Indeed, it is now widely acknowledged that girls and women on average do better in exams because of their greater ability to apply self-control compared with boys and men.

The historical record is littered with highly successful people, including people of considerable intellectual accomplishment, such as Alan Rusbridger, the former editor of the *Guardian* newspaper, Ben Pimlott, the late historian, Richard Blundell, the economist tipped for a Nobel prize, who failed their eleven-plus or equivalent life-determining exams or who performed poorly at school or college. A leading intelligence researcher in the US, Dr Scott Barry Kaufman, had a hearing disorder as a child and was classified as needing special educational support. Similarly, Robert Sternberg, mentioned earlier, now rated sixtieth most eminent psychologist of the twentieth century by the American Psychological Association, got a dunce-level IQ score in second grade.

Moreover, we also all know many people who are very capable in some areas of life and flail around in others – 'kinda dumb and kinda smart' as Bobby Goldsboro sang of his sadly deceased Honey – perhaps especially men, who sometimes score highly on cognitive functions but are emotionally stupid in ways that are damaging to themselves and those around them. And anyone who has spent time in a university will know that there are plenty of people with impressive academic credentials who do not seem very bright (what Nassim Nicholas Taleb has called IYIs: intellectuals yet idiots).

None of this is to deny that *g* captures *something* significant; nor is it to deny that there are real differences in more general intellectual aptitude between individuals. Just ask anyone who has had long experience of teaching people or indeed managing people.

The standard bell-curve for IQ in a country like Britain today has, as already mentioned, about 70 per cent of the population hovering around the average in the 85 to 115 range, with about 15 per cent highly gifted and 15 per cent struggling to keep up. Would we regard it as a successful outcome of our social and educational selection systems if most of the gifted 15 per cent, at least in IQ terms, were finding their way into the most important jobs? Toby Young, the journalist and educationalist, has written: 'All things being equal, a country's economy will grow faster, its public services will be run better, its politicians will make smarter decisions, diseases are more likely to be eradicated, and so on, if the people at the top possess the most cognitive ability.'[13] But surely that will not be the case if cognitive ability just means those who score highest on psychometric and IQ-type tests. Moreover, the 15 per cent will have a very similar experience of the world, and it will not be same as the 85 per cent, which is likely to be sub-optimal if you are creating policy for that 85 per cent.

A final observation in this section. David Robson, a British science journalist, described in his book *The Intelligence Trap* how very smart people, by test standards, often have real problems understanding risks and weighing up evidence. This, he argues, is not just about 'absent minded intellectuals', it is a case of 'smart people, by test standards, often lacking *rational* judgement and common sense'.[14] Indeed, people with high IQs can use their extra brainpower to rationalize erroneous beliefs and to dismiss the contradictory evidence that disagrees with their worldview, which is why climate change deniers and conspiracy theorists are often people of higher cognitive ability. Similarly, a Google engineer wrote a fascinating blog about the very smart, successful people around him whose over-confidence gave them the dangerous 'ability to convincingly rationalize nearly anything'.[15] And the idea that, even for highly educated people, our emotions and intuitions take precedence over our reason has become commonplace, thanks to the work of Jonathan Haidt (*The Righteous Mind*), Daniel Kahneman (*Thinking, Fast and Slow*) and others.

To summarize so far: cognitive ability is a real and measurable thing, but the cognitive ability-based sorting machine does not always get things right because of the difficulty of capturing something as elusive as intelligence in narrowly based tests. Moreover, many of the qualities that even advanced technological societies need to function well, and to do so fairly, do not feature at all in narrower definitions of intelligence – effort, empathy, virtue, imagination, courage, caring ability.

Perhaps part of the answer is in our use of language and labelling. It would surely be sensible to distinguish between what Linda Gott-fredson called 'test-taking smarts' and a broader notion of human capability. If we called the first 'cognitive function' and reserved the word intelligence for that broader notion of human competence and capability it would capture more accurately the kind of distinctions we want to make in selecting people for different roles. Entry into the higher levels of the cognitive class would still require a high level of cognitive function, but that would be a necessary but not sufficient condition of success. In the real world this is, in fact, what usually happens. Initial entry into an increasing number of jobs requires strong performance in exams and often IQ-type tests too, especially in the UK and US, but thereafter success in an organization depends on a broader notion of emotional intelligence and psychological aptitude.

I now want to consider two enormous questions. How heritable is intelligence? And how open is selection into the cognitive class?

NATURE AND NURTURE

First, to underline my main argument: whether a broad or narrow IQ-based form of intelligence is used to select for elites, whether intelligence (broad or narrow) is substantially heritable or not, whether or not we are moving towards a self-reproducing cognitive elite – these are all secondary issues compared with my main concern, which is to spread status and rewards more evenly across the Head, Hand, Heart range of human aptitudes. There has been a misallocation of both financial and psychological rewards to cognitive ability, broad *and* narrow. Establishing a fairer scramble to occupy the senior positions within the cognitive class does nothing to increase the status and pay of an exceptional care worker. The American conservative Charles Murray puts it well at the start of the chapter: high IQ does not equal wisdom or virtue.[16]

One might also want to argue that if the evidence shows that the cognitive ability that leads to success is substantially *inherited*, either genetically or culturally, from parents, then while society should not try to handicap the cognitively successful, in some parody of communism, neither should it excessively reward them as if the outcomes are merited purely by individual effort.

In the ancient argument between nature and nurture, nature seems to have stolen a march in the past few years. Physical traits such as height have always belonged to nature, but thirty years ago psychology and personality were thought to be mainly the product of environment. Yet genes are now said to account for around half of psychological differences, from depression to intelligence and school attainment, and even weight is about 70 per cent heritable, according to Robert Plomin, one of the leaders of the behavioural genetics movement.[17] These things, Plomin says, have been long established by twin and adoption studies, but now with the sequencing of the human genome we can detect the actual genetic basis of human difference, not through a single gene for this or that but through thousands of small differences that can be aggregated together to predict psychological propensities, so-called 'polygenic scores'.

This issue presents a challenge for our traditional thinking about many moral and political issues. The left's stress on the centrality of the social environment to individual outcomes and the right's ideals of personal responsibility are both discomforted by these findings.

Plomin himself is a politically liberal, softly spoken American, and when I met him recently he came across as anything but an old-school 'you can't buck nature' conservative. He strives to make us feel unthreatened by his claims by pointing out that if the first law of genetics is that like begets like, the second law is that like does not beget like, and genes are 'probabilistic propensities not predetermined programming'. He is, however, far too much of a genetic determinist for some fellow scientists, and a review in the journal *Nature* slammed his recent book, *Blueprint*, pointing out that in education the significance of good teaching as well as diet and home conditions 'have been established irrefutably'. And surely childhood trauma, such as losing a parent, and plain bad parenting, can leave a big mark too.

Plomin does not deny any of those points but the argument with the *Nature* reviewer arises out of that contentious history, mentioned earlier, that still makes many people wary of the discipline of intelligence research in general and behavioural genetics in particular. Many early researchers into the heritability of human traits in the nineteenth and early twentieth centuries were proponents of eugenics, and some were unashamed racists. The Nazi-eugenics association further discredited heritability research immediately after the war.

Then in 1963 an article in *Science* reviewed twin and adoption studies and concluded that genetic influence was important in IQ scores, tentatively restoring some respectability to genetic research into behaviour.[18] But this new respect for genetics was reversed in 1969 when the intelligence researcher Arthur Jensen published a paper that was sceptical about the impact of early years education – something that had widespread bipartisan support in the US to reduce race and class inequality – and he went further and suggested that IQ differences between races might be down to genetic factors. A few years later the American psychologist Richard Herrnstein argued in a magazine article that IQ differences between classes might be genetic in origin too. These publications caused outrage and entrenched the hard environmentalist position for two decades or more.

One beneficial side effect of the decades-long pariah status of behavioural genetic research is that it raised the quality threshold for research in the field. Many more rigorous large-scale twin and adoption studies emerged in the 1980s and 1990s showing substantial genetic influence on intelligence. This was through studying identical twins who share the same genes but have been raised apart in very different environments and yet often display similar aptitudes, interests and personality traits. The findings became hard to ignore and have been partly confirmed by the more recent sequencing of the human genome. As previously noted, among behavioural geneticists, if not in the wider society, it is now widely accepted that about half of the variance in measures of intelligence, as traditionally defined, is accounted for by genes.

In fact, for various reasons the genetic influence is only about 20 per cent in infancy, rising to 40 per cent in childhood and 60 per cent in adulthood. This is partly because of what Robert Plomin has called the 'nature of nurture', meaning that genes and environment interact with each other and that how we select, modify and create environments is also based on our genetic propensities. So even something like the amount of television watching that a child does, which used to be seen as the classic example of an environmental influence, turns out to be partly down to heritable traits too.

Critics point to methodological problems with twin studies and the obvious influence of class and family background. But geneticists do not deny a substantial role for environment or that normal child development requires a basic level of responsible care. Seriously deprived or abusive environments are bound to have a negative impact on development, including intellectual development. Indeed, Plomin, and other geneticists, stress that cognitive function is *only* about 50 per cent inherited and point out that the principle of 'reversion to the mean' means that very clever people often have only averagely clever children.*

It is also a commonplace among geneticists and intelligence researchers to claim that high IQ is robustly associated not only with measures of socio-economic status – education, occupational prestige and income – but health and longevity too. The main debate is about the direction of causality, or how much the economic investment of affluent, well-educated parents contributes to the IQ scores of their children.

An important recent study of the 'genetics of success' looking at genetic associations with educational attainment and social mobility provided a mixed picture. The study, led by Daniel Belsky, consisted

---

* The nineteenth-century polymath Francis Galton observed that the offspring of parents who lie at the tails of a distribution will tend to lie closer to the centre.

of five longitudinal studies testing 20,000 individuals in the US, Britain and New Zealand.[19] The authors concluded that participants with higher polygenic scores achieved most education and career success but they also tended to come from better-off families. Nevertheless, participants with higher polygenic scores tended to be upwardly mobile compared with their parents, and siblings with the highest polygenic score were the most upwardly mobile. So polygenic scores are not merely the product of advantages provided by background.

THE FLAWED MERITOCRACY

So one might say that it is not private tutors or genes that determine your success but both. It is indisputably true that educational and career success remains strongly connected with privilege and class background in all developed countries, though in some more than others. In Britain, although the dominance of the privately educated in the political, economic and cultural elite has weakened somewhat in recent decades, particularly in politics and business, it remains strong. And most social mobility researchers would agree that the main advantage conferred by a privileged background is a high floor for those of average or below-average ability. To express it as an equation: average cognitive ability + privilege = better chance of a high-status occupation. As James Bloodworth has put it in his book *The Myth of Meritocracy*, 'Environmental mechanisms exist that can turn a dull child into an average one and an average child into a successful one.'[20]

Nevertheless, there is also strong evidence for Britain being a more socially mobile and, indeed, meritocratic society than most people realize. The most recent research by Oxford sociologists Erzsébet Bukodi and John Goldthorpe finds that almost 80 per cent of adults move at least one class category relative to their parents, either up or down. Britain, they conclude, is not a low-mobility country.[21] A 2018 paper using the 1970 British Cohort Study also found that 63 per cent of people in the highest social class originated from lower down the social scale. And those in the top quartile of cognitive scores at age ten were relatively likely to achieve top social class positions (28 per cent) compared to those in the bottom quartile (5.3 per cent).[22]

Long-range mobility is, of course, harder than short-range mobility, and people from higher-class backgrounds do have a significant advantage in achieving high-status positions. But Bukodi and Goldthorpe also find a significant role for both cognitive and non-cognitive ability in determining mobility into the highest social classes. They find that there has been no significant fall-off in mobility in recent years, as is often claimed, but thanks to a slow-down in the number of new middle-class professional jobs there is 'less room at the top', so there has been more downward than upward mobility. Education, they argue, has not played a significant role in boosting mobility, and indeed may have restricted it, partly because higher education has been so dominated by the middle class and because better-off families can buy extra educational support of various kinds. Formal qualifications are used by employers as a signal of competence but seem to be less important for long-term career success than demonstrating capability on the job.

Economists from the LSE who looked at income, rather than the occupational position favoured by sociologists, found 40 per cent of children born in 1958 to fathers in the bottom income quartile rose to the top two, whereas for those born in 1970 the figure had fallen to 33 per cent.[23] That paper, published in 2005, helped to trigger a debate about a 'slump' in social mobility in Britain, when in fact what it revealed was a much higher level of it than most people would have expected. One of the main reasons given for the fall in upward mobility was a middle-class monopolization of higher education, yet one of the main policy levers favoured by politicians to *increase* upward mobility has been more higher education.

So, there are moderate levels of social mobility in Britain despite the fact that average-ability children from more affluent backgrounds do better than they should in a true meritocracy. According to mobility researcher Peter Saunders, about 41 per cent of middle-class children in the lowest IQ quartile end up in the top two social classes. But he also argues that almost 70 per cent of people in the top IQ quartile reach the top two classes irrespective of class background.[24] 'Performance in an IQ test at age 10 predicts a child's eventual social class destination about three times better than their parents' social class does. Class origins do have some effect on academic and occupational outcomes . . . but ability trumps class background,' according to Saunders.

So, if social mobility is at least partly driven by cognitive function and if, in turn, that is around 50 per cent inherited, one might already expect a proportion of people at the top to be there on cognitive merit and for many of their children to remain there too. One might also, therefore, expect average ability levels to start to vary between broad social classes and for Michael Young's nightmare of a *hereditary cognitive elite* to have come closer.

Young's dystopian futuristic fantasy *The Rise of the Meritocracy*, written in 1958 (and rejected by most publishers), describes Britain's progression to a radical meritocracy in the period 1870 to 2033 via extreme education reforms and annual IQ tests: 'By 1990 or thereabouts all adults with IQs of more than 125 belonged to the meritocracy. A high proportion of the children with IQs over 125 were the children of these same adults. The top of today are breeding the top of tomorrow to a greater extent than at any time in the past. The elite is on the way to becoming hereditary; the principles of heredity and merit are coming together.'[25]

This is in fact what psychologist Richard Herrnstein and political scientist Charles Murray *did* argue about the American experience in their controversial book *The Bell Curve* (1994). They said that the correlation between intelligence and socio-economic status has become stronger in America since the 1950s as access to higher education has become broader and more competitive and the economy has become more knowledge-based, and that this was particularly the case at each end of the IQ distribution curve. They did not claim that a person's IQ is the sole determinant of whether they succeed or fail, only that it's an increasingly important factor. 'Even as recently as mid-century, America was still a society in which most bright people were scattered throughout the wide range of jobs. As the century draws to a close, a very high proportion of that same group is now concentrated within a few occupations that are highly screened for IQ.'[26]

From the 1950s onwards college students were being selected ever more efficiently for their high IQ. By the beginning of the 1990s about

80 per cent of all people in the top quartile of IQ-measured ability continued to college after high school.

At the pinnacle of American society, they argued, there is a 'cognitive elite'. Typically, members of this group possess IQs of 125 and above, have postgraduate degrees from good universities and belong to a handful of 'high-IQ professions' such as accountants, engineers and architects, college teachers, dentists, physicians, mathematicians and scientists. According to their analysis, someone with an IQ of 130 has a less than 2 per cent chance of living in poverty, whereas someone with an IQ of 70 has a 26 per cent chance.[27]

Others have found similar relationships. Tino Sanandaji, from the Research Institute of Industrial Economics, has drilled down into a dataset tracking a representative sample of the US population and discovered that those with IQs above 120 typically earn twice as much as those with average IQs. Christopher Chabris, professor of psychology at Union College in New York state, estimates that a random person with above-average intelligence has a two-thirds chance of earning an above-average income, while a random person of below average intelligence has only a one-third chance.

So it seems that there is strong evidence that increased levels of cognitive selection into higher education and the higher professions has helped to shape a cognitive class over the past seventy years, reinforced by 'assortative mating' in which like increasingly attracts like in marriage and partnering. Bright men and women were attracted to each in the past too, but fifty years ago there were far fewer women at elite universities or in higher professional jobs, so the very brightest were less likely to meet up. Male doctors often married female nurses and male businessmen often married female secretaries.

According to *The Economist*,

In 1970 only 9 per cent of those with bachelor's degrees in America were women, so the vast majority of men with such degrees married women who lacked them. Now the numbers are roughly even (in fact women are earning more degrees) and people tend to pair up with mates of a similar educational background ... And in 1970, fewer than 5 per cent of American lawyers were female. Now the figure is 34 per cent, and nearly half of law students are female. So highly educated, double-income power couples have become far more common. The children of such couples have every advantage, but there are not many of them.[28]

There has been a similar pattern in other rich countries. Social class and educational background have tightened their grip on marriage in the UK in recent decades. According to research by the IPPR think tank, 39 per cent of women born in 1958 married a partner in the same social class, rising to 56 per cent for those born twenty years later.[29] David Willetts, the former Conservative minister, argued in his book *The Pinch* that such assortative mating has contributed to a slowing of social mobility. 'If advantage marries advantage then we must not be surprised if social mobility suffers . . . increasing equality between the sexes has meant increasing inequality between social classes. Feminism has trumped egalitarianism.'[30]

Charles Murray returns to this theme in his more recent book *Coming Apart: The State of White America, 1960–2010*. 'The reason that upper-middle-class children dominate the population of elite schools,' he writes, 'is that the parents of the upper-middle class now produce a disproportionate number of the smartest children.'[31] He says that 87 per cent of college-bound seniors who scored above 700 in their SAT in 2010 had at least one parent with a college degree, with 56 per cent of them having a parent with a graduate degree. He concludes: 'Highly disproportionate numbers of exceptionally able children in the next generation will come from parents in the upper-middle class, and more specifically from parents who are already part of the broad elite.'

The children of those in the top 4 per cent of earners in the US, those earning at least $200,000 a year, score on average 250 points higher on SAT tests than the children of people on median incomes who, in turn, score on average 125 points higher than those on low incomes. Princeton and Yale take more students from the top one per cent of the income distribution than the bottom 60 per cent.[32]

But it is the top 20 per cent in the US, not just the super-rich, who have enjoyed a disproportionate slice of the increased national income of the past forty years and dominated the highest rungs of the educational ladder, according to Richard Reeves. The children of the top income quartile are represented in the top 150 most competitive colleges in the US by a ratio of fourteen to one over those in the bottom income quartile.[33] It is a similar story in the UK: the most advantaged 20 per cent of young people are seven times more likely to attend one of the top Russell Group universities than the most disadvantaged 40 per cent.[34] So the US and the UK – where most of this research has been done – appear to have established very partial and flawed meritocracies. Higher socio-economic-status families tend to have higher polygenic scores on cognitive functions, which is what one might expect from a society that is at least somewhat meritocratic, given significant heritability of cognitive aptitudes *combined* with the ability of the affluent to invest in their children.

There is less of this kind of social mobility research in France and Germany. But the comparative work of Richard Breen looking at the US, France, Germany, the Netherlands and Sweden sees a broadly similar pattern between countries and, as in the UK, signs of the higher upward mobility of the 1960s and 1970s slowing down thanks to fewer new professional jobs being created.[35]

There is some other comparative work that suggests a lower correlation between parental socio-economic status and educational outcomes in Germany than in the US. In the case of France, as we will see in the next chapter, there is evidence of a strong hereditary meritocracy, with around two-thirds of students in the most prestigious Grandes Écoles coming from the highest social class.

There is, as one would expect, a weaker correlation between IQ and educational success for children from disadvantaged backgrounds. The ability of the privileged to tilt the balance in their favour by investing more in their children means they can thwart the emergence of a more fairly meritocratic society, as we have seen. But there appear to be natural limits on the extent to which the privileged can tilt the *genetic* balance in favour of their descendants. So the Michael Young nightmare of an ossified hereditary cognitive meritocracy is unlikely to fully materialize.

Murray estimates, in *Coming Apart*, that there will always be 14 per cent of children in the top 5 per cent of the IQ distribution curve who are the offspring of parents with below-average IQs. Others argue for much higher levels of genetic shuffling. Regression to the mean, meaning clever parents will sometimes have average children, still operates, even if it has been slowed somewhat by assortative mating and educational investment. Overall, the evidence for the emergence of a hereditary cognitive meritocracy remains tentative and is contested.

For example, Andrew Hacker, a teacher of political science and maths at Queens College, New York, writes: 'We know that well-off and otherwise accomplished parents can give their children a good start, or at least try. So the next question is how these presumably favoured offspring fare as adults. Such studies as we have suggest that early advantages don't always last.'[36] Ron Haskins at the Brookings Institution, following top-quintile youngsters, was surprised to find that only a little over half obtained college degrees.

A friend of mine who lives near Manchester, and is himself an educationalist, agreed with this observation based on his own experience:

> My third son is fifteen and goes to a selective grammar school. I am sufficiently in favour of selection to allow him to go, but sufficiently cantankerous about fair competition to refuse to pay for a tutor. He passed the exam and arrived at the school, and out of his whole year, only he and one other boy had not had a tutor, with parents often hiring them for up two years before the eleven-plus exam. But what subsequently happened is that some of the boys who passed the eleven-plus then struggled to keep up as they progressed through the school. They were already on the first rung of the cognitive elite ladder but in some cases were no cleverer than kids who failed the test.

Even for people who do score highly on IQ-type tests there are usually so many other things going on in determining whether someone enjoys a successful career or happy life that IQ-determinism is rarely justified.

David Robson, author of *The Intelligence Trap*, underlines the importance of factors other than cognitive function in successful careers:

> If you consider surveys of lawyers, accountants or engineers, for instance, the average IQ may lie around 125 – showing that intelligence does give you an advantage. But the scores cover a considerable range, between 95 and 157. And when you compare the individuals'

73

success in those professions, those different scores can, at the very most, account for around 29 per cent of variance in performance, as measured by managers' ratings.[37]

But the most convincing recent challenge to the *Bell Curve* analysis of a self-reproducing meritocratic elite comes from American sociologists Dalton Conley and Jason Fletcher.[38] They argue that Herrnstein and Murray simply did not have sufficient data on population genetics in the early 1990s to come to some of the conclusions they did about meritocracy ossifying into a sort of 'genotocracy'. Conley and Fletcher look at whether genetic traits relating to intelligence have become more heritable over the course of the twentieth century as assortative mating has increased. In 1960 32 per cent of men with college bachelor's degrees married women with degrees; in 2000 65 per cent did. But they conclude that there has been *less* sorting by genetic inheritance as educational opportunity has risen (they argue that is true of Sweden too). The Conley and Fletcher findings suggest that there is less genetic stickiness between generations than assumed in the *Bell Curve*.

So the question of how fairly selected for and how fluid the cognitive class is remains messy and complex. Nevertheless, a combination of genetic inheritance, parental support of various kinds and a much greater emphasis on educational selection processes for everyone is likely to be shaping a somewhat more entrenched cognitive meritocracy than fifty years ago. To many meritocrats, and many of those who thrive in a knowledge-based society, this just seems like common sense. The meritocracy may always be tilted somewhat towards the affluent and well-connected but so long as it is sufficiently open, the most able people will rise into the higher cognitive roles, benefitting themselves and the wider society.

But is that just the self-interest of a nascent cognitive caste speaking? The alternative view is put pithily by American philosopher Tim Sommers: 'Even if you don't mind the tyranny of the talented, just wait, it will become the tyranny of the talented's children.' And, in any case, even a relatively open cognitive meritocracy still leaves a significant minority, if not a majority, in knowledge-based societies feeling excluded or with non-cognitive aptitudes that do not command sufficient respect and reward. What is to be done? One way of considering the issue is through listening in to a cross-generational debate within the Young family.

THE COGNITIVE VEIL OF IGNORANCE

Toby Young, the British journalist and educationalist quoted earlier, has recently taken an intense interest in these debates on a different side to his father, the late socialist intellectual Michael Young, author of both the radical 1945 Labour Party manifesto and then twelve years later the anti-meritocracy satire *The Rise of the Meritocracy*. Young Junior is a pugnacious fifty-five-year-old, educated at state schools and Oxford, who for the first part of his career was a troublemaking journalist. In recent years the bespectacled Young has appeared to want to follow in his father's intellectual footsteps, albeit espousing very different views, and has become a more serious, if controversial, figure in the London educational and political world and set up his own state school in the capital.

Michael Young was an egalitarian who opposed the idea of equality of opportunity because it was about the opportunity to be unequal. He argued, like other egalitarians such as philosopher John Rawls, that the intelligence and capability you are born with is the result of a 'natural lottery' and no more deserved than the wealth that a rich person might inherit. Toby Young is a classical liberal who believes in equal rights, equal treatment and equal opportunities, but not equality of outcome, because he believes the latter can only be achieved at too high a human cost. 'I like meritocracy for the same reason that my father disapproved of it: because it helps to secure people's consent to the inequalities that are the inevitable consequence of limited government. I say this not as someone fond of inequality but as someone who believes limited government is preferable to a large coercive state.'

How does he believe that meritocracy achieves this goal? First, by creating a society which is dynamic and wealthy because talents are put to good use. Second, by allocating wealth and prestige in a way that at least appears to be fair, or fairer than the alternatives. Third, by creating opportunities for at least some people born on the wrong side of the tracks. But there is also a danger that a creeping hereditary

meritocracy and an overshoot in the status attached to cognitive aptitudes could destroy the consent for a free society just as his father
predicted in the closing scene of his book *The Rise of the Meritocracy*,
when the resentment of those excluded from the cognitive class boils
over, and they rise up violently against their oppressors.

So which Young is right, the elder or the younger? Looked at
through one lens, the knowledge society, the expansion of higher
education and the creation of a large cognitive class of almost one-
third of the population is a process of opening, democratization and
inclusion. And looked at in both historical terms or internationally
– just consider the recent success of Singapore and China, which
has been driven at least in part by the principle, if not the practice,
of cognitive meritocracy – it should surely be considered a success.*
But, as Michael Young was keenly aware, one person's inclusion is
another's exclusion. The psychological pain and resentment created
by that exclusion, combined with the higher democratic expectations
of modern citizens, is one of the factors behind the current political
alienation.

Generally speaking, high cognitive ability is a desirable attribute.
Indeed, it is such a desirable attribute that it might be said to be
its own reward. The ability to understand one's environment and to
pick up new skills quickly does not necessarily require the additional
rewards that society has been granting the cognitively able in recent
decades. In any case, to repeat, high intelligence may be a highly
desirable attribute but it is not the only one. It does not make anyone
a good or likeable or honest or conscientious or compassionate or cou-
rageous or contented person. And yet increasingly parents will go to
great lengths to ensure that their children can pass into the graduate
class even if they do not have the cognitive ability or personal attributes to properly benefit from a three- or four-year degree course. This
is creating an epidemic of square pegs in round holes.

---

* According to Professor David Goodman of the University of Sydney, a joint study
conducted by researchers at BeiDa and Australian National University found that
Chinese women's occupation, status and wealth is almost completely determined
by their father's occupation and status. For men, that determination is about 80
per cent.

If respect for intelligence were tempered by a broader valuing of human abilities, then it might also be easier to be more honest about some of the discoveries about human aptitude emerging from genomics research. And that could, in turn, make it easier to help to fit people's cognitive and psychological propensities, as revealed by that research, to the most suitable jobs and occupations and for society, more generally, to be more accepting of people for who they are.

Natural abilities are distributed unequally, but in rich democracies the outcomes of such inequality are constrained by our moral and political beliefs and institutions, above all our belief that all humans are morally and politically equal. A gradual rearrangement of current trade-offs to produce a more even distribution of status – while avoiding false egalitarian extremes – is the most desirable direction of travel for rich countries.

The philosopher Kwame Anthony Appiah has put it most eloquently:

> The goal is not to eradicate hierarchy and to turn every mountain into a salt flat; we live in a plenitude of incommensurable hierarchies, and the circulation of social esteem will always benefit the better novelist, the more important mathematician, the savvier businessman, the faster runner, the more effective social entrepreneur. We cannot fully control the distribution of economic, social and human capital, or eradicate the intricate patterns that emerge from these overlaid grids. But class identities do not have to internalize those injuries of class. It remains an urgent collective endeavour to revise the ways we think about human worth in the service of moral equality.[39]

In *The Rise of the Meritocracy* a fictional Chelsea Manifesto is drawn up by opponents of the new meritocratic order that asks for a society with a different system of valuation.

> Were we to evaluate people, not only according to their intelligence and their education, their occupation and their power, but according to their kindliness and courage, their imagination and sensitivity, their sympathy and generosity, there could be no classes . . . Every human being would then have equal opportunity, not to rise up in the world in the light of any mathematical measure but to develop his own special capacities for leading a rich life.[40]

Meritocracy, like all social arrangements, is based on the idea of reciprocity: what you put in is connected to what you take out. But, as Appiah points out, meritocracy then elides two different things: capability and human worth.

> I know what it is for my life to go better or worse, but it doesn't make sense to ask whether my life is better than yours. And that means there is no comparative measure, no single scale of human worth . . . Indeed, because each of us faces a distinct challenge, what matters in the end is not how we rank against others at all. We do not need to find something we are best at; what is important is simply that we do *our* best.[41]

The egalitarian political philosopher John Rawls invented the idea of the veil of ignorance, asking people to imagine the social arrangements they would be most likely to favour if, behind the veil, they did not know what their position or status in society was going to be. This idea has often been applied to income distribution, class, race and gender. But it should apply to cognitive ability too. And if it were to be so applied, most people would surely choose meritocratic *selection systems* for the most important jobs to ensure that society made best use of bright people's talents but not a meritocratic *society* that sharply divides winners from losers. This is a vital distinction, analogous to wanting a market economy but not a market society (in the phrase of French socialist Lionel Jospin). Obviously, we want some of our most competent statisticians running the government statistical service. There is a commonsense case for cognitive meritocratic selection in education, science, professional organizations and so on (and indeed for non-cognitive meritocratic selection in sport and other areas of human endeavour). And Young himself said this: 'It is good sense to appoint individual people to jobs on their merit. It is the opposite when those who are judged to have merit of a particular kind harden into a new social class without room in it for others.' This is the crux of the matter and much easier said than done, maybe impossible. There will always be hierarchies of ability and competence across all fields of human endeavour, and that means hierarchies of status too. But accepting that there is no single scale of worth can help to dilute the over-concentration around Head capabilities and spread it more widely. People want opportunities, but not always the same kind of opportunities.

In politics and representative organizations there is a particularly strong case for cognitive *diversity* – for people with a range of aptitudes and experiences to be making decisions and having their experiences taken into account.

This chapter has tried to navigate a route between describing some of the scientific consensus about cognitive ability and questioning both the possibility and desirability of a cognitive meritocracy. A cognitive meritocracy is welcomed by most people as preferable to the hereditary ruling class of the recent past. But these are not the only two alternatives for democratic societies, and, as this chapter has shown, a *fair* cognitive meritocracy is almost as hard to achieve as a fair hereditary ruling class, because it is also too easy to pass on cognitive advantage through education, upbringing and genes.

The other big problem with the cognitive meritocracy is that in a world that requires a diverse range of aptitudes to function well it selects for and rewards – both psychologically and materially – just one cluster. The next three chapters will describe how that one cluster has become so dominant in the past two generations, in what I call the cognitive takeover.

PART TWO

The Cognitive Takeover

4

The Era of Educational Selection

Where is the wisdom we have lost in knowledge? Where is the knowledge we have lost in information?

T. S. Eliot

Most people, certainly most politicians, regard more formal education as an unquestionable good that helps economies to grow faster, societies to become more civilized and individuals both to earn more and somehow to become better people. There is also a general sense that a more educated population is part of a teleological story of human progress; that we all started as primitive people dominated by instinct, then reason began to play an ever-larger role in human affairs. This was initially led by a small, literate elite, but gradually literacy became the norm, at least in rich societies, followed by mass primary, secondary and now higher education.

Given how much humanity has benefitted from knowledge and its application in the last 200 years it seems counter-intuitive to argue that education, and in particular higher education, can produce diminishing returns. Yet the central claim of this book is that, at least in rich countries, we are now approaching 'Peak Head' and that guiding more and more school leavers into academic higher education is neither politically nor economically rational. Expanding higher education made sense for a few decades in the latter part of the twentieth century and early twenty-first centuries, but that time is now past. Most of the conventional assumptions about higher education and the benefit for individuals and whole societies are now at best only half-right – consider the fact that, just as the graduate share in the workforce has been sharply increasing, productivity has been slowing in most developed economies, inequality has been increasing (or at least not declining) and political polarization has been rising.

The ideal that many of us might think of when we consider education in the abstract – say studying medicine, combining vocational and academic learning with a view to an obviously useful and well remunerated professional career – is a very long way from the reality for most people, most of the time. Many of the academic qualifications that people are working towards have a far more tenuous connection to future employment and are often a form of *credentialism*, signalling to employers where you stand relative to others rather than evidence of mastery of complex cognitive skills.

There can, of course, be valuable intellectual inquiry that is neither signalling nor vocational. A friend of mine says he studied the philosopher Kant for a year at university and now could not write a coherent sentence about him but he thinks it did help him to think – a kind of intellectual gymnasium. But outside of core vocational subjects such as medicine or engineering there is plenty of evidence that many students do not learn, or at least retain, much from their studies and whether they learn to think critically is hard to measure.

Education can be 'what is left after you have forgotten everything you were taught', in the old saying. The problem is this. Education is in many circumstances a cultural good and an economic investment both for individuals and for society. But it is also a signalling arms race that sorts people into different occupational streams. It usually makes sense at the individual level to invest in it, but some of the investment can be misallocated at the social level.

If, thanks to an oversupply of graduates, advertisements for teaching assistants or accounting technicians begin to routinely require a degree, it is common sense for individuals who wish to work in these fields to obtain one. But it would be better for both individuals and society if the arms race could be called off and access to such jobs restored to conscientious school leavers, as used to be the case. It is not that we are investing too much in education in general, but too much may be going on signalling efforts for the higher-level exam-passers and not enough on the vocational, professional and technical skills, and indeed the lifelong learning, that most of the population, and the economy, need to flourish. It is a bit like acquiring a state-of-the-art nuclear weapon while your tanks and artillery decay.

And it is worth recalling just how much our ancestors achieved in the nineteenth century and early part of the twentieth, most of them having received only the most rudimentary education. This was true as recently as the 1960s. As Mark Bovens and Anchrit Wille put it in their book *Diploma Democracy*, 'The idea that success in school was the only road to achievement was absent in the 1960s. Many people who failed in school succeeded later, while the idea of success was broad and varied.'[1] By making academic achievement the only gateway to success we are shutting out some of the most talented future leaders of our police force, legal profession, civil service and private enterprise.

In 1972 more than 40 per cent of pupils left school in the UK with essentially no qualifications (some with the basic Certificate of Secondary Education).[2] The figure was a bit lower in the US – around 25 per cent. Even the elite public schools in the UK sent only about half of their pupils to university at that time.[3] The year I left Eton, in 1974, many of my fellow pupils were going directly into family businesses, professions or the armed forces. Today the elite public schools send 90 per cent or more of their pupils to top universities.

In the early 1970s most exams were still only for a minority, even in developed countries. At that time in England just one-third of pupils took O levels (the main school exam for sixteen-year-olds) and about 15 per cent took at least one A level (the school-leaving/university entrance exam taken at age seventeen/eighteen). There were only about thirty universities, and 9 per cent of school leavers went to them.

In 1988 GCSEs, designed for a wider ability range, replaced O levels, and *all* pupils took them. Today about 47 per cent of pupils take A levels and nearly half of the school-leaving cohort go on to some form of higher education according to the Department for Education. That has inevitably led to some dilution in standards, an A at A level or a first-class degree from most universities is easier to achieve than in the 1970s.

The period since the Second World War, and especially since the 1970s, has become the *era of educational selection*. In the second half of the twentieth century many developed countries, led by America, moved from being countries of mass literacy and numeracy, and mass primary and secondary education, to being countries of mass *higher* education.

It was the 1944 GI Bill for returning servicemen that set the US onto the path to mass higher education. Rewards for veterans were an established part of American politics, and the sense that the First World War package had been a miserly one prompted Roosevelt to agree to a much more generous package of benefits in 1944, including not just funding for college education but also cut-rate mortgages and medical care. Nobody knew how many veterans would take up the offer, but well over 1 million did, doubling the already high number in higher education, at least compared with Europe, to 2 million in 1951, compared with barely 100,000 in the UK at the same time. The number had doubled again to 4 million by 1961. By the 1970s about 40 per cent of high-school graduates were experiencing some kind of higher education, but only around a quarter were taking four-year bachelor's degree courses, with the rest doing two-year courses at community colleges. By 2018 the percentage had risen to around 50 per cent in total but with only around one-third taking full four-year bachelor's degree courses.[4]

This expansion of the cognitive class in all rich countries was, initially, a welcome and necessary change. The economy and the expansion of the public sector required more Head jobs, and relatively fewer Hand ones, and as we shall see in the next chapter the income returns to knowledge and education began to take off in the 1970s after almost a century of income compression between Head and Hand.

Frederick Winslow Taylor's theories of scientific management, developed in the US before the First World War, had produced the giant mass-production factory by ending skilled workers' monopoly of production know-how and breaking it down into easy-to-perform functions. This required less manual skill but some degree of literacy and numeracy. Taylorist standardization and specialization hugely increased productivity, and by the 1970s many corporations were employing many more people with college degrees in marketing, sales, engineering, IT and management than on the increasingly auto-mated production lines. There was also a big increase in professional, high-cognitive employment – doctors, scientists, teachers, lawyers, accountants – as the proportion of the workforce involved in broadly professional work rose from low single figure percentages at the turn of the nineteenth and twentieth centuries to between 30 and 40 per cent today. This was a common trend across all developed countries, but there were also distinctive attitudes to knowledge and to the relationship between Head and Hand in different national traditions (as described in Chapter 2).

England, as we have already seen, opted at the dawn of the twentieth century for a socially exclusive, national higher education system – dominated by Oxford and Cambridge – which imposed its ethos through exam boards and scholarships on the rest of the nascent education sector. Central to the ethos in higher education was the principle of the *residential* university.

This was partly inherited from the way that upper-middle-class families educated their children, as Nick Hillman, director of the Higher Education Policy Institute, has explained:

> Children sent away to boarding school as young as eight are unlikely to return home for undergraduate study on turning 18 because they have long ago cut their mother's apron strings. Indeed, they are more likely to travel further afield to cement their independence. Boarding school headteachers used to say that upper-middle-class children travelled south to school and north to university.[5]

That was certainly true in my case, I travelled from London about 80 miles south to Broadstairs in Kent at the age of eight to go to prep school and then, aged nineteen, travelled 200 miles north to go to York University.

The English ethos (Scotland was somewhat different) was not only socially exclusive, it also favoured the generalist-academic over the specific-vocational at every turn with the partial exception of medicine and engineering. The domination of theoretical reasoning over knowledge of facts or practical expertise went furthest in the Anglo-Saxon countries, thanks in part to the cultural influence of Oxbridge in Britain and to John Dewey in the US. Germany, Austria, the Netherlands and the Scandinavian countries have continued to attach greater prestige to vocational and technical education.

Education in technical and manual skills in Britain had been regarded as a lower-status option since the origins of compulsory education in the late nineteenth century. The universities established in industrial towns like Sheffield, Manchester and Leeds provided new courses in things like metallurgy but, as we have seen, did not establish an alternative style or ethos of higher education to challenge Oxbridge.

The 1944 Education Act in the UK reinforced the separation of Head and Hand. It proposed a tripartite system of grammar schools, technical schools and secondary moderns, but in most parts of the country the technical schools never emerged. The decision in 1992 to convert the thirty-five polytechnics – institutions, established in 1965, that had given some prestige to technical skills – into universities represented another tilt in the direction of academic/analytical aptitudes.

Mass higher education in England was elite academic higher education writ a little larger, as higher education policy expert Guy Neave has put it. And since the postwar expansion – from just 4 per cent of school leavers going to university in 1962 to almost half today – the school system has become more and more focused on nurturing academic, analytical ability.

Academic A levels have been the one prestigious constant in the school curriculum as different vocational qualifications have come and gone. A levels were developed by universities themselves in order to decide who to admit. But, as David Willetts, former UK Universities Minister, puts it: 'A finely tuned device for producing mini-scholars has become a de facto school-leaving exam, shaping the character of mass secondary education.'[6] Willetts and others rightly complain about the early specialization, with young people choosing just three A level subjects at the age of sixteen, something unique to the UK. It contributes to the damaging gap between the 'two cultures' of the arts and sciences, Britain's notorious weakness in foreign languages and to few people pursuing maths after the age of sixteen. 'Employers are unhappy: young people, they object, are force-fed for narrow academic excellence without a wider range of necessary subjects and skills,' Willetts writes.

But despite the abolition of most grammar schools, the school ranking system has become increasingly focused on the number of pupils schools are able to send to top universities. By contrast, those not in the academic A level stream and not heading to university have little incentive to apply themselves.

In countries such as Germany, Austria and the Netherlands, where academic schooling is combined with strong vocational tracks, and an institutionalized school-to-work transition, pupils at the lower end of the academic ability spectrum still have incentives to work hard in order to get into the best vocational schools or to have the widest possible choice of apprenticeship. By contrast, in general skills systems, such as the US and the UK, there is a big divide in the secondary-school population between those in the academic stream and those with a much less certain future in either the job market or some other form of post-school education. Many of them will already regard themselves as failures.[7]

It is easier to move from the cognitive environment of the school to the cognitive environment of a college or university than into the non-cognitive environment of an actual job, as Paul Collier has pointed out, and yet in Britain there has been far more financial and institutional support for the first than the second.

By common consent non-academic, post-school education remains poorly funded, complex and often inadequate, in both the UK and US. The Hand has been sorely neglected in school and post-school education, which has made both economies unusually dependent on foreign labour. One in ten adults in England have a technical qualification compared with more than one in five in Germany.[8] Meanwhile university expansion continued unabated in most rich countries in the first part of the twenty-first century, at least until the Covid-19 crisis, which is likely to slow or even reverse the expansion. In 2015 the British government abolished the cap on university numbers and allowed almost anyone who wanted to become an undergraduate to become one. Universities have a big financial incentive to cram in as many students as possible, lowering entry standards, inflating degree awards, reducing direct contact time with academics, and in the case of some of the newer universities, which tend to attract less research funding, struggling to remain solvent. Germany is also now fast increasing the proportion of school leavers going on to university which might over time weaken the broad appeal of its apprenticeship system.

UNIVERSITY OR BUST

The rise and rise of academic secondary education, and then higher education, really began in the UK with the aforementioned 1944 Education Act. It was the 1944 Act that first introduced the exam principle into most households in the country with the eleven-plus exam, determining entry into the academic grammar schools attended by 20 per cent of the age cohort.

The eleven-plus was an intelligence test rather like an IQ test, with verbal and non-verbal reasoning, based partly on the work of Cyril Burt, the influential educational psychologist with a strong belief in the heritability of intelligence. (Burt is a controversial figure who is considered by some to have falsified his research results.) During the late 1960s the eleven-plus and grammar schools were phased out in most of the country, partly thanks to the influence of Michael Young's meritocracy scepticism on Labour Education Secretary Tony Crosland. Young may have won this battle but he lost the war, as cognitive-based meritocratic selection increasingly became the symbol of national modernization – symbolized by Harold Wilson, the technocratic grammar school boy from Huddersfield who won the 1964 general election for Labour and became Prime Minister.

The early 1960s saw the first big postwar expansion of higher education, with seven new universities established to accommodate the surge of pupils coming out of the new grammar schools. The British universities had had a 'good war',[9] with university scientists playing a prominent role and academics occupying senior positions in Whitehall. And there was belated postwar political pressure to broaden the social base of higher education and catch up with the US. The university sector was still tiny in 1945 with just eleven full universities with a further 150 technical colleges run by local authorities.

The 1963 report on the future of higher education, led by the economist Lionel Robbins, provided justification for further expansion with a view to making it available to all of those qualified 'by ability and attainment'. Robbins wanted more room at university for people not from elite backgrounds and pointed out that 'working class grammar school boys' might not perform as well at admissions interviews as their more polished middle-class peers. Robbins was largely endorsing and justifying a significant expansion that was already under way along with the beginnings of a national system of student grants and loans and a national university application system. But Robbins also reinforced a traditional 'Oxbridge' view of disinterested study for its own sake.

Indeed, Robbins provided a useful definition of what is distinctive about specifically *academic* learning.

> While emphasising that there is no betrayal of values when institutions of higher education teach what will be of some practical use, we must postulate that what is taught should be taught in such a way as to promote the general powers of the mind. The aim should be to produce not mere specialists but rather cultivated men and women. And it is the distinguishing characteristic of a healthy higher education that, even where it is concerned with practical techniques, it imparts them on a plane of generality that makes possible their application to many problems – to find the one in the many, the general characteristic in the collection of particulars. It is this that the world of affairs demands of the world of learning.[10]

It is not at all clear that this is what 'the world of affairs' does demand from the world of learning. But the universities that emerged in the 1960s borrowed heavily from Oxbridge in their structure and intellectual ethos – Sussex was nicknamed 'Balliol by the sea' – focusing on research as well as teaching, being overwhelmingly residential, and in most cases with a college system and a tutorial system and an offer of subjects that mimicked Oxbridge. Eric Robinson, an adviser to Education Secretary Tony Crosland, complained that the new universities were established by people seeking to 'reaffirm the boarding school principle'.

In one significant departure from Robbins's recommendations, Crosland created in 1965 another tier of higher education – thirty-five polytechnics – that were technical and vocational in focus: engineering, computer science, management, architecture, town planning and so on. They differed from universities not only in their STEM and vocational focus but also in the fact that they were not mainly residential, were governed by local authorities, did not (at least initially) do research, catered for part-time and mature students and offered diplomas rather than degrees.

The university–polytechnic divide was also found in France, with both the specialist technical elite Grandes Écoles and the Instituts Universitaires de Technologie, in Germany, with its Fachhochschüle, created in the early 1970s as distinct technical institutions of higher education, and, in a slightly different way, with the US community colleges.

The British polytechnics did not survive long enough to establish a tradition of excellence, and their distinct mission was in any case gradually eroding as the polytechnics drifted towards traditional academic subjects and away from their vocational STEM subject focus. By 1987 the proportion of students studying engineering and technology had fallen from 44 per cent to 18 per cent, and some polytechnics had become partly residential.[11] The directors and senior staff of the polytechnics, themselves often Oxbridge trained, began to lobby for the higher prestige and greater independence of the classical university. And in 1992 Kenneth Clarke, then Conservative Education Secretary and himself Cambridge-educated, saw no reason to deny them this privilege. This left the UK as an outlier among rich countries in having no dedicated institutions of higher technical education.

This was the moment of real take-off for higher education in the UK, as the number of official universities rose from forty in 1990 to around 130 today, while over the same period the proportion of young people going to higher education rose from 20 per cent to nearly half – overtaking most other developed countries in relative participation rates. The internal hierarchy of prestige within the university sector in both teaching and research also became more overt. In order to distinguish themselves from the former polytechnics, or 'new universities', the so-called Russell Group of the most selective and research-intensive universities was established in 1994, eighteen universities initially (now twenty-four), accounting for about 20 per cent of all undergraduates – a larger version of the American Ivy League or French Grandes Écoles.

As noted, raising the overall educational level of the population and selecting the most cognitively able to go into an expanded higher education system were the two principal goals of the education system in all rich countries from the 1970s. Those two goals can, however, conflict, and schools, especially in the UK and US, have been increasingly judged in official league tables by the second goal, their ability to find the most able pupils and send them on to top universities.

Between 1970 and today the UK's spending on education has risen from around £30 billion in today's prices to more than £90 billion (and as a proportion of total spending it has risen about 20 per cent since the 1960s).[12] There has also been a step change in direct state involvement from the 1980s with the creation of a national curriculum and then, in the 1990s, national accountability systems, notably the Ofsted inspection regime and the publication of exam league tables. The spending increases have been similar in the US, Germany and France, with all four countries now spending between 5 and 6 per cent of GDP on education, though as a proportion of public spending and per capita spending the overall spending numbers are a bit higher in the UK and US, probably because of the higher level of spending on higher education.[13]

More and more, education came to be seen by politicians, who were now almost all graduates, as the answer to everything from a more productive economy to social mobility, if not equality (150 years of mass public education has proved a disappointment to egalitarians). Tony Blair's famous 'education, education, education' mantra of 1997 evolved two years later into the plan to send 50 per cent of young people into academic higher education, at a time when only about 30 per cent were then attending.

This headlong rush into mass academic higher education, leapfrogging even the US, happened faster in the UK than in most other comparable countries and it seemed to happen on automatic pilot, with remarkably little thought given to either the economic or social consequences. And in the Anglo-Saxon countries, which have long had weaker traditions of vocational and technical training, a status gap opened up which sucked much of the remaining purpose and prestige out of non-university, post-school education. This was much less true in Germany, and to a lesser extent France, where there were still respected alternatives to higher education, but in the UK and US almost all the bright and ambitious kids now had only one goal – university.

In the UK the academicization of education and careers for something between a third and a half of the younger population was a quiet revolution. Yet the only thing about this revolution that was closely debated was the level of fees that UK students should pay. There was a recognition that truly mass higher education in the UK could not be solely funded by the state, especially given the economic benefits of a university education to the individuals concerned, and tuition fees were introduced and raised rapidly to a ceiling (that became the norm) of £9,000 a year. But the loan and funding arrangements meant that university was free at the point of use, and the typical student is currently estimated to repay only a little over half the roughly £50,000 in loans that they are likely to acquire for tuition and living expenses.[14*] Higher education is now open to almost anyone who wants it, and, contrary to expectations, the number of full-time students from low-income backgrounds has been going up, not down.

One reason that the rapid expansion of higher education, to half of school leavers, seemed self-evidently desirable to those in the room when the decision was made is that all of them were graduates. One man in that room and closely involved in discussions over the Labour government's 50 per cent target was David Soskice, the charismatic and original LSE political economist and son of former Labour Home Secretary Frank Soskice. When I spoke to him in his north London home about the target he can remember nobody in government involved in the decision raising any objections. The economy seemed to want more graduates, judging by the graduate income premium, and university was regarded as a ladder of social mobility for those from middle- and lower-income groups.

What I call the 15/50 problem does not seem to have been considered: the idea that when 15 per cent of people in your class or school or town go to university and you don't it does not create a 'left behind' problem, but when 50 per cent go to university and you don't it does create such a problem.

---

* The current repayment terms mean that a student who studies an economically worthless degree and gains no career benefit from it will repay nothing, meaning the taxpayer provides the greatest subsidy to the least beneficial degrees.

Soskice himself, an influential analyst of different models of capitalism, was convinced, with good reason, that there was no point in Britain trying to copy the highly regulated German market economy with its apprenticeship system and commitment to long-term investment in manufacturing technology. Britain, thought Soskice, should play to its strengths in innovation, finance and the service sector, and he saw university expansion as producing the professional and managerial generalists to run the service economy. This, he said, was merely going with the grain of the route that Britain, like America, had chosen back in the 1980s: the post-industrial route of deregulated, flexible labour markets and the teaching of general, transferable skills rather than the continental European model of more regulated, company-based skill training. In Britain apprenticeship training never really recovered from the wave of de-industrialization in the 1970s and 1980s, and school-based vocational qualifications could never compete with the prestige of academic A levels.

Yet just fifty years ago Britain had a vocational training system that was patchy but worked pretty well, and followed a common European pattern: the largest bloc of school leavers went into employer-led apprenticeships; qualifications called BTECs provided a respectable classroom-based alternative to A levels; there was a dual higher education system with polytechnics alongside universities offering a range of higher technical and vocational qualifications, with FE colleges offering lower-level vocational qualifications. This system has now largely disappeared. The apprenticeship system was the weak link in the chain and was seen by the free market enthusiasts of the early Thatcher era as a source of protectionist labour movement power and also far too narrowly focused on disappearing manual skills. When it collapsed in the 1980s, it was replaced with low-level alternatives such as NVQs or diplomas designed by independent training providers, not by employers. The NVQ system reflected a characteristically British over-rigid separation of Head and Hand, white collar and blue collar, in its sharp distinction between 'knowledge' and 'doing' focusing on very narrow areas of specific competence.

The dramatic expansion of higher education from the early 1990s then obliterated the higher manual qualifications, particularly the sub-degree qualifications at so-called levels 4 and 5.* Higher National Diplomas (HNDs) and Higher National Certificates (HNCs), the qualifications taken since the 1920s by technicians, non-university engineers and skilled trades people such as electricians and plumbers, were being taken by 64,000 and 49,000, respectively, as recently as the year 2000, and the numbers were even higher in the 1980s. In 2016/17 just 15,000 students in England were registered for HNDs and 19,500 for HNCs. Just 4 per cent of twenty-five-year-olds in England hold a sub-degree technical qualification as their highest qualification compared with more than 20 per cent in Germany.[15] The numbers have been falling further despite recent concerns about technician shortages. In 2009/10 there were 510,000 people enrolled on level 4/5 courses overall; by 2016/17 that had fallen to 190,000 largely because of the way that funding and incentives in post-school education currently work hugely in favour of classical university degrees.[16] Meanwhile, anything between 30 and 50 per cent of graduates in England are in non-graduate employment five years after graduating.

Supporters of the current version of mass university education in the UK argue that around 40 per cent of university courses, and even more in the new universities, are essentially vocational – whether traditional, high-prestige, vocational courses such as medicine, law and engineering, or newer university degrees such as nursing, quantity surveying or marketing. Yet thanks to its student-demand-led higher education funding system the UK was in the bizarre position, in the 2011–17 period, of increasing university teaching funding in physics by just 6 per cent per student, compared with 27 per cent for business degrees and 34 per cent for sports sciences.[17]

It is true that many of the new universities do an impressive job. Standards vary enormously, but some of them have retained a distinctive polytechnic-technical ethos and are good local colleges serving local students and the local economy. And what they lack in research success they often make up for in teaching quality: in *The Times Good University Guide* for 2018 Loughborough had the highest satisfaction

---

* The international classification system for educational levels, first developed at the UN in the 1970s, runs from 1 (primary school) to 8 (PhD), with level 3 being an A level in the UK and level 6 a bachelor's degree.

for teaching and the lowest rating for research. There are specialist colleges such as Harper Adams in agriculture and many with strong ties to local employers such as Sunderland, Teesside, Lincoln and Coventry, as well as more general success stories such as Northumbria and South Bank in London. They often add more educational value than the elite Russell Group universities with their high proportion of students from selective or private schools.

The people who run these new universities bridle at the suggestion that they should abandon their university status and form a more distinctive 'technical' or 'applied' sub-set of higher education, yet they choose to play in a league where they are bound to be the losers, in part because they attract so little research funding.

THE MISSING MIDDLE

The relevant question in most rich countries is this: is a classical university – with its bias towards the academic, and lecturers who are often researchers first and teachers second – the best place to deliver the kind of higher vocational skills that many individuals want to acquire and that the economy, especially in the UK and US, so badly needs? Public opinion in the UK clearly does not think so. A large-scale survey by the think tank Onward found that 66 per cent of respondents agreed that more people going to university and fewer gaining technical qualifications had been bad for the country overall; 34 per cent said it was beneficial.[18]

Yet the current incentives in the UK, from very tangible financial ones to less tangible cultural ones, focus on three- or four-year full-time courses for eighteen–nineteen-year-olds, usually at residential universities, old or new, which is very expensive both for the country and the individuals concerned and not always an effective use of someone's time. And those incentives tend to discourage part-time study, mature students, shorter diploma-type higher vocational courses, sandwich courses and the more spread-out lifelong learning that is set to become increasingly important.

And the content of courses at universities leans towards academic/ analytical, essay-writing methods even in the vocational courses that many of the new universities in the UK teach. In the case of something like a construction management degree course the emphasis is on general cognitive skills, critical thinking and management theory, rather than field-specific experience. And many readers may be surprised to learn that it now requires an A and two Bs at A level to obtain a place at university in the UK to study midwifery, an essential occupation for which the average graduate starting salary is £23,000 a year. There is actually a strong case for graduate nurses and midwives, but there ought to be other routes into these vital jobs too that do not exclude the less academic, especially when there is a national shortage of both (see Chapter 8).

The overall economic effects of mass higher education present a mixed picture, but one thing that is worth noting here is that much research has shown that the *technician gap* in middle- and higher-skilled manual occupations – a particular problem in the UK and US – cannot easily be filled with graduates, partly because they have different expectations of work after studying for a degree.

Paul Lewis of King's College, London, has studied UK employers who have responded to shortages of genuine technicians by recruiting science and engineering graduates to fill technician roles. This is especially common in the case of laboratory and manufacturing technician roles in the chemical industry, industrial biotechnology and cell therapy/regenerative medicine. But the use of over-qualified graduates often causes significant problems, and non-graduates are still preferred in many jobs such as air traffic control. As Lewis puts it:

> First, whilst graduates may possess a higher level of *theoretical* knowledge than is needed to fill a technician role, they are also often *under-skilled*, because they lack the *practical* skills required to do the job well. Second, graduates often quickly become dissatisfied, both with the mundane, highly routinized nature of technician work and also with their relatively low wages, and so often leave relatively soon after joining their employer. The education system is producing the wrong mix of skills, with too many graduates and too few technicians being educated in some STEM disciplines.[19]

David Willetts, when he was Minister for Universities in the UK's 2010 Coalition government, illustrated a similar point with an anecdote told to him by the director of a German energy company. The director praised British electrical engineering graduates for often having better theoretical knowledge than their German equivalents but he said he would not trust them on a night shift at a power plant with few experienced people about because they knew much less about how the equipment worked.

Meanwhile only about 65 per cent of young people in Britain have a level 3 qualification, and most of them are academic A levels; by contrast, in most comparable European countries the figure is closer to 90 per cent, and a good proportion are non-academic qualifications, including many of the celebrated German apprenticeships taken by about 52 per cent of school leavers (some are higher than level 3).[20]

The section of society most let down by the under-investment in decent non-academic skill training does not have a loud voice: the parents of young people on low-level apprenticeships or taking unsatisfactory courses at Further Education (FE) colleges are not heard in the corridors of power, and those colleges themselves – often described as for 'other people's children' – have none of the funding or lobbying power over public policy that the university vice-chancellors enjoy.

In 2017–18, despite high tuition fees paid by students, over £8 billion in public funding was spent supporting 1.2 million UK undergraduates, compared with just £2.3 billion of public funding for 2.2 million full- and part-time Further Education students. Thanks in part to this funding squeeze, the number of adult learners in FE, people retraining or trying to raise their skill levels, dropped from 4 million to below 2 million between 2005 and 2016.[21] The *average* salary of an FE lecturer is £30,000 a year, which will soon be the starting salary of a primary and secondary-school teacher.[22]

Meanwhile FE colleges are supposed to teach not only post-school vocational education but remedial education for those who have not managed enough basic GCSE qualifications in school. And they end up having to deal with all the worst-performing school students because of the magnetic pull of more academic, middle-class, sixth-form colleges and university for the rest. In the quest for budget cuts in 2010 civil servants even suggested closing the whole FE college network, 'because no one would notice', as reported by the then Secretary of State, Vince Cable.[23]

Employers, for their part, have become part of the problem in the last twenty years in the UK with a sharp cut in training budgets[24] and increased dependence on immigrant labour, or 'free' graduates, to deal with skill shortages. Since the 1980s much off-the-job training has been delivered not by employers themselves but by private training providers offering training in a bewildering range of functions and qualifications and certificates, several thousand in all.

Everything in the UK points to university by default, as one of the country's leading economic commentators, Paul Johnson, discovered for himself when his second son, Tom, decided after getting modest A level results that he didn't want to go to university.

> An apprenticeship looked like a good option for son number two. The government is promoting this as an alternative route. So I spent a large part of the Christmas holidays helping him to apply for higher and degree-level apprenticeships. It is staggeringly hard even to find the right opportunities. Just 1,800 18-year-old school leavers started any form of higher apprenticeship in 2016, roughly the same number that started at Oxford and Cambridge.[25]
>
> My son wants to be a computer programmer or software developer. Apparently this is a shortage occupation. You wouldn't know it from the scarcity of openings. By comparison there are hundreds of relevant degree courses, all clearly advertised . . . Our education system is designed for students who go straight from A levels to university. Their route is clear. It's much tougher for the rest. The other routes are opaque.[26]

Johnson ended up making a BBC radio documentary about this experience with Tom, who did eventually get the software apprenticeship he was seeking. One of the most revealing moments in the programme was when Johnson took some teachers from Tom's school to the local FE college, which they had never visited before and where they were surprised to see so many of their former pupils. Schools boast about the number of pupils they send to university but rarely mention those who have gone on to good apprenticeships or acquired useful vocational qualifications at FE colleges. Too many people in Britain and America, and increasingly in France and

Germany too, are being sucked into higher education because of the prestige and the promise of professional security even when it is clearly not suitable.

A friend of mine has a nephew called Roger, who studied physics at university. He did science A levels at a state school in Leeds, where the only option presented was university; indeed the sixth form was given evidence of the higher earnings of graduates, and positive presentations were given by undergraduate ex-pupils. He chose his university partly because of its sporting focus, as all he ever really wanted to do was play football for England. The university has great sports facilities, and he spent too much of his time playing sport. But he also complained that too much of the course was essentially memorizing equations, and there was no intellectual enjoyment in his studies. He failed his second-year exams and had to retake a year and then failed his final exams. So he owed four years of fees and living expenses and still had no degree. He then did an unusual apprenticeship in fund-raising at a charity and now has a job, which he loves, working for a sports charity with young kids. He plays serious football every weekend and also coaches a women's football team.

He is just one case but says he knows of many others who in retrospect realized they were pressurized into going to university by their schools and parents and the wider culture when it was not the right choice. A 2017 YouGov poll in the UK found that 35 per cent of recent graduates disagreed that the cost of university had been worth it in terms of career prospects.[27]

The result is not just many frustrated individuals but that glaring 'missing middle' in the economy's skill base and the neglect of Hand that has left severe skill shortages in STEM-related areas, the skilled trades and technician-level jobs, especially in construction, health and information technology from coders to web designers. UK employers in 2017 complained that they had trouble filling more than 40 per cent of skilled trades vacancies.[28] (Many Commonwealth countries, especially in Africa, that followed the UK down the path of university expansion are also now worrying about the weakness of their vocational skill base.)

THE US, FRANCE AND GERMANY

This failure is part of a bigger training and retraining failure, especially in the UK and the US, in response to the export of large slices of manufacturing industry to lower-cost countries. Robert Reich, Bill Clinton's Labour Secretary, argued in his book *The Work of Nations* (1991) that workers in rich countries should accept the great wealth-producing machine of globalization so long as responsible governments retrained them for the jobs of the future. Steel workers would become IT technicians. This retraining simply did not happen on any significant scale in either country. And according to Richard Reeves, prior to the 2017 Tax Bill for every $1 the US government spent on trade adjustment assistance for workers it spent almost $25 on the tax subsidies for the endowments to elite colleges.[29]

At the zenith of American industrial power in the 1950s and 1960s a significant proportion of young people did some Hand education at school and then served apprenticeships in local factories and offices, often then rising to senior positions. But formal apprenticeships, combining work and off-the-job training, have always been relatively rare in the US: in 1975 there were just 292,000 formal apprenticeships, compared with 1.4 million in West Germany. In 2018 240,000 people began apprenticeships in the US and only 6 per cent of young people are in formal technical or vocational training. According to official figures there were just 15,000 apprenticeship places in 2018 for the whole of manufacturing. Daniel Markovits, author of *The Meritocracy Trap*, says that the average US firm today spends less than 2 per cent of its payroll budget on training.[30] And since the 1970s the US, like the UK, has seen schools downgrade their 'shop classes' – metalworking, woodworking and so on – as they came to be judged by how many pupils they sent to college (see Chapter 7).

In recent years, and partly inspired by populist political alienation, there has been a recognition that governments need to think harder about the non-university 50 per cent-plus of school leavers, and there is noisy political support for more investment in post-school vocational and technical education in the US and UK.

Governments have not been completely idle. The UK introduced an apprenticeship levy on bigger employers in 2017. On the missing middle of higher manual and technician training there was the Sainsbury review of 2016, which also informed the creation of T levels, a new attempt to create a valued, classroom-based vocational alternative to A levels, due in 2020.

In the US too there has been plenty of political speech-making about vocational education, and President Trump passed an executive order in 2017 to expand apprenticeships, but the state of play is probably better summed up by President Obama's bid for a $12 billion boost to community colleges, which was whittled down by Congress to just $2 billion.

The ability of academic higher education to set the tone and priorities for the whole education system, especially in the UK and US, remained undimmed at least until the Covid-19 crisis. And one reason why the Anglo-American academic generalist approach has taken root is that it goes with the grain of modern school teaching methods. A child-centred teaching style took hold in the 1970s and 1980s, especially in the US and UK, that downplayed drilling and practice and the acquisition of specific knowledge in favour of uncovering the pupils innate talent and creativity through learning general, analytical skills such as 'decision making' or 'handling information critically'. Those of middling or below average ability have not in the main been helped by this shift in focus, and, according to the Sheffield Report of 2010, about 17 per cent of pupils still leave secondary school in the UK functionally illiterate and innumerate.

In the UK and elsewhere what one might call the 'traditionalist avant-garde', led by people such as former Education Secretary Michael Gove, has been pushing back against a child-centred, generalist skills approach, armed with the work of the American educationalist E. D. Hirsch. Hirsch started his career in a US community college wondering why black boys performed badly in SAT tests. He concluded it was all about cultural knowledge. They didn't know enough of the right things to make the connections when reading complex texts, so they would miss nuance and allusion and the depth of meaning in a text and score poorly when asked about it. The solution was to address their knowledge deficiency.

Supporters of the child-centred approach reject this and argue that we don't need to know particular things any longer because we can look it up on Google; what we need is a generic ability to acquire knowledge and think critically. By contrast Hirsch insists that knowledge is cumulative: we have to build knowledge in order to think and be creative.

In the UK the popularity of generic skills also grew out of the particular de-industrializing circumstances of the 1980s. David Willetts again:

> In my constituency in the 1970s you went to school and you knew that when you left you would do an apprenticeship in the Portsmouth dockyard. And the school had a reasonable sense of what you needed to know to work in the dockyard. But then the dockyard closes, the steel works closes, the car plant has just gone bust. We don't quite know what these 17 year olds are going to do but we are pretty sure it is not the old jobs in mass manufacturing. So they need some stuff that is broader and more flexible for a more flexible labour market.[31]

So *general* skills came to be regarded by much of the educational and political establishment in the UK and US as the most relevant education and training for a complex and fluid modern world. As the American author Matthew Crawford puts it in his book *The Case for Working with Your Hands*, the manual trades are now given little honour in the US school system because of the fear 'that acquiring a specific skill set means that one's life is *determined*. In college, by contrast, many students don't learn anything of particular application; college is the ticket to an *open* future. Craftsmanship entails learning to do one thing really well, while the ideal of the new economy is to be able to learn new things.'[32] Crawford argues that today's preferred role model is the management consultant, who swoops in and out and whose very pride lies in his lack of particular expertise. 'Like the ideal consumer, the management consultant presents an image of soaring freedom, in light of which the manual trades appear cramped and paltry: the plumber with his butt crack, peering under the sink.'[33]

In the US, like the UK, a single route into the cognitive class via high SAT test scores and selective higher education has replaced the multiple routes of the recent past. In the US before the Second World War you could 'read' law in a lawyer's office and take the bar examination without a law degree. By the end of the 1970s in medicine, law, accounting and other professions a college degree was increasingly necessary. Business was one of the main routes open to ambitious but non-academic people. 'And the rags to riches ascent (or, more accurately, clerk-to-capitalist, if one follows the career of a Rockefeller, Harriman or Carnegie) required drive and ruthlessness rather than education and skills,' writes Daniel Bell in *The Coming of Post-Industrial Society*.[34]

> Within the corporation, as managerial positions have become professionalised, individuals are rarely promoted from shop jobs below but are chosen from the outside, with a college degree as the passport of recognition. Only in politics, where position may be achieved through the ability to recruit a following, or patronage, is there a relatively open ladder without formal credentials.

(Bell turned out to be wrong about politics, which by the twenty-first century had also become dominated by the credentialized cognitive class, see Chapter 6.)

The US story of rapid expansion of secondary and then higher education, as I described in Chapter 2, preceded the expansion story in Britain, though it has recently run out of steam thanks partly to high costs and cuts to the federal funding of public universities. Both countries, as we have seen, have shown a somewhat similar neglect of vocational and technical education. After the GI Bill surge there was further expansion of higher education in the US in the 1950s and, especially, the 1960s. Cold war competition and Soviet success in sending a man into space produced more public funding for higher education in the shape of scholarships and student loans, and by the 1970s, as noted, nearly half of young people were going into higher education of some kind.

The US system is more differentiated than Britain's. At the pinnacle are the Ivy League private universities and liberal arts colleges, highly prestigious and expensive, and then the somewhat less expensive state or public universities, both usually offering four-year degree courses. Combining tuition fees and residential costs, Ivy League colleges are now costing over $70,000 a year, private four-year colleges about $50,000, public four-year colleges $38,000 (for those coming out of state) and around $22,000 for those from within the state.[35] Entry to the elite colleges, as in most countries, is skewed towards those whose parents attended them, with the added bias in the US of the 'legacy admissions' students who are more likely to get a place at a top college because their family has been donating to the college. (Against that, many colleges are trying to become less dependent on SAT scores and give more weight to social context and potential of a student.)

Lower down the chain are the community colleges, closer to Britain's FE colleges or former polytechnics, but counted as part of the higher education system. Nearly two-thirds of all undergraduates are currently studying in one of the 980 community colleges; most of them are doing vocational two-year 'associate degrees', more than half part-time and often training for jobs in the health sector or public services, such as a registered nurse or an appointments manager at a health clinic. Anyone can attend a community college if they have graduated from high school – nearly 6 million students were enrolled in 2016 – and the colleges are far cheaper than four-year state or private universities, annual tuition fees averaging about $3,000 a year.[36] It is also possible to transfer after two years at community college for a final two years at a four-year university course.

Partly because so many people use community colleges as a way of making a four-year liberal arts or humanities degree more affordable, there has been a drift away from more technical and vocational courses. So in 2016–17 easily the largest category of community college graduate (386,658), representing more than one-third of all graduates, were studying 'liberal arts and sciences, general studies and humanities'. The next biggest group, at 186,299, was 'health professions and related programs', and after that, at 108,353, came 'business management, marketing and support services'.[37]

In 1982 the average high-school graduate graduated with 22.1 credits, rising to 26.6 in 2013. Academic credits have increased from 14.4 to 19.6 while vocational credits have declined from 4.6 to 3.4.[38]

The 60 per cent-plus of the US adult population who have only a high-school education or less have seen their incomes stagnate since 1980, so it is no surprise that 90 per cent of high-school students want to go to college (numbers are similar in the UK) and about 70 per cent do now go to some kind of post-school education. But, to repeat, only 35 per cent do a full four-year degree and only 9 per cent go to a highly selective college. About 13 per cent of Americans have postgraduate qualifications and study at 'grad schools' of many kinds that have long been more common in the US than Europe, though Europe is catching up.

Overall entry into higher education in the US peaked in 2010 and is now in decline thanks to spiralling debt and a more brutal repayment scheme for the 45 million indebted students than in the UK, which has a lower cap on tuition fees and writes off more debt. It is little wonder that student debt is a big political issue in the US, with all the Democrat candidates for President supporting some version of abolition of student fees.

To some analysts it is the fact that America slipped back from being the leader in mass secondary and higher education that is the cause of its great income and status divergence since the 1970s. Claudia Goldin and Lawrence Katz argue that when college attendance no longer kept up with the pace of technological change it started to sharply increase the demand for and pay of the most highly educated.[39] This, surely, downplays other factors promoting inequality, such as the disappearance of middle-income jobs thanks to trade openness, technology and the decline of organized labour. Also, if there is such demand for graduates, why are so many working in non-graduate jobs?

American higher education, like the British, also struggles to combine two functions – mass opportunity and elite selection – and both end up favouring the latter, perhaps because it is inherently simpler. Nicholas Lemann in his critique of the SAT test, *The Big Test*, accuses it of being fundamentally un-American.

> The idea of educating everyone at public expense ranks with political democracy as one of the United States' great original social contributions. Both ideas rest on a belief that ordinary people are capable of more than the leaders of previous societies would have thought possible . . . Our apparatus of meritocracy is not part of this tradition. Rather, it belongs to an older, less distinctively American tradition of using tests and education to select a small government elite.[40]

In Germany and France, at least until recently, the story has been a somewhat different one to the US and UK. In recent decades universities have carried less prestige partly because there have been attractive post-school alternatives – about 50 per cent of German school leavers still go straight into an apprenticeship and in France, while about 40 per cent of school leavers achieve the academic Bac Général, another 15 per cent achieve a Bac Technologique, and 25 per cent a lower-level Bac Professionnel, which lead to non-university technical colleges of various kinds. Also, because universities are largely non-selective, once a student has achieved the school-leaving exam, the Abitur in Germany or Baccalauréat in France, they have a right to attend university (though some courses have quota restrictions).[41]

The unselective university system in France is flanked by the *highly selective* Grandes Écoles, which take the top 3 to 4 per cent of students but receive about 30 per cent of state funding for higher education.[42] There are about 250 Écoles overall, some quite general such as the École d'Ingénieurs or École de Commerce, some much more specialized. After passing the Bac Général, students aiming for one of the Grandes Écoles undertake a gruelling two-year preparatory course, known as the *prépa*, followed by a competitive national exam. Those who pass, about half, then have three to five years study at a Grande École before, in most cases, going on to staff the French political, administrative, academic and business elite.

The École Nationale d'Administration (ENA), established by General de Gaulle in 1945 as a symbol of meritocratic modernization, is the most notoriously exclusive of them all. The annual intake is just eighty, but it has produced four of the last eight presidents and eight of the last twenty-two prime ministers. It has now become a symbol of an ossified elite, and proposals to abolish it, most recently by Emmanuel Macron, are made from time to time.

The most prestigious Grandes Écoles – the École Polytechnique and ENA – take about two-thirds of their entrants from the children of the highest professional and managerial class, and in 2015 only 1.3 per cent and 4.4 per cent, respectively, from working-class backgrounds. Looking more broadly at all those taking the *prépa*, the numbers from the highest social class fall back to about 50 per cent. About 7 per cent of young French people go straight into an apprenticeship, although the Macron government has been talking them up in recent years. The roughly 40 per cent who pass one of the technical Bacs take either a technician qualification, the Brevet de Technicien Supérieur (BTS) or the Diplôme Universitaire de Technologie (DUT).[43] That leaves around 30 to 35 per cent of school leavers going into the mainstream university system.

Germany is unlike the UK, US and France in having *no* elite higher education institutions comparable to Oxbridge, the Ivy League or the Grandes Écoles, though many elite children go abroad to study. Like France and the US, it has a more differentiated higher-education system than the UK – and has preserved the specialist technical colleges, again somewhat similar to the UK's former polytechnics, known as the Fachhochschüle. There are about 210 Fachhochschüle (now classified as universities) educating about 22 per cent of young people compared with 120 traditional universities educating 38 per cent.[44] As in France, more than half of students go to a *local* college or university, though some may live in student halls.

As the country that pioneered the modern research university, Germany remains deeply respectful of academic traditions but has managed to combine that with an appreciation of what one might call the practical intellect. Around half of school leavers, including nearly 20 per cent of those who pass the Abitur, go into a traditional apprenticeship lasting between two and three and a half years. This national 'dual system' of apprenticeships, combining low-wage employment in a company with time in vocational schools, is embedded in all three levels of government (federal, state and local) and in the social partnership system. It trains people in just 325 different occupational categories (compared with thousands in the UK) that are drawn up by employers, and every schoolchild receives the *Beruf Aktuell* book giving details of the jobs the apprenticeships lead to and pay levels they might expect. About 20 per cent of German companies offer apprenticeships, and about two-thirds of apprentices are taken on by their companies.[45]

Many of the longer apprenticeships include a substantive theoretical content. A plasterer, for example, will have to do complex calculations on heat loss. Some apprenticeships are the equivalent of a level four or five in terms of the international education grading system. By comparison, the modern British apprenticeship is much more basic and generally lasts just one or two years. The funding rules encourage providers to focus on shorter, cheaper, lower-level programmes in subjects such as business administration.

The German apprenticeship system still has considerable prestige. I know middle-class, professional German families where it is still completely normal for a child to do an apprenticeship before probably moving on to do a further qualification. There is a sense in Germany that all qualifications are on the same spectrum, at least in status. Jens Spahn, the German Health Minister (at the time of writing in September 2019) and one of the brightest sparks in Angela Merkel's government, did a bank clerk apprenticeship before going to technical college and then university. It is not an untypical story for political and business leaders.

On a recent visit to Germany I met someone who had just witnessed the importance that many employers attach to the apprenticeship system. He had been at an official dinner in Berlin with Reinhard Zinkann, who runs the Miele home appliances company and was going to meet him again the following day at a meeting in the German capital. But Zinkann left dinner early that evening to be driven from Berlin to Gutersloh (about four hours) to be at his company's apprentice graduation ceremony at 8 a.m. the following morning before returning to Berlin.

The system is seen by some as too inflexible; it took seven years, for example, to agree the most recent addition to the apprenticeship job function, an e-commerce sales role. Some of the more traditional apprenticeships, and those that require anti-social hours, are increasingly hard to fill. And there has been more poaching of recently trained staff than in the past, thanks to a tight labour market, at least pre-Covid. But the biggest threat to the standing of the system is now the reformed university system. German university degrees used to last at least five years, and young graduates would often not start their careers until they were twenty-eight or even thirty. This is one reason why according to the OECD only 31 per cent of German 25–34-year-olds had higher educational qualifications in 2017, compared with 52 per cent in the UK, 48 per cent in the US and 44 per cent in France.

But recent reforms have copied the UK's three-year bachelor's degree (or four to five-year master's), and the government has been encouraging more people to go to university, with the participation level now rising close to 50 per cent (including the Fachhochschüle). It is also attracting more international students.

With the encouragement of the OECD, Germany is being pushed to swap its specific skill-based system for a more Anglo-Saxon generic aptitudes system based in higher education. But employers complain, as in the UK, that graduates' expectations make them poorly motivated employees. There is also a 35 per cent dropout rate from degree courses, with most people falling back on an apprenticeship.

Over the next few years we will discover whether Germany can sustain an apprenticeship system that has succeeded in giving status to many middling and even quite low-skill jobs or whether it will opt for UK-style mass higher education with what seems to be its attendant squeeze on higher manual and technical skills.

TOO MUCH SIGNALLING?

Our societies would not work properly if people only had the education levels of the early nineteenth century. But that does not mean more academic education is always the answer to our ills. As Alison Wolf has demonstrated in *Does Education Matter?*, there is no clear link between education and economic growth, except perhaps in the early stages of industrialization. Countries with similar levels of educational attainment can exhibit very different productivity and growth performances. Conversely, rich countries with very different numbers of graduates can produce very similar growth and productivity numbers. It is true that the UK saw a productivity surge in the 1980s and 1990s, as graduate numbers were rising, but that was largely thanks to the elimination of the least productive companies and even whole sectors. There is an extraordinary amount of magical thinking about the beneficial impact of higher education on productivity, economic growth and social mobility, (Alison Wolf compares it to the Soviet Union's irrational belief in capital goods).[46] In fact all of these things have been stagnating in the years that university enrolments have been roaring ahead (in 2017 an average of 44 per cent of 25–34-years-olds in OECD countries had a higher-education qualification).* The American economist Robert Gordon, in his book *The Rise and Fall of American Growth*, says that innovation has been nose-diving in the era when there has never been more investment in research universities. Productivity has been in particularly sharp decline in those parts of the economy that are graduate-dominated. And some analysis even sees professional bureaucratization stemming from mass higher education as an active drag on productivity.[47]

Moreover, higher education has done nothing to reduce inequality and, as Wolf suggests, its expansion in recent decades may actually be one cause of our political divides. Education, from an employment point of view, turns out, at least at higher levels, to be not so much about what you have actually learned but what your level or place of education will signal to a potential employer about your general academic aptitudes and your character and attitudes. It is a ranking system and, in the UK, it is reinforced by the physical and social separation of the residential universities. And the sorting hat of higher education creates a qualification treadmill requiring ever more differentiation. When more than one-quarter of students in the UK receive a first-class degree, it encourages more people to differentiate themselves with a master's degree: the number of adults with a post-graduate qualification rose from 4 per cent to 11 per cent between 1996 and 2013.[48] As the American sociologist Randall Collins has put it: 'The process of credential inflation . . . feeds on itself. As educational attainment has expanded, the social distinctiveness of a degree and its value on the occupational marketplace has declined; this in turn has expanded demand for still higher levels of education.'

A friend who is a senior psychologist, having done the necessary master's degree to enter the profession in the UK in the late 1980s, says that now it would be unthinkable for someone to rise to her level without a PhD. Indeed, most people at work address her as 'Doctor' because they assume she must have one. And I know of a prestigious recruitment firm which, as a matter of principle, does not take people without master's degrees.

---

* One high point of magical thinking was reached in 2002 when Estelle Morris, then UK Secretary of State for Education, wrote an article in the *Guardian* newspaper claiming that a one percentage point increase in the proportion of graduates in the workforce led to a 0.5 per cent increase in GDP.

This also creates its own interests and demarcations much like the old trade union demarcation disputes. A former colleague of mine who runs a historic building in Scotland had an ugly dispute with his deputy, who has an MA in museum studies, when he wanted to recruit a very capable and experienced person who did *not* have that qualification.

But if academic education is partly a way of signalling the right aptitudes to employers then, as Bryan Caplan argues in his book *The Case Against Education*, there might be less time-consuming and costly methods of achieving the sorting than our current system of higher education.[49]

There is certainly plenty of evidence that students forget much of what they have learned at college, and, as noted earlier, transferable skills such as 'critical thinking' are hard to measure. Indeed, there is an increasing body of research that finds that many students are learning almost nothing at college. Richard Arum and Josipa Roksa argue in *Academically Adrift* on the basis of surveys and studying test results that a significant proportion of US college students demonstrate no improvement in a range of skills including critical thinking, complex reasoning and writing.[50]

Further, the hours that students devote to study have been in sharp decline in the US. In the early 1960s students spent roughly forty hours per week on academic work (combining studying alone and class/lecture time), which has now fallen to twenty-seven hours per week, and studying alone has fallen to just thirteen hours. (A recent paper found that vocabulary among American adults had declined across all educational levels since the 1970s with the largest declines among those with a bachelor's or graduate degree.)[51]

The situation in the UK is not very different. According to surveys conducted by the Higher Education Policy Institute, about 25 per cent of students admit to working less than twenty hours per week. If it is still possible to be awarded a 2:1 doing so little work, it cannot be a very demanding or rigorous course.[52]

The rapid expansion of higher education in the UK combined with the incentive for universities to recruit as many fee-paying students as possible has inevitably eroded degree class standards, especially in the humanities. Only seven per cent of students achieved a first in 1994; the figure is now 29 per cent, and 79 per cent get a first or a 2:1.

'We have got to protect ourselves from complaints,' Natalie Fenton of Goldsmiths College in London told the *New Statesman* magazine. 'It's an endless process of dealing with students who haven't been able to buy the grade they wanted.'[53]

The grade inflation is also true of the A levels that students need for university entrance, though many universities are now offering 'unconditional' offers, as they are so desperate to fill places. According to professor of education Robert Coe, those who were receiving D and E grades in the late 1980s were being given Bs and Cs by the mid-2000s.[54]

In a 2016 OECD report on basic skill levels among recent graduates from twenty-three countries, England ranked in the bottom third despite the endless boosterism about 'world-class' higher education. And after all the huffing and puffing about the knowledge society and the importance of sending as many school leavers as possible to university, it turns out that what many employers are looking for in graduates is not the little they have learned at college but rather 'soft' social skills – application, concentration, ability to cooperate with co-workers, and so on – learned primarily in the family (especially the middle-class one). Indeed, some humanities graduates often have to *unlearn* the style and rhetoric they have painstakingly acquired in their essay-writing years in order to be of any use to their employer. I vividly remember as a trainee journalist on the *York Evening Press* being put through the mill by an exasperated managing editor whose job it was to expel all the pompous circumlocutions from the new intake of graduate trainees. Writing in simple, direct prose and learning to put the most interesting facts first in the story can be surprisingly hard after three years of absorption in post-modern discourse!

It is true that people without decent levels of basic academic skills are at a permanent disadvantage in today's world. And society would not work without the higher academic skills of doctors, engineers, scientists, mathematicians, computer scientists, bio-technologists and some of their counterparts in the humanities and social sciences. But, to repeat, education should increasingly be regarded as a 'positional good' – one which gains much of its value from whether you have more than other people. 'The rewards your education brings are as much to do with being labelled a 'top' or 'near-the-top' sort of person as they are to do with the curriculum you studied,' as Alison Wolf puts it.[55] As we saw in Chapter 3, you have a much better chance of being a 'top' or 'near the top' sort of person if one or both of your parents graduated from a good university and you are also more likely to possess those relevant non-cognitive skills that employers like. You are likely to progress, without fuss, into the cognitive class, as my own four children have, three of whom have good degrees from Russell Group universities.

Moreover, whereas in previous generations children from less privileged backgrounds would have been judged, and would have judged themselves, by different standards of capability, there is now, as already noted, thanks to the expansion of academic higher education, something like a *single, common cognitive class* with everyone measured by the same cognitive standard. In the past the talented and ambitious were more randomly scattered about geographically and occupationally and were judged according to a wider range of aptitudes.

There is no longer a working-class intelligentsia thanks to the widening and democratization of society's *general* cognitive class. But, as Andrew Hindmoor, professor of politics at Sheffield University, has pointed out, this has the effect of skewing the geographical distribution of cognitive talent.[56] The Labour MP Angela Rayner gave an interview to the *Spectator* magazine a few years ago and told the story of how a Tory MP had once approached her, saying: 'You should be one of us, Ange! You've done well, you've climbed out!' She used this episode to explain why she could not be a Conservative, but such views are just as common, albeit using the language of upward mobility meritocracy rather than aspiration, on the centre-left.[57]

As already observed, English working-class towns such as Barnsley, Doncaster and Wakefield each year suffer a brain drain, losing thousands of their academically brightest eighteen-year-olds to university towns and metropolitan centres such as Leeds and Sheffield. Many of them never return there to live permanently. Almost one-quarter of all UK new graduates end up in London at least initially, while big cities such as Manchester, Birmingham and Belfast retain about half of the students who studied there.[58] According to a recent study drawing on the 450,000 people enrolled in the UK Biobank, this is now creating a 'gene drain' in left-behind areas, with those who are healthier and brighter leaving for urban centres. 'If these processes continue the biological inequalities we observe may grow larger each generation, as like keeps marrying like,' said David Hugh-Jones.[59]

The same brain/gene drain occurs in the more depressed parts of the US, Germany (especially eastern Germany), France – the 'France Périphérique' described by social geographer Christophe Guilluy – and elsewhere in Europe. In Britain the lack of prestigious local technical colleges, the dominance of residential universities and the London effect make the social and geographical imbalances even worse. The gap between the richest and poorest regions in the UK is almost twice as large as in France and three-quarters larger than in Germany.[60]

Also, with the single university-shaped funnel into the professional and business class and the increased dependence of employers on the signalling effect of a university degree there has been a sharp fall-off in promotion from below in recent decades (see more in Chapter 5). As noted earlier, as recently as 1991 only about half of senior people in professional and managerial positions had a university degree, and it was possible for ambitious people without extensive educational credentials to rise inside a company or professional organization.[61]

FLYING THE NEST, INTO THE MIDDLE CLASS

There is a final important point about the expansion of higher education – the social experience, particularly for *residential* students. Some people, such as David Soskice, argue that this is the single most important thing about it.

> The key element of the modern university is the social skills that people acquire often living away from home for the first time and mixing with people from different backgrounds. It's not so much the going to lectures but the ability to organize a meeting or work cooperatively with other people to achieve a social goal that matters.

This is a new version of the very old idea of joining a community of scholars and thereby becoming a better and different kind of person, more refined, more knowledgeable, closer to God. In more recent history the private boarding school similarly included a character-building and character-changing offer to parents who sent their children there.

The modern case for the residential university experience might be seen, in part, as a more egalitarian way of spreading the magical confidence that is often thought to attach to young people emerging from elite private boarding schools. Though the often-quoted 'polish', charm and soft skills associated with the privately educated are surely inculcated at least partly at home.

It is true that social skills are increasingly essential to many professional jobs as the more routine intellectual calculations and judgements are automated. It is assumed that three or four years away from home can breed confidence, self-reliance and openness to different people and situations. That is no doubt the case for many students. And it is certainly the case that in an increasingly multi-ethnic, but often quite ethnically segregated, society, universities bring people from different ethnicities into close contact often for the first time.

Set against that, the residential university experience also seems to be responsible for a sharp rise in mental stress among students. The *Guardian* newspaper in the UK reported in March 2019 an online survey of nearly 40,000 students that found very high levels of anxiety and thoughts of self-harm, with fully one-third saying they had experienced a serious psychological issue for which they needed help.[62]

In the academic year 2017–18 around 80 per cent of full-time British students left home for study. The most affluent and those going to the most elite universities generally travel furthest. Many poorer students either continue living at home or at least stay in their home region.[63] But even if you just move the 15 miles from Mansfield to university in Nottingham you are still likely to adopt what one vice-chancellor described to me as the 'leaving mentality'. Every autumn 1.5 million British teenagers take part in this mass migration, dividing the country into a residential university class of mobile, professional people, and a more rooted non-graduate group. This has surely exacerbated the country's value and social divisions and anti-London feeling, revealed in the Brexit vote.

Mass *residential* higher education remains a very British phenomenon (and even more so in England than in Scotland); it is less common in continental Europe (apart from Scandinavia) and the US, although the trend is for it to decrease somewhat in Britain – partly because of more students from less mobile low-income and ethnic minority backgrounds – and increase in the rest of the rich world. (If the Covid-19 crisis reduces mobility both within and between countries, the growth of residential higher education may be checked.)

In the US, although the residential system was imported from Britain at the start of the twentieth century, at least for elite colleges, more than 40 per cent of college students live at home and 77 per cent attend college in their home state. In Ireland about half of students live at home, similarly in Australia. And only about 18 per cent of students in Europe live in student accommodation, although a bit less than half are thought to live away from home, with many, as in the US, remaining in their home town.[64]

On the positive side of the balance sheet, the expansion of residential higher education in the past thirty years in England has played a big role in rejuvenating post-industrial cities such as Manchester, Leeds, Sheffield, Newcastle and Liverpool. Some of these cities are now primarily university towns. According to Chris Husbands, who runs Sheffield Hallam University, in 1976 Sheffield had 45,000 steel workers and 4,000 students, in 2017 it had 3,000 steelworkers and 60,000 students.

There is an element of unintended, redistributive regional policy too. A lot of relatively affluent and disproportionately southern English students move north for three years, bringing with them many tens of thousands of pounds to spend in tuition fees and living costs each year, and quite a few of them then stay permanently. But these economic benefits have been bought at a price. Anecdotally, graduates in the UK are far less likely to have close friends who are non-graduates compared with the US and continental Europe. One FE college principal I know said this: 'When you ask most graduates what happened to the people they went to school with who didn't do A levels, they have no clue.'

Soskice and others, such as David Willetts, remain unapologetic about the 50 per cent university target despite conceding that the 'left-behind' 50 per cent issue has contributed to current political alienation. Willetts says he wants to see a continuing increase in university attendance but does not believe in a target. Some Scandinavian countries have reached 75 or 80 per cent of young people going into higher education.

But to build an entire, expensive edifice of residential, academic higher education on the grounds that the extra-curricular activities *might* have a positive effect on some students' social skills seems like an irresponsible allocation of national resources, especially at a time of significant skill shortages in caring and technical jobs and a Covid employment shock. And both the US and German economies out-perform the UK economy, at least in productivity growth, without such large numbers going into *residential* higher education.

Indeed, the Soskice argument overlaps with the Caplan (and Arum and Roksa) claim that many students effectively learn little specific of value at college and employers are more concerned with both the signal of general academic ability sent by getting to university in the first place and the subsequent acquisition of non-academic aptitudes once there. Caplan, however, draws the opposite conclusion to Sos-kice and Willetts and argues that there is no case for public subsidy of higher education, and much of it, beyond technical and vocational specialisms such as medicine and engineering, could be closed down or done in other institutions without any loss.[65]

One might not want to go that far, but there are surely other ways, short of sending almost everyone to residential universities for three years, of enabling young people to develop social skills. It could be in a revised secondary-school curriculum with more stress on social skills or in residential apprenticeships or forms of national service – a 'gap year for all' volunteering on farms or in hospitals – that could replicate the horizon-raising and social mixing experience of the resi-dential university at its best, and help to provide some of those soft skills that not everyone gets at home. It is true that longer, residential courses are popular with students – many are naturally attracted to three years fun and freedom away from parents at age eighteen/nine-teen – but the high cost (both for the individual and the taxpayer) and disappointing returns is starting to shift attitudes. And if Covid-19 is going to mean a permanent reduction in the flow of international students, whose high fees have helped to subsidize the system in the UK, this middle-class rite of passage may be a luxury the UK can no longer afford.

Universities are, in the main, full of decent people. The institutions exist in part to challenge tradition and authority and in recent years they have become overwhelmingly dominated by what French economist Thomas Piketty playfully calls the Brahmin left (as opposed to the merchant right), especially in the social sciences and humanities. The academics and administrators therefore find it hard to see themselves as part of the establishment, the gatekeepers of modern society's new class system.

According to the intelligence researcher Noah Carl, in 1960 about one-third of academics in the UK supported the Conservative Party and 45 per cent Labour, but by 2015 it was 11 per cent who supported the Tories and about 70 per cent left-wing parties. The figures in the US are even more politically skewed.[66] Partly because of this political bias public opinion has become more hostile and increasingly thinks that universities have got too big for their boots, especially in the US. According to Pew almost 40 per cent of Americans think that universities are having a negative effect on the country, including a large majority of Republican supporters.[67]

Many people in the universities realize that they must do more than credentialize the new mass elite and build lots of shiny new buildings, if they want to show that they are of use to the local people who do not attend them. In September 2019 I attended a conference on this very subject at the University of Manchester, with the grand title of the Global University Engagement Summit. I had been invited to the conference to present a sceptical view of higher-education expansion. And I was challenged, as I have been many times before, with the 'kicking away the ladder' argument. I went to a Russell Group university, as did three of my four children, so how come I want to stop others enjoying this advantage, especially young people from much less privileged backgrounds than mine or that of my own children? Wanting anything less than this for everybody opens one to accusations of an exclusionary elitism. 'This indignation . . . carries all the moral weight of egalitarianism. Yet it is also snobbish, since it evidently regards the trades as something "low",' as Matthew Crawford puts it.[68]

The point is that university does not produce the best outcomes for everyone. It makes no sense for many young people, from all social classes, who do not flourish in the rigorous academic environment that a university *should* be. And it makes even less sense for an economy that requires a range of skills and aptitudes many of which are better acquired in workplaces or other kinds of post-school educational institution.

And it is surely just self-defeating to assume that the answer to the education-based status (and income) divides is to send ever more people to university. People from all backgrounds, especially less privileged ones, should be encouraged to go to elite universities *if they have the aptitude for it*, as spelled out by Lionel Robbins in his report. But in my experience too much of the case for mass higher education is based precisely on an indiscriminate spirit of not wanting to kick away the ladder. It is a decent instinct but it can also be, as noted earlier, a kind of narcissism that says: be like me, pass exams at school, go to a Russell Group university and enjoy a successful professional career. But there are strict limits on the number of people who can do that, even if everyone in the society had exactly the same level of cognitive ability! Isn't it better to widen the sources of achievement and try to raise the status of 'not university' rather than send as many people as possible to university, and in the process raise expectations of professional success that in many cases are likely to be disappointed, while starving the economy of the middling, technical skills it needs?

I would not advocate closing universities, though some, at least in the UK, would certainly benefit from rebranding themselves as technical or applied universities and offering something shorter and more vocational than the standard university degree course. But thanks to the imminent demographic bulge of eighteen-year-olds in the UK, the country would need another thirty to thirty-five universities over the next couple of decades, an extra 300,000 places, if we were to keep up the present proportion of school leavers going into higher education. So the simple answer is: do *not* create these universities and let the proportion going into higher education fall back while investing in and raising the visibility and status of other forms of post-school education and training. This can help prevent academic standards falling further and provide a more socially useful balance between analytical and practical forms of knowledge – between Head and Hand.

5

Rise of the Knowledge Worker

There is a war for talent, and it will intensify.

Steven Hankin

At the age of eight most children want to be firefighters or cooks, nurses or bus drivers, or people who work in shops – obviously useful occupations that serve other people and make daily life possible, as we were reminded during the Covid-19 crisis. Yet by the time they leave school most children have been guided away to less hands-on, cognitive-based jobs. The vast majority of British and American parents want their children to go to university, according to surveys that higher-education lobby groups take great pleasure in quoting. This is not surprising when everyone from politicians to school teachers to employers have been telling them for the past three decades that it is the only way to a secure, middle-class future for their offspring.

As we will see in Chapter 9, this is actually ceasing to be the case, as the mass production of graduates has weakened the economic advantage of a degree, especially from less prestigious universities, and there is even some evidence of rising wages at the bottom and middle of the skill range. Many of those parents would be better advised to encourage their children – unless they are heading to one of the top universities – to take a high-grade apprenticeship or train as a technician, at least from a purely economic point of view.

Nevertheless, until very recently, the widely shared assumption that academic qualification equals cognitive achievement and a respected, well-paid job has been hard to argue with and is one of the cultural factors driving the continuing 'graduatization' of the labour market. To some extent this has been true since the start of the modern age.

What has happened in rich countries since the 1980s is that this logic, which for 100 years applied to just a small elite, started to apply to *everyone*. That in turn was caused by the decline of the old industrial Hand economy and the shift to a more Head-based knowledge economy as a result of more open, global trade and new technologies, particularly computer technologies, that replaced a lot of middling administrative/secretarial jobs and skilled manual jobs.

This 'hollowing out' of the labour market which is often associated with periods of technological change saw the start of what some economists call the 'great divergence' – a growing number of well-paid Head jobs for the highly qualified and Hand and Heart jobs often with stagnant or declining wages for the rest, especially in the US. Technological change does not have to result in this kind of divergence. Indeed, the period from what is called the second industrial revolution at the end of the nineteenth century – associated with steel, chemicals, electricity and automobiles – right up to the 1970s is often called, in the US, the 'great compression' because differentials between Head and Hand narrowed significantly.[1] In the US in 1900 a university professor was paid four times more than an unskilled worker; by 1960 this had fallen to twice as much, though both were a lot richer. Overall inequality between blue- and white-collar Americans declined from 1900 to 1970.

In Britain the income share of the top 5 per cent, which included all of the best-educated people, fell from 40 per cent at the end of the nineteenth century to 20 per cent by the 1970s.[2] 'The drop in inequality reflects the fact that labour finally started getting scarce at the same time as innovations started making labour especially productive. It is also surely important that this second phase corresponded, after World War 1, with a rise in workers' negotiating and voting power,' writes Richard Baldwin in *The Globotics Upheaval*.[3] But there is now overwhelming agreement among economists that this relatively egalitarian period ended in the 1970s and 1980s and mutated into one of greater labour market polarization, with jobs 'increasingly concentrated in high-education, high-wage occupations and low-education, low-wage occupations at the expense of traditionally middle-skill career jobs', as the American economist David Autor puts it.[4]

In the UK the share of middle-skill occupations, measured by the share of all hours worked, fell from 58 per cent to 40 per cent between 1981 and 2008. Across the OECD as a whole middle-skill jobs fell as a share of total employment by ten percentage points between 1995 and 2015.[5]

The hollowing-out story has been an even bigger one in the US. In 1970 US jobs were more or less evenly divided between *low-skill* (manual and basic service occupations) at 31.4 per cent of all hours worked, *middle-skill* (production, office and sales occupations) at 38.4 per cent and *high-skill* (professional, technical and managerial occupations) at 30.2 per cent. Over the next forty-five years the middle-skill hours fell steeply from 38.4 per cent of hours to just 23.3 per cent, with most of those hours switching from middle- to high-skill occupations, which grew from 30.2 per cent to 46.2 per cent of hours.[6]

So far, so good, one might think. And for those with a college degree that is broadly true, with around 60 per cent in high-skill occupations. But for non-college workers it is a very different story. According to Autor, in 1980 the employment of non-college workers was roughly split between low- and middle-skill jobs, with 42 per cent in the former, 43 per cent in the latter. Over the next few decades the share of non-college employment in middle-skill jobs fell sharply by 14 percentage points from 43 to 29 per cent, and *almost all of this is explained by the movement of non-college workers from middle-skill into low-skill work.*[7]

This single statistic illustrates the stark reality of the declining status of so much non-graduate employment and the political reaction against it of recent years in the US and elsewhere. It also illustrates how the relative wage stagnation at the bottom end of the labour market has worked. People have not, generally, been experiencing a cut in wages; rather they have lost a middle-skill/middle-pay job and can then only find a lower-skill/lower-pay job.

In his work on so-called deaths of despair in the US – the sharp increase in suicide, and death by drug overdose and alcoholism – the economist Angus Deaton talks about the 'the man who loses his decent $28 an hour job at General Motors and ends up working as a parking lot attendant' and in the process loses his health insurance and maybe his partner too.[8]

In broad terms the pay differentiation story has followed a similar pattern throughout the rich world. It is not just about the graduate premium, the higher incomes graduates receive relative to non-graduates – though that is most visible and most quoted in the academic literature – it goes all the way up and down the qualification range. And it is predicted by a branch of economics that has emerged to account for the higher returns to skill and education called human capital theory.

The theory, developed in the 1950s and 1960s at Chicago University by several economists, most notably Gary Becker, is that education directly increases an individual's stock of 'human capital', productivity and earnings potential.[9] Other things being equal, additional units of education (years of study, qualifications gained) will be rewarded with increased earnings. The assumption is that employers respond to the increase in supply of high-skilled workers by altering production processes to take advantage of this new supply of skilled workers. In any case, at least until recently, the demand for skill has kept pace with the much greater supply, one of the factors behind the pay differentiation story (though this is now changing, as we will see in Chapter 9).

It is not actually clear that higher pay for graduates is always the result of higher productivity as opposed to social convention and inherited differentials between blue collar and white collar. Moreover, measuring everything by qualification can have perverse outcomes and leads to what one might call 'cognitive creep'. A job comes to be judged, and paid, by the qualifications you need to get it rather than how productive or demanding it is or how well or badly you do it. For example, many jobs in the care sector need few, if any, qualifications but great patience, skill and emotional intelligence to do well. Similarly with some driving jobs that appear from the outside to be quite basic. Consider this description of a London bus driver.[10]

> Boarding an overcrowded 109 bus to Brixton (south London) at 8 a.m., dinging my pass on the yellow disc, I glance . . . at the driver. Although she appears to be looking straight ahead, she's checking what's happening on both decks, in the queue at the front door . . . whether passengers are trying to sneak aboard through the back door because they can't get on at the front, and deciding when to close the doors because the bus is already seriously overcrowded.

In the space of a few seconds, the driver makes many decisions: whether to stop in the first place, if and when to open the front doors and how many passengers to allow on before closing them; whether to ask the man who's just got on at the back to get off again; and whether to move off when the bus is now so full that passengers obscure the view to the nearside mirror. The driver makes a series of difficult decisions at nearly every stop on the journey between Croydon and Brixton.

In addition to these decisions, the driver has to make decisions to drive the bus! When to pull out, to overtake, to slow down, to stop or carry on at an amber light, to allow traffic to cross from a side road, to take special care of cyclists and pedestrians, some of whom dice with death as they weave in and out of the dense, slow-moving traffic. Driving a large vehicle with nearly 100 people crammed tightly into it requires great skill; the responsibilities are onerous and the technical expertise is considerable.

Since 1975 the hourly pay of bus and coach drivers in the UK has risen just 22 per cent (in 2017 prices) compared with a 111 per cent rise for advertising and public relations managers. In the US a bus driver has actually seen average hourly pay *fall* by 20 per cent in that period.[11]

In any case, fair or not fair, there is no escaping the broad trend on pay differentiation since the early 1980s. David Autor divides the recent history of pay in the US into three phases: 1963 to 1972, when real wages rose robustly and evenly among all education groups; 1973 to 1979, when following the first oil shock real earnings stagnated for everyone; and finally the era of rising wage inequality from 1980 onwards, where wages rose robustly among the most educated and fell in real terms among the least educated, most strikingly among men with less than a bachelor's degree.[12]

And it is worth remembering, again, how recently the less-well-educated dominated developed societies. As late as the 1990 census in the US whites without a college degree were more than 60 per cent of the adult population.

The divergence story has also been true of the UK and continental Europe, though less so in terms of pay because of high minimum wages and stronger unions – median pay in the UK has risen 78 per cent since 1975, 63 per cent in Germany and 30 per cent in France, while it has remained flat in the US, partly thanks to rising health costs for employers.[13]

The increase in the high-skill wage bill has been steeper in the US and the UK than in much of Europe between 1980 and 2004, reflecting sharper income dispersal. It rose by 13.9 percentage points in the US and 16.5 points in the UK. Contrast this with rises of 6 to 8 percentage points for France and Germany.[14] But in Europe as a whole there has been a similar growth in professional and associate professional occupations and a sharp decline in more routine 'good jobs' in administrative/secretarial and skilled manual roles – just think of the medium-sized engineering company of the 1970s and 1980s with its small army of white-collar office workers and skilled manual workers who have marched off into history.

It is worth briefly recording the speed and scale of that march. Between June 1978 and September 2018 the proportion of UK jobs in manufacturing and mining fell from 26.4 per cent to 7.9 per cent.[15] The fall was slightly less sharp in Germany, which is down to 15 per cent and France to 10 per cent.[16] In the US the fall was from about 22 per cent to around 9 per cent.[17] In the UK in the last twenty years alone there have been further sharp falls in printing trades (minus 69 per cent), metal forming, welding and related trades (minus 56 per cent) and secretarial and related occupations (minus 42 per cent).[18]

These declines carry within them a story of the radical diminishment of working-class power and institutions. I was a witness to the dying days of that power as a labour reporter on the *Financial Times* newspaper in London in the early 1980s. I was one of five journalists who had a whole page of the broadsheet newspaper to fill every day with stories of pay deals, strikes and trade union politics. We never had any trouble filling the page: there was still a last gasp of life in the unions and their centralized pay negotiation institutions. Union membership in the private sector was in the process of collapsing, thanks in part to the closure of plants with high union density, and overall union membership fell in the UK from around half of the workforce in 1983 to 23 per cent in 2017, and most of the latter was public sector and professional workers.[19] Starting from a lower level, the decline in the US was also sharp and now stands at just 10 per cent of employees, mainly in the public sector. Government legislation in the UK and US in the 1980s hastened the decline, as did suicidal strike action, particularly Arthur Scargill's year-long miners' strike in the UK in 1984–5.

Union involvement in training and apprenticeship systems and management decisions and pay bargaining gradually disappeared, at least outside the public sector and one or two niches in the private sector, and the era of the deregulated labour market, at least in the UK and US, was ushered in – with a corresponding rise of the knowledge worker and the graduate premium. The slice of income that workers had once laid a claim to through their collective power now seeped upwards to be claimed by the graduates with their cognitive qualifications in the offices.

The destruction of union power was mainly a British and American story. The social partnership system remained intact in Germany, and union power remained significant in key sectors in France, though some of the same trends in income distribution emerged in milder form.

But this is also in part a surprisingly happy story of more 'lovely' than 'lousy' jobs. Between 2001 and 2018 in the UK jobs in the bottom three deciles of the earnings distribution have declined as a share of employment while those in the top three have increased.[20] Many of the most unpleasant jobs have been exported to low-income countries, which is probably one reason why, despite the negative commentary, people tell opinion surveys that life at work has been improving. In 2015 71 per cent of British employees said they had a good job compared with just 57 per cent in 1989, according to the British Social Attitudes Survey.[21] In the US too only 15 per cent of employees say they are somewhat or very dissatisfied with their job, according to a recent Pew survey.

Meanwhile, the share of graduate level jobs has been expanding fast in the UK at a bit less than one percentage point a year since 1986 (though it has slowed since 2012) and is now estimated at almost 40 per cent.[22] It is a similar story in other rich countries; in the US 47 per cent of jobs are now classified as 'managerial, professional, technical or associate professional'.

UK employer demand for the highest school-level qualification, A levels, peaked in the late 1960s (when overall participation in higher education was below 8 per cent). Thereafter A level recruitment was for lower-status managerial and technical roles, though many of the largest banks continued to prefer A level students well into the 1980s.[23] (This is now coming back into fashion as more employers – including prestigious consultancies such as EY and KPMG – realize that, apart from the very top graduates, the level of ability dividing a bright A level student from an equivalent graduate may be negligible.)

As noted, the 'great divergence' on pay in the UK and the rest of Europe has been less dramatic than in the US, but real enough. The most recent pay data comparing hourly pay in 1975 and 2017 in the UK (in 2017 prices) finds a 137 per cent increase for company financial managers and 86 per cent for actuaries and statisticians, compared with 21 per cent for welders and 9 per cent for refuse collectors. In the US the figures for the same period at the bottom end are *minus*: minus 12 per cent for sheet-metal workers, minus 16 per cent for truck drivers, minus 34 per cent for butchers, minus 42 per cent for bakers.[24]

Numerous OECD reports have noted a sustained fall in relative wages of less-educated workers from the 1980s onwards. According to one of the most recent reports in 2018, those who have attained only upper-secondary education will on average earn 65 per cent of their graduate contemporaries' salaries across all OECD countries, although there is a great deal of variation across countries and course types.[25]

More or less in line with human capital theory, the differentiation works all the way up and down from the highest forms of postgraduate qualification to the lowliest school qualification. About 10 per cent of jobs in the UK now require a postgraduate qualification of some kind and they bring with them significant earnings returns relative to the next rung down the qualification ladder, 8.9 per cent for men and 10.3 per cent for women.[26] (In the US postgraduate qualifications are even more common, and postgraduates experience a 30 per cent lower probability of being unemployed than those with bachelor's degrees.)[27]

The basic 'graduate premium' in earnings has been declining with the expansion of the graduate class but remains significant, at least from elite universities. In the UK at the age of twenty-nine the average man who attended university earns about 25 per cent more than the average man with just five good GCSEs. For women the gap is even more at 50 per cent thanks to the relatively lower pay of women in non-graduate, often Heart, jobs.[28] Even at the bottom end those with A levels, GCSEs and apprenticeships achieve significantly higher lifetime productivity and pay compared with those without.[29]

The story is a similar one in the US and France, and the graduate returns to higher education are even higher in Germany, partly because the expansion in numbers has been, until recently, less rapid than in the UK. According to the latest figures from the OECD, someone in Germany with a bachelor's or equivalent degree earns on average 63 per cent more than someone with upper-secondary education. With a master's, doctoral or equivalent it is 83 per cent. For France the figures are 47 per cent and 110 per cent (reflecting the higher salaries of those who go through the Grandes Écoles system), and for the US, 64 per cent and 131 per cent.[30]

PERMISSION TO THINK

This forward march of the knowledge worker and the income divergence associated with the knowledge economy are now a well-known story. But two aspects of the cognitive takeover story are less visible. First the extent of the privileging of key cognitive employees that has been emerging in big multinational companies. Second, the extent of the spread of *graduate-only* jobs in recent years.

Higher returns to qualification have also been reinforced by other developments in modern economies such as the so-called 'war for talent' and winner-takes-all markets. Both are the product of technology and global openness. The war for talent was a phrase coined by Steven Hankin of the management consultancy McKinsey in 1997 to describe more intense competition among top companies for recruiting and retaining key knowledge workers.

The prediction that the modern market economy combined with certain new technologies would generate a new layer of superstars was made a few years ago by two American academics, Robert Frank and Philip Cook. In *The Winner-Take-All Society* they describe how technology allows a few stars to corner a disproportionate level of earnings in a particular market.[31] Frank and Cook quote Rabo Kara-beckian, the only moderately good painter in Kurt Vonnegut's 1987 novel *Bluebeard*:

> simply moderate giftedness has been made worthless by the printing press and radio and television and satellites and all that. A moderately gifted person who would have been a community treasure a thousand years ago has to give up, has to go into some other line of work, since modern communications has put him or her into daily competition with nothing but the world's champions . . . The entire planet can get along nicely now with maybe a dozen champion performers in each area of human giftedness.

Now that most of the music we listen to is pre-recorded, the world's best soprano can be everywhere at once.

> And since it costs no more to stamp out compact discs from Kathleen Battle's master recording of the Mozart arias than from her under-study's, most of us listen to Battle. Millions of us are willing to pay a few cents extra to hear her rather than another singer who is only marginally less able; this allows Battle to write her own ticket.[32]

The focus on the most talented people at the top of organizations, combined, especially in Britain and America, with intense pressure to reduce costs and maximize shareholder returns, has also been reshaping the way that big corporations operate in what is some-times called the 'Future of Work' transformation. Back in the 1980s the so-called GMNs (global multinationals) began introducing enterprise-wide IT systems and turned routine administrative work into specialist centralized 'shared services centres' that supplied a standard service to all business units. As this work was classified as non-strategic and non-value-creating, it could even be outsourced and offshored to low-wage countries. GMNs reduced their head-count and produced much better-looking labour productivity ratios. This opening phase of the Future of Work, established a sense of 'core' work and work that could be contracted out to the 'contin-gent' labour market. A friend of mine who designs remuneration systems for big companies, and therefore has to remain anonymous, described to me the next phase.

The next phase is driven by the GMNs fear of the new wave of small, agile, digital disruptors. Many of these new firms are well funded start-ups who have no baggage to preserve and no patience. Given a choice of waiting decades to climb a job grade ladder or work in a start-up offering instant status, reward and power, many bright young people are choosing *not* to join the GMN graduate training schemes. They choose, instead, to join a small organisation where everything is out-sourced except the stimulating work of idea origination, design, IP protection and marketing. They can try many things, fail fast and follow what works. Digital start-ups can get products to market very quickly, even in something as traditional as razor blades.

By comparison the GMNs look at themselves and see rigid job definitions, turf wars, a command level that got there over time and is out of touch with the latest skills and technology. Their middle rank employees are risk averse. They move slowly to protect their CV from failure. Their career is built on long-term progress up a professional hierarchy rather than the success of the immediate mission.

The new business structure consists of three layers: elite core full-time employees; contingent professionals; and contingent service staff, cleaners, security and so on, many in the gig economy.

The core of the business is the elite talent who are trusted with the 'secret sauce'; the secret ingredients behind competitive advantage. The elite are considered exceptionally talented. The only ones clever enough to create new value. Logic suggests that these are the only people the firm needs to directly motivate and retain.

Beneath that elite there will still be a lot of complex technical and professional work that requires human input, but can be bought in at standard rates as needed from the external contingent labour market. Their role is seen as definable and standardized. This might include highly technical specialists such as project managers, scientists, engineers.

My friend describes the core talent in more detail:

Careers will still start with a top degree from a prestigious university and specialist qualifications, but hierarchies within specialisms will be replaced with agile teams which are highly motivated and autonomous

. . . You will be encouraged to see yourself as a one-person business or entrepreneur who markets their talent to the highest project bidder within the organization, and if the organization undervalues your talent you will leave.

What my friend is describing overlaps with the work on Digital Taylorism of Phil Brown and Hugh Lauder that will be explored in more detail in Chapter 9.[33] Brown and Lauder break down service jobs into three categories of Developers, Demonstrators and Drones, with only Developers – typically 10 to 15 per cent of the workforce – given a degree of autonomy and cognitive judgement.

It is worth noting that this strict demarcation of those with 'permission to think' and the functionaries providing contracted-out services seems to be a product of western business schools and, paradoxically, has not been adopted by the more authoritarian-communitarian Asian business cultures. Several decades ago Japan surprised western manufacturers by showing the value of asking all workers to think about process and quality, in what was called Total Quality Management. The Future of Work strategy does not seem to have learned this lesson.

IF YOU CAN'T BEAT 'EM, JOIN 'EM

The relentless graduatization of the labour market is another trend that has been making it harder to achieve a wider spread of income and status. In the UK in 2017 23 per cent of jobs required no qualifications on entry, while around 38 per cent of jobs needed at least higher-education qualifications.[34] There is quite widespread popular hostility to the graduatization of jobs like nursing, police officer, project manager and even prison officer. And yet it continues inexorably with powerful professional lobbies pushing it in many rich countries. Most of the above jobs are not yet exclusively graduate entry, but the graduate entry channel is becoming more central to the ethos of the organizations involved, and non-graduate entry routes are increasingly seen as a permanent slow lane rather than an alternative route in.

But people seldom stop to ask whether the graduate pay premium actually reflects greater value produced by the graduate. Is it just the graduate class awarding itself a premium? If university education was abolished tomorrow, how many tasks could not be completed because people would lack the skills? Is the trend being driven by traditionally non-graduate jobs like nursing and policing just wanting some of the higher status associated with being a graduate profession?

Peter Cheese, head of the UK's Chartered Institute of Personnel and Development, the professional body for HR people, sees 'high graduate supply creating its own employer demand', and so long as parents believe that going to university and getting a graduate job is the path to safety, and maybe even success, for their children, that supply will keep coming. This also creates, according to Cheese, a 'herd' effect: 'If everyone else is only hiring graduates, then you assume that you should do that too.' But one of the issues in hiring too many young people who have exam-passing ability but little experience of life is that they may be weak on the non-cognitive aspects which are actually required for most jobs – leadership, communication, judgement and dealing with difficult people and situations.

Cheese says he has advised various different organizations with high levels of graduate entry but who need help providing people with a kind of remedial training in basic human skills. He thinks we need to find ways to embed more clearly into education at all levels the recognition of core 'human' skills that are essential in the workplace. (This might just be a polite way of saying that there are far too many plausible middle-class people with good social skills, now credentialized with degrees, who are quite poor at what they do. The people they manage can see this, and it undermines legitimacy in the organization.)

Nevertheless, the case for graduatization is sometimes a strong one. As we will see there is evidence that graduate nurses, for example, improve the overall quality and effectiveness of health care. Yet there is the balancing anxiety, just mentioned, of lack of real-life experience combined with unrealistic expectations and disdain for the more basic aspects of, say, nursing or policing.

As so often in the cognitive takeover story, the graduatization of the labour market, even in the upper echelons, is a surprisingly recent thing. Managers, directors and senior officials (the highest category in the UK's nine-level Standard Occupational Classification) have historically employed most graduates, but the proportion was just 53 per cent in 1991, rising to 78 per cent in 2014.[35] In managerial, professional and technical occupations (the second-highest occupational class) there are now nearly as many graduates as non-graduates, while only about one in every six workers in these occupations was a graduate at the start of the 1990s.[36]

The official definition of a 'graduate job' in the UK is anyone working in the top three occupational classes (in that nine-class Standard Occupational Category schema). However, many of these managerial, associate professional and technical occupations have, historically, not required a degree and include jobs such as dancers and choreographers, fitness instructors, youth and community workers and IT user support technicians.

The remaining occupations (so those in Standard Occupational Categories four to nine) had a near insignificant share of graduates in 1991, but this share has increased to 21 per cent for administrative occupations, 13 per cent for both sales and personal service occupations and 8 per cent even for the lowest-skilled elementary occupations. Only the manual occupations, skilled trades and semi-skilled process operatives have seen less significant rises.[37]

The evolution of nursing into a graduate profession in the UK has crystallized the debate on the advantages and disadvantages of graduatization. The idea that the nurse should be 'a professional among equals . . . and not a handmaiden to other professionals' goes back many decades, but it was not until 2013 that nurses officially required a degree. Today's division between the graduate nurse and the more junior nursing associate actually mirrors the old distinction between the SRN (state registered nurse) and the SEN (state enrolled nurse), with the SRN requiring a higher level of knowledge and qualification. There have been some graduate nurses since the 1970s, but back in the 1980s it was decided that registered nurses should study for a diploma rather than a degree, which left them as the poor relation of other health professionals, who were mainly graduates. In 2009 the Nursing and Midwifery Council finally decided to establish all-graduate entry for registered nurses.

The 2012 Willis Commission found no evidence 'that degree level registration was damaging to patient care'. But it did also say that there should be a diversity of entry points and career pathways into nursing.[38] A 2014 article in the *Lancet* that looked at hospital mortality in nine countries found 'growing evidence from across Europe and the US that a better-educated nursing workforce delivers better patient outcomes, in terms of morbidity and mortality'.[39] But the language used in much of the debate assumes that without a degree-level of training people are somehow incompetent. When the decision was made in 2009 to establish an all-graduate nursing profession, Christine Beasley, then the Chief Nursing Officer, said this: 'We need to make sure that not only do nurses need to care and have compassion, but they also need to have real ability to think, to make critical decisions and have technical skills.'[40] The idea that before 2013 nurses were unable to think and make critical decisions is a bizarre one, especially coming from the Chief Nursing Officer, which suggests that this is just as much an argument about the relative status and prestige of nurses relative to doctors.

The Willis Commission found that non-graduate nurses, nursing associates or care assistants do about 60 per cent of the hands-on care but often do not have the consistent training that went with the old SEN role. For graduate nurses almost half of the training is delivered in real situations in hospitals; nonetheless the Commission found that many nurses needed a lot of extra support immediately after qualification.[41] The Commission also reported that nurses with degrees are more likely to say that nursing did not live up to their career development expectations, compared with registered nurses without a degree. The answer (in line with human capital theory), 'a clear postgraduate development pathway must be put in place'. The National Health Service (NHS) professional bodies and, of course, the universities who put on the degree courses are convinced of the benefits of graduatization, yet the public remain sceptical, and the academics seldom find significantly higher levels of skill from the graduate route in general.

Ken Mayhew, an Oxford professor of education, summarizes: 'A few studies identified benefits of degree programmes in terms of enhanced competencies and qualities such as creativity, innovation, leadership, critical thinking, reflection, transferring knowledge, and better research skills . . . . However, [other] research demonstrated that there were no marked differences between skills and competencies developed by the different routes.'[42]

In 2018 the UK's statistics body the Office for National Statistics (ONS) reported that only 57 per cent of young graduates were in high-skilled employment, a decline over the decade since the 2008 crash of 4.3 percentage points.[43] The proportion of older graduates in high-skilled employment was only slightly higher at 65 per cent. The Department of Education speculates that this could reflect 'the limited number of high-skilled employment opportunities available to younger individuals and the potential difficulties they face matching into relevant jobs early in their careers'. Graduatization, in other words, doesn't always mean new professional skills but can just be a way for employers to screen for more able candidates. Consider the graduatization of the UK police force. Around one-third of police officers are already graduates (up from just 1.6 per cent in 1979),[44] but it was announced in 2015 by the College of Policing that all new officers in England and Wales will have to be educated to degree level by 2020. Chief Constable Giles York, of the National Police Chiefs Council, said this would 'improve our ability to attract and retain really good people'.[45] York also said that it was 'fair and right' that officers receive the recognition and accreditation they deserve as professionals. As with nursing this reflects the deep cultural bias in favour of the academic along with a desire for *recognition*.

The better class of candidate that the College of Policing is seeking turns out to be someone with a different set of attitudes rather than professional skills as such. It says it wants: 'improvements in both academic skills (such as critical thinking, reflection, communication, critical analysis, independent judgement and research skills) and "soft skills" such as tolerance, willingness to embrace alternative perspectives, empathy, and moral and ethical reasoning'.[46] The College cites research that graduate officers are better at dealing with complexity, had a wider understanding of their role in society, used force more appropriately and had wider belief systems. They also argued in their consultation that 'many in the policing workforce already take decisions in complex and unpredictable settings, with limited information, meaning they tend to operate at the equivalent of . . . graduate level.'[47] But the graduate argument put like this is based on a logical fallacy. The fact that graduate officers are better at dealing with complexity does not mean it is *because* they went to university. The most intelligent police officers who deal best with complexity are likely to have been in the academic track at school and gone to university but they might have dealt just as well with complexity without higher education. Higher education correlates with but does not necessarily cause higher performance.

The plans have been criticized by the Police Federation (the staff association for police in the UK), who are concerned with access and diversity as well as disputing whether 'graduate-level study is needed to perform the job given that many are currently able to effectively deal with its growing complexity despite not having a degree'.[48] (In July 2019 Lincolnshire police authority launched a legal challenge to the College ruling, claiming it would reduce frontline police numbers by 10 per cent.)[49]

Supporters of graduatization claim, with sometimes limited evidence, that it raises skill levels as well as the more obvious uplift to status. Critics say that concrete skills relating to research, organization and IT can be learned, and in some cases are already being learned, in settings other than universities. And to the extent that it is about soft skills it represents a cultural shift that is not necessarily welcome and which can exclude too many potentially good recruits. Moreover, for the capable non-graduate graduatization can produce a double whammy: not only is promotion from below without a degree now much harder beyond a certain level in many organizations, but you are also likely to be pushed down by people who may do your job less well than you.

An acquaintance who is a management consultant recalls helping to reorganize a government agency a few years ago. Part of the reorganization involved regrading and reclassifying jobs. He tells this dismaying story:

> I remember a thirty-something guy who worked in accounts payable matching invoices to purchase orders. He was a long-term employee. He was fastidious and reliable in a repetitive clerical job. It was low-grade, lowish pay, but he dressed in a suit and had a briefcase and looked for

all the world like a manager. The job was due to be reclassified as a graduate position. A graduate would be bored and offended by the routine, errors would increase, turnover in the position would increase, a decent human being is discarded and degraded for what? Satisfying a misguided theory about social mobility?

This echoes the 'missing middle' problem of the unsuitability of graduates for many middling jobs, described by Paul Lewis in the last chapter. As does a 2016 report for the UK think tank the Resolution Foundation on 'the 'forgotten 40 per cent' of the workforce – mid-skilled workers without a university degree.[50]

The Foundation organized focus groups for members of that forgotten group who reported that the influx of graduates into their occupations had reduced their progression prospects. A woman in her forties explained: 'I've got a friend who works at a company he started at when he left school at sixteen. Went straight in the back office at sixteen. He's my age and he now recruits for his back office and won't take anyone who isn't a graduate.'[51]

In some sectors, a degree was viewed as essential in order to reach a management position. While sometimes this reflected the additional technical knowledge required, in the view of another focus group member it was more of a cultural decision, as extensive training was provided. And for him, it resulted in better people being overlooked for promotion:

> In my industry, I've been held back by not having a degree. I've seen people who have a degree move on into better positions. They don't care what the degree is in, they just take them on and pass them through. They're absolutely useless at their job. Having a degree just opens the door, it doesn't matter what it's in. I've had to fight my corner and use my experience.[52]

This connects with the work of Amanda Goodall and other academics on 'domain specific knowledge' which finds plenty of evidence that the best managers tend to be technical experts not generalist managers.[53] Yet in recent years the idea that the 'really good people' (in Chief Constable Giles York's phrase), who can turn their hands to almost anything, are to be found graduating with good degrees from top universities has been reinforced by the success of organizations such as Teach First.

Teach First, modelled on Teach for America in the US, was designed to tempt top graduates of top universities back into the teaching profession, which they had largely deserted since the 1960s. It offers a short-cut training and demands at least two years' commitment to working in usually challenging schools. It is regarded as a big success and continues to attract many talented and idealistic young people, a good proportion of whom stay in the teaching profession (my eldest daughter is one of them). In the UK it has also been copied in social work (Frontline) and in the prison service (Unlockedgrads).

But we should be cautious about contributing to the cult of the elite university graduate. Clearly some of the value of Teach First has been in attracting more able young people with top degrees back into teaching, but wherever it has been tried it has usually been accompanied by other changes such as breaking the monopoly of teacher training in education faculties and generally disrupting group-think in public service professions.

A concluding observation: the knowledge worker is increasingly a female worker. The rise and rise of the knowledge worker in the last three decades is also, in part, about the rise and rise of the female professional. Women in the UK have not only caught up with, but overtaken, men in jobs that require higher education. In 1997 28 per cent of men and 23 per cent of women were in such jobs. In 2017 it was 36 per cent for men and 40 per cent for women.[54] Universities, law schools and medical schools are now at least 50 per cent female, and although few women are CEOs of top companies, roughly half of the jobs in the top managerial and professional class are now taken by women.[55]

The top end of the labour market has been almost completely gender desegregated, but the middle and bottom end remains highly segregated, with women overwhelmingly concentrated in the caring sectors such as primary education, nursing and social care. This is one reason why the graduate premium is considerably higher for women than for men because of the bigger earnings gulf between professional women and often part-time women workers in the lowest-paid corners of the economy. Men in low-skill jobs such as refuse collection or postal delivery tend to be better paid than women in low-skill jobs, partly because the jobs have historically been unionized.

Employment status is usually more strongly connected to well-being in men than in women.[56] Women on average place a higher priority on home and children than men, and household income is a stronger predictor of well-being among women. These changes have thus had a greater impact on status feelings of non-graduate men, as I will spell out in more detail in Chapter 7. And because women have partly swapped work in the home for work in the public economy the home has experienced higher income but higher stress too, as we will see in Chapter 8.

The rising status of women need not necessarily contribute to a corresponding decline in the subjective social status of men. Many men have welcomed such developments or at least not seen them as negatively impacting their own status. 'However, because social status is based on a rank ordering, it is somewhat like a positional good, in the sense that, when many others acquire more status, the value of one's own status may decline,' write Noam Gidron and Peter Hall in a 2017 paper on the politics of social status.[57]

Over the last thirty years the female graduate has been one of the main winners, and the male skilled manual worker one of the main losers, from the rise of the knowledge economy – maybe something Hillary Clinton's campaign managers should have been more alert to. But, as we will see in Chapter 9, the era of the ever-expanding knowledge worker class is now drawing to a close.

6

The Diploma Democracy

Comrades! You do not imagine, I hope, that we pigs are doing this in a spirit of selfishness and privilege? Many of us actually dislike milk and apples . . . Our sole object in taking these things is to preserve our health. Milk and apples (this has been proved by Science, comrades) contain substances absolutely necessary to the well-being of a pig. We pigs are brainworkers. The whole management and organization of this farm depend on us. Day and night we are watching over your welfare. It is for YOUR sake that we drink that milk and eat those apples.

George Orwell, Animal Farm

John Adams, the American Republic's second president, thought that the new American legislature should be 'an exact portrait in miniature' of the population. The French revolutionary Mirabeau also thought the French National Assembly should represent the people as accurately as 'a map represents a landscape'.[1] In pre-democratic politics in Europe in the eighteenth and nineteenth centuries politicians were mainly drawn from the land-owning or capital-owning class that dominated the small enfranchised elite, though their interests were often represented by lawyers who formed a disproportionate slice of the political class. One of the main demands of the labour movements and parties of the left that emerged in the nineteenth century was that working men should have the means to represent people like themselves and sit in parliaments and legislatures.

Should politicians resemble, and reflect the views of, the people they represent? Adams, Mirabeau and early labour movement politicians have a formidable adversary in Plato, who argues in

The Republic that the best government is one guided by philosopher kings, able to rise above the atavistic demands and interests of ordinary people. One consequence of our current political turbulence likely to be reinforced by the Covid-19 crisis is that traces of Plato's views are resurfacing among sections of today's cognitive class, some of whom are suspicious of mass democracy (particularly when it produces results that they dislike, such as Brexit and Trump) and would prefer more decisions to be taken by unaccountable experts.

An important strand of the democratic tradition, going back to Athenian democracy, has been the concept of 'lay politics', the idea that anyone can be a politician and the political class should be a collection of ordinary, and socially representative, people – ordinary people doing an extraordinary thing.

In the early decades of mass democracy in the twentieth century, when socio-economic cleavages dominated politics, this ideal was partly realized in the social composition of political parties; labour parties tended to be represented by working-class people with low levels of formal education, though allied with a large minority of middle-class idealists, and similarly, liberal and conservative parties tended to be represented by the affluent and better-educated.

In recent decades, following the loosening of the class structure and a greater professionalization of politics, the idea that it is desirable for politicians to be *like* the people they represent had begun to weaken – at least for class, if not for race and gender. But the most recent wave of political alienation has returned this question to the centre of the democratic conversation.

An exasperation with the existing political elites was a significant factor behind Brexit, the election of Donald Trump and the national elections in France in 2017 and Italy in 2018. In almost all cases politicians were rewarded for their *lack* of political experience and, at least in some of those cases, for their 'blokeish' lack of deference towards so-called politically correct speech – consider the reluctance of Boris Johnson, Donald Trump or Matteo Salvini to be constrained by the normal rules of official discourse. But, of course, as that list also underlines, the idea of politicians as like ordinary people will always be a fantasy. They will always be different from the great mass of voters. As Jonathan Sumption, the former British judge, put it in his final 2019 Reith lecture:

Representative democracy necessarily produces a political class separated by life style and outlook from those who vote for them . . . Few politicians will ever be like the generality of the electors even if they began that way . . . Getting elected calls for exceptional levels of ambition and commitment, government calls for high levels of information, experience and skill . . . The uncomfortable truth is that all political systems are aristocracies . . . Democracies are only different in that the aristocracies are installed and removeable by popular vote.[2]

But *how* politicians differ from the great mass of voters matters. And in recent years one thing above all has distinguished the political class from at least two-thirds of voters: almost all of them are *highly educated.*

Mark Bovens and Anchrit Wille express it succinctly in their important book *Diploma Democracy*:

Most contemporary democracies in Western Europe are governed by a select group of well-educated citizens. They are diploma democracies – ruled by those with the highest formal qualifications. University graduates have come to dominate all relevant political institutions and arenas, from political parties, parliaments and cabinets, to organised interests, deliberative venues, and internet consultations.

. . . In the British House of Commons, after the 2015 elections, nine out of ten MPs were university graduates . . . In the 2013 Bundestag, 86 per cent of the MPs had attended an institute of higher education . . . After the 2012 elections, almost 97 per cent of the members of the Dutch Tweede Kamer had attended college or graduate school. In Denmark, Belgium and France, between 75 and 90 per cent of the MPs have the equivalent of a college or a graduate degree. This is not because everybody goes to college nowadays – over 70 per cent of the electorate in Western Europe is still only educated up to secondary level, at the highest.[3]

During President Obama's second term 93 per cent of House members and 99 per cent of Senators held at least bachelor's degrees compared to a national average of 32 per cent. (And a large majority in both Houses have further degrees.)[4]

Cabinets and governments, as one might expect, tend to be even better educated than ordinary politicians. Of the fifteen ministers in

Angela Merkel's third cabinet, fourteen held a master's degree, nine had a PhD, seven had worked at universities and two had been professors. In David Cameron's two cabinets, in 2010 and 2015, 69 per cent and 50 per cent, respectively, were Oxbridge graduates.[5]

In France the political, media and business elite is still drawn overwhelmingly from the Grandes Écoles, which educate just 4 per cent of all students. Between 1986 and 2012, 36 per cent of members of the government had graduated from these top schools, above all ENA (the École Nationale d'Administration). At the time of writing (in June 2019) both the President and the Prime Minister are so-called Énarques as are: the heads of the Central Bank, the Finance Ministry, the Presidential Office, the Republican Party, the external intelligence service, the state railways and several top private-sector companies. Moreover, recruitment to ENA has become narrower, not wider, in recent years, with the share of graduates from blue-collar backgrounds down to around 6 per cent.

ENA's annual intake is just eighty but, as noted earlier, it has produced four of the last eight presidents and eight of the last twenty-two prime ministers. Eleven of the fifteen postwar British prime ministers graduated from Oxford (which takes 3,000 undergraduates a year) and six of thirteen postwar US presidents attended either Harvard or Yale (both take around 2,000 undergraduates a year).

In many countries the takeover of politics by the cognitive class, like the rise of educational selection that we noted in Chapter 4, and the increased economic returns to a large knowledge worker class described in Chapter 5, is a relatively new phenomenon. In the UK's 1964 general election graduates were still a minority in the British parliament, reflecting a country where most people still left school without qualifications. (And in the mid-twentieth century many of the most significant British politicians had little formal, post-school education: neither Winston Churchill, nor Ernest Bevin nor Aneurin Bevan, who between them played key roles in victory in the Second World War, the formation of NATO and the creation of the National Health Service, attended a university.)

In the nineteenth and early part of the twentieth centuries political elites were based on class and property. They were usually better educated than the average citizen, but this was not the source of their power. As Bovens and Wille put it: 'In the information society, however, knowledge and information are the most important social goods. Political power is concentrated not among the landed gentry, patricians, or manufacturers, but among the "symbolic analysts", "creative professionals", and all those other citizens with ample capacity to process information.'[6]

This cognitive class takeover of politics does not apply just to politicians but also increasingly *to the whole apparatus of political parties and political activism*, and the voters themselves are increasingly divided along educational lines.

Bovens and Wille have produced a useful summary, drawing on many national and international surveys, of the political participation story in six European countries,* with the population sub-divided into low-educated, middling-educated and high-educated. Their political participation 'pyramid' ranges from informal participation (reading about and discussing politics) to voting in elections, to conventional participation (lobbying an official) and protest participation (joining a demonstration), to party membership and, finally, standing for political office. With the single exception of watching politics on television the highly educated outscore the less-well-educated in all political activities, in all countries, in some activities significantly. The political activism gap is especially large in France and the UK. As the authors point out: 'For many highly educated people, writing letters or emails, engaging in debates, and running meetings are all in a day's work. Yet they can be intimidating for people for whom these are not regular activities.'

Pathways into politics have changed too in recent decades, in ways that benefit the educated. Mass political parties, trade unions, churches and traditional women's groups have all been in decline, while pressure groups, NGOs, advocacy groups, internet political forums of various kinds have expanded their membership. But whereas the former were usually rooted in particular communities, the latter tend to require a pre-existing commitment or membership of a community of ideas. Barack Obama is a case in point: he moved from an elite university to becoming a community activist, quite unlike an elected trade

* Belgium, Denmark, France, Germany, the Netherlands and the UK.

union official of the old days. Community activists, you might say, appoint themselves to represent the communities they judge unable to represent themselves.

Mass political parties and trade unions, with membership and interest often passed down through family connections, provided basic political education to the less-educated. The smaller 'cadre' parties of today are often run by people who became involved in politics at university and then went on to a job with a political connection – working for a lobby group, or in the media, or a think tank/policy organization or even as an aide to an MP – providing useful experience and networks. The number of Belgian MPs who had previously worked as a parliamentary aide rose from 10 per cent in the early 1970s to 35 per cent in 2010.

The background of the two main party leaders in the 2015 UK election is also emblematic of this shift. Ed Miliband is the child of two academics and as a teenager worked as an intern for a family friend, the iconic socialist MP Tony Benn. After Oxford he became a Labour junior policy adviser, then after a master's at the LSE and some teaching at Harvard he became a special adviser to Gordon Brown and was then elected to parliament in 2005. David Cameron, from an upper-class background, graduated in PPE from Oxford with a first (Ed Miliband only managed a 2:1 in the same subject, though his brother David achieved a first) and began working for Norman Lamont, then Chancellor of the Exchequer and later Home Secretary Michael Howard. He briefly left politics for a job in public relations before becoming an MP in 2001.

Modern forms of political participation such as online discussion groups, public consultations and e-petitions show, according to the UK's Hansard Society, an even bigger divergence between those with high and low education than old-fashioned political activities such as party political meetings and attending demonstrations.

Why is the takeover of politics by an educated elite, the old Platonic dream, a problem? Does it not make sense to have the most intelligent or at least the best-trained people running our political institutions? Up to a point. But there are two big, related, problems with the cognitive class takeover of politics. First and most serious is that the cognitive class tends to pursue its own interests and intuitions even while believing sincerely that it represents the wider common good. Second, it turns out that a university degree is not necessarily the best training for a life in politics.

Of course, it is true that bright and ambitious people have always been drawn to politics, and many of those who went into politics before mass higher education would have had degrees today. Yet the cognitive class in general has become more homogeneous and parochial in recent decades through the shared experience of residential higher education, partnering together and tending to live in the same places while often sharing the same interests and values. Americans seem to be dividing themselves into alarmingly homogeneous residential communities reflecting their educational backgrounds and beliefs.[7] According to German sociologist Heike Wirth, there has also been an increase in the social distance between the high and low education groups.

There are many issues, of course, where the interests of the highly educated and less-well-educated overlap, above all in competent management of the economy, public services and crises like Covid-19. And there is no inherent reason why the highly educated cannot represent the interests of the less-well-educated, particularly on traditional left–right socio-economic issues on which there has been some convergence in recent years, as, broadly speaking, the middle class has become less right-wing and the working class less left-wing.

On socio-cultural matters such as immigration, multiculturalism, globalization, national sovereignty and European integration, it is a very different story and we have seen a well-documented divergence between people with different levels of education in most rich countries. As noted earlier, about 75 per cent of people with minimal educational qualifications voted for Brexit and about the same proportion with degrees or more voted to remain; a similar electoral divide was seen in the Trump vote in 2016.

The highly educated – who are usually more affluent and liberal than the average – also have a disproportionately loud voice in the political system and have used it to shape a society at least partly in their own interests. Martin Gilens, in his study of public policy and public preferences in the US between 1964 and 2006, finds a fair amount of common ground across voter groups, but when preferences diverge the affluent and educated almost always carry the day, on everything from free trade to social policy. Other studies in the US, such as that by David Kimball, have found that the lobbying agenda does not reflect the policy priorities of the public.[8]

There has been a friendly, symbiotic relationship between modern liberal Anywhere values and the rise of a large class of cognitive Head workers, people who generally prioritize individual success, self-actualization, openness, novelty, autonomy, mobility and generally find social change comfortable. Economic openness has usually been the priority of the highly educated of the centre-right, and social and cultural openness has been the priority of the centre-left. The two often combined in recent decades in the default 'double liberalism' of the new centre represented by the New Democrats, New Labour and others – against which modern populism is in revolt. This 'double liberalism' did win elections in both the US and the UK but with a fair economic wind behind it and when openness seemed to be producing more winners than losers, and even then the broadly liberal preferences of most of the cognitive class were not endorsed by a large minority, even a majority, of the population.

Today in the UK a bit less than half of the population support the death penalty.[9] Around two-thirds think that immigration has been too high or much too high in recent years.[10] Around half the population supported leaving the EU.[11] About 60 per cent think that Britain 'sometimes feels like a foreign country'.[12] 58 per cent of people think that newcomers are not integrating well.[13] Most British people broadly support gender equality but only around one-third of women identify as feminists.[14] Similarly, in the US more than half the population want stricter limits on legal immigration,[15] 54 per cent support the death penalty for those convicted of murder,[16] a bit over one-third of women identify as feminists,[17] and nearly half of white working class Americans agree that 'things have changed so much that I often feel like a stranger in my own country'.[18]

Yet most of the people who voted for Brexit and Trump are what I call 'decent populists'. They have accepted the great liberalization of recent decades on race, gender and sexuality, even if those issues are not of primary concern. They are, in the main, social conservatives not social authoritarians and do not generally conform to traditional values in their own lives. And yet if you survey the political scene in the UK and the US over the past twenty-five years prior to the votes for Brexit and Trump it is hard to find many policies that reflect these small-c conservative views. (The only political party represented in the UK parliament to support leaving the EU was the Democratic Unionist Party.) On the other hand, it is easy to list half a dozen policy areas (mainly drawing on UK experience) that have been at a sharp angle to the expressed preferences of many of the less-well-educated: openness to global trade and the de-industrialization it has led to; promotion of a knowledge economy and the 50 per cent target for university attendance (discussed in Chapter 4) and relative neglect of vocational and technical training; openness to large-scale immigration and the embrace of multiculturalism, with its attendant ambivalence about majority identities; the social and geographical mobility that strips many communities of their most able people; a family policy that downplays the private realm of the family and gives priority to both parents working; and finally the embrace by the cognitive class of a more technocratic, global politics that has stressed international integration, climate change, human rights, and sex (and sexuality) equality, and downplayed national social contracts and national democratic sovereignty.

On global trade, as noted earlier, Robert Reich, Bill Clinton's Labour Secretary, in the early/mid-1990s, argued in his influential book *The Work of Nations* that workers should not resist the wealth potential of globalization but should roll with it and an activist state would help them retrain. The factories closed in both the US and UK but the retraining barely happened at all (it did happen to a greater degree in the Germanic and Scandinavian lands).

A knowledge economy works, by definition, in the interests of the highly educated and requires a thriving higher-education sector. Yet in both the UK and the US remarkably little thought was given in recent decades to the reduced status of so much non-graduate employment or the vocational and technical training needs of former industrial areas. Politicians, who are almost all graduates and whose children mainly attend elite universities, encouraged the school system to focus overwhelmingly on sending students to college and, as we saw in Chapter 4, non-academic post-school training has become a Cinderella sector. And, especially in the UK, with its 50 per cent university target, little thought was given to the psychological impact on those not going to college or to the impact on the economic geography of the country of encouraging the geographical mobility of the most academically able.

The immigration story is also one of an openness-inclined cognitive class choosing to follow its own intuitions and essentially ignore the sentiments of more than half the population for more control and more modest inflows. In Germany and France the lack of a tough line against immigration from any of the mainstream parties in the 1990s and early 2000s was a big recruiting sergeant for populist parties. Angela Merkel's decision in 2015 to allow more than 1 million refugees to settle in Germany is often seen as an act of great political courage, but it deeply divided her country.

In the US, before Trump, there was only a debate about *illegal* immigration. But legal immigration running at more than 1 million a year is considered too high by more than 50 per cent of Americans, a mainly less-educated voice that was hardly ever heard.[19]

In the UK around two-thirds of the adult population has considered immigration too high or much too high for most of the last twenty years, since the number rose sharply after 1997 (though its level of salience to voters has shifted about, and immigration anxiety has declined since the Brexit vote). Yet immigration has continued at historically unprecedented levels for two decades.

The most telling moment in the recent immigration story in the UK came in 2003, when a Labour government dominated by the highly educated decided to ignore the views of its less-educated voters and allow people from the former communist countries immediate access to the British labour market when their countries joined the EU in 2004. In a speech in Poland in 2000 Tony Blair had talked about 'popular but misplaced fears that freedom of movement means massive shifts of population'.[20]

The UK was the only big EU economy not to use the seven-year transitional period allowed under EU rules. Tony Blair wanted to repay the support in the Iraq war from many former communist countries, and business was lobbying hard for easier immigration, yet the decision remains a remarkable example of how centre-left parties have come to reflect the priorities of liberal graduates rather than less-well-educated workers, many of whom have subsequently ceased voting for them.

The same is true of family policy, which has favoured the public realm of work over the private realm of the family itself. Policy has reflected the priorities of highly educated professional women concerned with competing on the most equal possible terms with men in their careers. At the middle and bottom end of the labour market most women with young children want to and need to work but would prefer to do so part-time or even not at all when children are very young, yet the UK state provides little support to make it easier to stay at home. As Alison Wolf has written:

> Today's female workforce features a professional elite for whom a career is as central to personal identity as it is for elite men. It also features a female majority whose work patterns are very different. They do jobs. And they do jobs which fit with and around their family responsibilities and priorities. They are, therefore, very often part-time. Part-time work is both the norm and a preferred option for vast proportions of the female workforce. It is also the main reason for the notorious 'pay-gap'.[21]

Social mobility, as I argued in Chapter 1, is another idea and policy that has been relentlessly promoted, at least rhetorically, by cognitive class governments of centre-left and centre-right, especially in the UK and US, with little nuance or sense of its costs for those who are not mobile. For the politicians of the centre-left equality of opportunity is preferable to an unachievable and unpopular goal of equality of outcome, and for the centre-right the stress on mobility helps to protect them from accusations of defending privilege. Yet less-well-educated people often hear speeches from highly educated and successful people about social mobility as exhortations to become more like them. Especially as, in the UK at least, getting on often means a ladder *out* and leaving your roots behind – you have to 'leave to achieve'. Some people do want to fly away, but others would prefer good, well-paid jobs in their locality that would allow them to lead successful, happy lives in settled communities close to relative and friends.

More rooted individuals have, in the past, been able to achieve status and recognition through work as *service* to their family and community. As the sociologist the late Geoff Dench put it:

> It is the knowledge that they are being useful to their families and communities that assures ordinary people of the self-respect they need to carry on leading productive lives even when this does not result in great success and public recognition . . . Mobility does have a place for talented individuals and as an escape from a group experienced as oppressive. But when promoting mobility becomes a state objective, this seems likely to produce a profoundly discontented and unstable society.[22]

TECHNOCRATIC DEPOLITICIZATION

The argument over the more technocratic style of politics of the post-Cold War era also divides along educational lines. After the 2016 Brexit referendum there was certainly a quiet undercurrent of support, on the part of more extreme Remainers, for the idea of an epistocracy: the rule of the well-educated. This is David Runciman in his book *How Democracy Ends*:

> Living in Cambridge, England, a passionately pro-European town and home to an elite university, I heard echoes of that argument in the aftermath of the Brexit vote. It was usually uttered sotto voce – you have to be a brave person to come out as an epistocrat in a democratic society – but it was unquestionably there. Behind their hands, very intelligent people muttered to each other that this is what you get if you ask a question that ordinary people don't understand.[23]*

* There is some evidence that more intelligent people are on average more to the left politically. Ian Deary, a professor of Psychology at Edinburgh University, has found that higher general intelligence at aged ten is correlated with anti-traditional attitudes at thirty. His study confirms the general finding that people with higher intelligence tend to have less traditional moral values. But Noah Carl, another intelligence researcher, partly disagrees or rather argues that those with more open personalities are more likely to pursue careers in academia, or similar, which *then* skews their views in a left-liberal direction.

And pretty open contempt for Leavers has been a recurrent theme. Matthew Parris, a former Conservative MP and *Times* columnist, wrote about the people of Clacton, Essex:

> Only in Asmara after Eritrea's bloody war, have I encountered a greater proportion of citizens on crutches or in wheelchairs . . . this is Britain on crutches. This is tracksuit-and-trainers Britain, tattoo-parlour Britain, all-our-yesterdays Britain . . . I am not arguing that we should be careless of the needs of struggling people and places such as Clacton. But I am arguing – if I am honest – that we should be careless of their opinions.[24]

And Vince Cable, then leader of the Liberal Democrats, said the Brexit vote was 'driven by a nostalgia for a world where passports were blue, faces were white, and the map was coloured imperial pink'.[25]

Parris and Cable are both decent, liberally minded people, but sophisticated, highly educated people often see the political preferences of the less-well-educated as morally wrong or irrational and contrast them to the rational deliberations of experts, who can see a question in all its complexity. And there is a widespread view that politicians are often swayed by short-term electoral cycle and pork-barrel motivations and that public policy is of a higher quality when it is conducted by clever technocrats, insulated from political influence.

These sentiments are not always wrong, and experts can usefully inform political debate in specialist areas of knowledge, such as how best to analyse and defeat a virus epidemic. But there is no expert who knows 'objectively' whether you should be left-wing or right-wing, liberal or conservative, a risk-taker or security-lover. Moreover, there are two bigger problems with this approach to politics. First, it often assumes that highly educated people are more rational than less-educated people. But the opposite is often the case in my observation, because educated people are more likely to have absorbed political ideologies into their personal identity and thus find it harder to look dispassionately at political options.

The political philosopher John Gray explored this issue in a recent BBC radio talk:

The ignorance of the learned can be a great deal more dangerous than the common or garden variety. Over time the errors of ordinary people can be corrected by their everyday experience. The ignorance of the learned, in contrast, tends to be invincible. They like to think they have a clearer view of the world; in fact they are often more easily taken in by mass delusions than the rest of human kind. Those who have studied to degree level and beyond have often embraced ideas and projects that many less educated folk instinctively recognize were dangerously absurd. Something like this happened in Britain in the 1930s. Much of the intelligentsia was ready to junk democracy in Britain for a new order that they felt was coming into being somewhere else.[26]

Second, a drift towards *technocratic depoliticization*, with more and more aspects of life – from control of interest rates to immigration – being removed from the national democratic contest ends up contributing to a populist reaction. And this is surely exactly what we have experienced in the past twenty-five years.

After the initial optimism about the spread of democracy at the end of the Cold War some influential figures have been quite open about preferring the constitutional to the popular aspects of democracy. The writer and columnist Fareed Zakaria argues that the western model is best symbolized not by elections but by the impartial judge and says that 'what we need in politics today is not more democracy but less'.[27] Similarly Alan S. Blinder, then deputy head of the Federal Reserve Bank in the US, published an influential article in *Foreign Affairs* in 1997 arguing that the independent central bank model should be extended to other areas of policy, including health and welfare, with decisions being removed from elected politicians and handed to independent experts.[28]

The late Peter Mair in his book *Ruling the Void*, on the hollowing-out of western democracy, talked about the anti-politics politicians such as Tony Blair – who once described New Labour as 'the political wing of the British people' – and set himself up as a leader above political partisanship. 'In an ideal world, it seemed, politics would rapidly become redundant. As one of his close cabinet colleagues, Lord Falconer, was later to remark, "depoliticising of key decision-making is a vital element in bringing power closer to the people".'[29]

This is one reason for the popularity of the European Union among the political classes of Europe. As Mair puts it: 'The EU has become . . . a protected sphere in which policy-making can evade the constraints imposed by representative democracy.'[30]

Highly educated technocrats usually believe that national self-government is unable to solve many of today's most complex problems – the nation-state is either too big for local problems or too small for global ones, as the cliché has it. They are happy to pool or transfer sovereignty to make markets and politics work better in a relatively interdependent world.

This does not just mean majority voting in the committees of the EU or WTO. It's also true of domestic politics: think of independent central banks or a more activist judiciary striking down the decisions of politicians. All of these things that shrink the space of democratic accountability may be justified in their own terms, but it is invariably true that when policies are removed from the national democratic arena, they are decided according to the values and priorities of the cognitive class; namely, international openness, income maximization, individualism, diversity and so on.

It is also the case that, on a personal level, many highly educated people are comfortable relinquishing sovereignty. They think they appreciate the trade-offs and benefits in GDP growth or in greater cooperation to combat climate change and through their own friends and networks they may have connections to power. They also tend to have quite a high degree of agency in their own personal and professional lives, so feel less directly diminished by the erosion of agency in the national political sphere. Most less-educated people have no political influence other than their vote.

In the recent book by Will Hutton and Andrew Adonis, *Saving Britain*, national sovereignty is described as merely 'notional'.[31] Technocratic politics, in other words, is experienced as expansive and empowering by cognitive elites and narrowing and disempowering by non-elites, whose response can mutate into populist rejection. As the former head of the UK representation to the EU, Ivan Rogers, has written: 'If you evacuate many domains of public policy of any real element of choice at the citizen level . . . then the only way to voice opposition becomes to voice opposition to the *whole system* and to argue that it needs to be demolished rather than changed from within.'[32]

The decisions by Tony Blair's Labour government to target the sending of 50 per cent of school leavers to university and to accept immigration from the former communist countries of central and eastern Europe seven years before it was necessary illustrate both a cognitive-class lack of emotional intelligence and a social distance from less-well-educated citizens. The same political instinct seems to have informed the extraordinary decision of Tony Blair, and many leading Blairites, to reject the referendum result and actively campaign for its reversal, rather than lobby for the softest possible version of Brexit.

In the light of such decisions it is not surprising that less-well-educated voters have lacked confidence in contemporary politics. Many of them stopped voting at all, and withdrew from political participation more generally, on the grounds that from their perspective all the main parties appeared to pursue the same technocratic liberalism.

Robert Putnam's famous book *Bowling Alone*, on the breakdown of civic life in America, notes that voter turnout has declined by around 20 percentage points since the 1960s, while likelihood to attend a public meeting about local affairs was down by one-third between 1973 and 1994.[33]

More recently, some voters have been prepared to support anti-system politicians such as Donald Trump. Just as the 1960s and 1970s gave rise to a generational revolt and a new type of liberal and left politics of the highly educated (Green parties in Europe have the highest educational profile of any), so populist parties have emerged in the past generation as a kind of counter-weight for the less-well-educated.

It is, however, as Bovens and Wille point out, one of the curiosities of the new political stratification that new political parties do not *explicitly* articulate the interests of lower- or higher-educated citizens – one reason why Donald Trump's famous phrase after victory in Nevada in the 2016 Republican primary, 'I love the poorly educated', attracted so much attention. There is no Liberal Graduate Party or Union for the Poorly Educated.[34] There would be too much stigma attached to the latter and egalitarian embarrassment attached to the former.

These cultural-educational divides in politics did not exist until quite recently. In the UK, Labour's decision on east European immigration would have been unthinkable in the 1980s, as would the Conservative decision to legislate for gay marriage.

If one goes back even further to the immediate postwar period, the current cleavages become even more unimaginable. The two front benches in the UK parliament in the 1950s would have disagreed fundamentally about socio-economic issues but would have held broadly similar views on race, nation, gender and so on. Moreover, their views would have overlapped with the average man or woman on the street. Nations then were far more culturally homogeneous and conservative.

In the US as recently as 1972 almost 80 per cent of *Democrat* Party voters agreed marijuana should be illegal, against just 22 per cent today, 78 per cent agreed same-sex sexual relations were almost always wrong, against 28 per cent today, and almost 40 per cent opposed interracial marriage, a question that is no longer even asked today.[35]

In the past, the cognitive class was too small to have its own interests and divided along other lines, primarily socio-economic. Now it has become large enough to have its own interests, which are expressed within the existing party-political forms, taking a distinct centre-left and centre-right form.

One way of mitigating today's divides and retaining a sense of the broad-church party is simply through a wider range of people being represented. Your own life experience matters when it comes to understanding the experiences of others, a point often made by race campaigners.

This is Paul Johnson, whom we met in Chapter 4 struggling to find a decent apprenticeship for his second son Tom, reflecting on how the experience changed him:[36]

> Our failure to get enough young people into high-quality, job-based training at eighteen years old creates our skills shortages, low wages and productivity problems. If there is a problem with our universities it occurs when students fall into low-value courses by default because that's the easiest thing to do.

I have known this for years. You can see it in the data. But it is not until it is part of your experience that you really feel it. Here's an admission. Having done well by the exam system myself, if I'd stopped at one son I would always have had that little voice at the back of my head telling me that if I could do it, and if he could do it, then everything is fine. Maybe everyone else should just buckle down and get on with it. That little bit of extra experience with my son Tom has changed the way I think. That, by the way, is why I believed David Cameron's claim that the treatment received by his son Ivan brought home to him the value of the NHS in a way that mere theory never could.

This self-knowledge has also shaped my view about the importance of having people with a diversity of experience at the top of politics. Perhaps it shouldn't matter if they have all been to public school and Oxbridge and are comfortably off. That doesn't make them worse people. They are perfectly capable of understanding the evidence and sifting the options. But human nature is such that different experiences will lead them to understand that evidence, and weigh those options, differently. Perhaps this is most true of education policy, where we are all too much influenced by our own, dimly remembered, schooldays.

Many less-educated voters do say they want people more like themselves in politics, though they seem to make an exception for people at the very top, like Donald Trump or Boris Johnson, who are allowed to be *sui generis*. According to British political scientist Oliver Heath: 'All else being equal, people with a given social characteristic prefer candidates or leaders who share that characteristic: women are more likely than men to vote for female candidates, and black people are more likely than white people to vote for black candidates.' Similarly, other researchers Nicholas Allen and Katja Sarmiento-Mirwaldt, find that there is 'good evidence, from Britain and elsewhere, that citizens generally want representatives who are 'like them', either in appearance or thought, who are local and who have experienced what they have experienced.'[37]

They are also more likely to want politicians to directly reflect the views of those they represent: a 2019 YouGov poll found that 80 per cent of British MPs think they are elected to exercise their own personal judgement, while 63 per cent of voters think that MPs should act according to their constituents' wishes, and just 7 per cent think MPs should exercise their own judgement.[38]

The overall implication is that there are far too many graduates in the UK parliament for the taste of a substantial section of the electorate. Political scientists Rosie Campbell and Philip Cowley were dismayed to find that in response to a questionnaire people preferred to vote for a sixteen-year-old school leaver rather than someone with a PhD. 'Perhaps because we spend our lives working in universities, the finding that respondents seemed noticeably to prefer a candidate who had *not* been to university surprised (and depressed) us somewhat.'[39]

It is not, however, by any means obvious that people with a university education do make better political leaders. It is difficult to test this, and few political scientists have tried. But American political scientists Nicholas Carnes and Noam Lupu have attempted to check the claim by looking at economic performance of countries, performance of members of the US Congress (staying in office, passing more bills and winning re-election) and levels of corruption of Brazilian mayors. They conclude: 'Politicians with college degrees do not tend to govern over more prosperous nations, are not more productive legislators, do not perform better at polls, and are not less likely to be corrupt.'[40]

In my own observation of friends and colleagues from elite academic institutions who have gone into politics it is clear that the knowledge they have acquired and their ability at abstract reasoning is only one part, and not always the most important part, of what is required to be a capable politician.

Charlotte Leslie is a high-flying Oxford graduate and was one of the youngest British Conservative MPs from 2010 to 2017. I spoke to her in Bude, Cornwall, where she used to work on the beaches as a lifeguard. She told me:

> Whilst many of my Balliol friends were doing internships in law firms, banks and consultancies, I spent my holidays from Oxford working on the beach as a lifeguard in Bude. At the time I thought I was being a drop-out and a bum. But I now know that what I learned from working on the beach has been, without doubt, more valuable to me for a career in politics than what I learned at Balliol, or what I could have learned in any London office.

There I was, a privately educated, cosseted Oxford undergraduate amongst a team of experienced Cornish and Australian lifeguards on the dangerous Atlantic coast. It was tacitly understood that because I was 'academic', I might be a bit back-of-the-class on the commonsense scale. And I was. But everyone was very kind and treated me as someone with a distinct educational disadvantage. If I did something a bit stupid, they would often laugh: 'It's all right, Charlotte,' they would say. 'You're an academic!'

She remembers feeling at the bottom of a huge learning curve among the lifeguards and found her glittering academic career helped very little in many of the tests and exercises she had to undertake.

I was a former national-level competitive swimmer, and I was OK with the physical fitness requirements and the academic elements of the first aid. But I struggled with translating what I knew on paper into actual sand-spattered, rain-soaked, wind-buffeted action. Which knots to use, and when, I was pretty useless at. And the scenario tests – how would you rescue someone from a rock in these circumstances – again, pretty poor. Being fairly proficient at analysing Virgil's Augustan encomium poetry turns out to have very little to do with being practically useful in an emergency. I definitely wore the dunce's hat in that lifeguard hut.

Leslie believes that her lifeguard boss and mentor in Bude, Martin (Mini) Fry, was probably more important to her education in growing into the sort of person who could become a good MP than her university tutors. 'Mini and my lifeguard friends have taught me so much. I am profoundly grateful for their influence in my life. Yes, MPs need a good analytical ability, but politics is more like fixing the boiler than writing an essay. I think academic people can easily forget that.'

And her main lesson from that experience: 'If you want an improvement done well, ask the people who do it for eight hours every day. Not the person wearing the suit.'

I remember one day a man in a suit arriving on our beach. He was all the way from Wadebridge. He was from the council. The man in the suit spent about half an hour looking at 'our' beach. At the end of it, he informed us that what we really needed were railings around the open-air sea-pool and no-diving signs.

No, no, we advised. The kids will jump off the railings at high tide and this will cause issues, and they'll slip on the no-diving signs. But the man in the suit was having none of it. His recommendations were fulfilled, and so were our predictions. At great cost to the public purse. I remember thinking 'If ever I find myself as the person in the suit, I will listen to the people who spend eight hours every single day on whatever is the equivalent of our beach.' I took this memory with me to parliament. I always tried to remember how little I knew about the areas I was required to legislate about.

Another example underlines the context-dependency of ability and the limits of academic intelligence in the rough and tumble of politics. It concerns the former British cabinet minister Ed Balls. I used to know Balls when we were both working on the *Financial Times* in the early 1990s. He had just arrived from Harvard University to write leaders and was widely regarded as one of the brightest young economists in the country, which is why in 1994 Gordon Brown plucked him from the *FT* to become one of his closest advisers for the next ten years. But several years later, in the run-up to the 2005 election, he moved from being a government adviser to being a politician in his own right. And he was dreadful. I remember hearing him on the BBC Radio *Any Questions* show and cringing as he spoke. He was wooden and charmless and inarticulate. What it revealed to me was that being a politician, and speaking well in public, is a craft that you need to work at, and just being clever and well informed, and probably in possession of a high IQ, is not enough.

To be fair to Balls he was able to learn from his early mistakes, which may have been exacerbated by a stutter, and over the years he worked at the craft of political rhetoric and became reasonably good at it before losing his seat in 2015. (He then went on to win more national popularity for his performances on *Strictly Come Dancing* than he had ever achieved as an academically accomplished politician.)

Academic ability can be useful in politics, as in many other walks of life, but evidently it is neither a necessary nor a sufficient condition for success. Yet the cultural bias towards higher cognitive aptitudes seems to have had some influence on the selection of front-rank politicians in recent decades, especially on the centre-left. Consider the elevation of the academically luminous Miliband brothers, Ed Balls and even Gordon Brown himself. They were all known for high ability but not the human touch.

A cabinet colleague of Alan Johnson, the former postman and Home Secretary, told me Johnson would almost certainly have made a better, and more popular, Prime Minister than Gordon Brown but, surrounded by highly trained academic minds, he felt he wasn't up to it.

There are many explanations for the current wave of political alienation sweeping across western societies. One way to think about it is that politics has a demand and supply problem. Voters are more demanding and less deferential to authority of all kinds. They have high expectations, and a click-button consumerist world has made people less patient of public realm inefficiency. They are also better educated and have the internet and social media to help them challenge their leaders.

Yet at the same time that the democratic demand has been rising, the democratic supply has been faltering. Globalization has increased inequality in the west, while appearing to require a more technocratic, less national politics that makes many people feel less in control. The Iraq War debacle, the financial crisis and subsequent austerity, the inability to control immigration, the belief that life will not be better for our children, the increasing stratification by education, these have all reduced faith in the political class, stoked resentment and encouraged people to vote for anti-system parties.

This period of relative political failure, compared with the immediate postwar period, has coincided with the entrenchment of cognitive class domination of western politics. This is not to say that the former has been caused by the latter, but a rapid growth in the graduate share in the population in most countries, and the almost complete domination of politics by graduates and the interests of graduates, has not made our politics function more smoothly or rationally or, indeed, tolerantly. Instead it has become another source of popular resentment.

It was noticeable that a global survey tracking declining satisfaction with democracy published by the University of Cambridge's Centre

for the Future of Democracy in January 2020 found that among countries bucking the trends were those – such as Poland and Hungary
– which have self-consciously rejected the liberal graduate-centred
politics of western Europe.

The graduate/non-graduate divide is not a sharp one on all issues or
political preferences but according to YouGov Profiles data there are
significant differences in values and worldview. The Profiles contain
some 330,000 questions across a very large panel of nearly 1 million
Britons. This typically yields a sample of around 50,000 individuals
per question, which ensures a strongly representative sample and high
statistical power. Here are some of the traits where the two groups
differ.[41]

While 71 per cent of graduates agreed with the statement 'I like
to surround myself with a diverse range of cultures and ideas', just
51 per cent of non-graduates did so. Non-graduates are more rooted
than graduates, valuing locality and family more. 43 per cent of
non-graduates said they preferred to listen to local radio stations,
compared to 29 per cent of graduates. By a 73–62 margin, non-grads
are more likely than graduates to agree that 'family is everything'.
Indeed, when asked what they would like to be named after them, a
theory, grandchild or mountain, 54 per cent of non-graduates replied
'grandchild' compared to just 33 per cent of graduates.

Graduates identify heavily with their educational qualifications. 73
per cent of graduates said they 'learned important things through my
school education', while only 51 per cent of non-graduates agreed. By
a 73–44 margin, grads are more likely to say their education helped
them get ahead in life. 19 per cent of grads, but only 6 per cent of
non-grads, offer 'well-educated' as one of their defining traits. In a
three-choice question, 46 per cent of graduates say their 'head tends
to rule the heart', and only 31 per cent the heart ruling the head. For
non-graduates the numbers are nearly reversed, with 42 per cent opt-
ing for heart over head, and 31 per cent for head over heart. This spills
over into the importance of work: 47 per cent of graduates say they
'love my job', but only 34 per cent of non-graduates agree.

Graduates are more achievement-oriented and seek a more this-
worldly sense of control over their lives. By a 36–20 margin, they're
more likely to agree that 'having goals' helps motivate them to get

through the day. For having 'a challenge', there's a similar gap. 'Accomplishing', 'learning', 'challenging' and 'adventure', all associated with more open personalities, register 10–15 point premiums in favour of graduates. Non-grads are between 10 and 20 points less likely to exercise, say they are healthy or emphasize physical appearance and weight loss. And while only 46 per cent of graduates said they don't 'plan too far into the future', 60 per cent of non-graduates avoid long-term planning. This taps into a greater sense of fatalism among non-graduates. Witness the fact that 36 per cent of them believe in fate or destiny compared with 22 per cent of graduates. And non-grads are between 10 and 15 points more likely to believe in religious concepts such as reincarnation, life after death or ghosts, while being 10 points more likely than grads (72–62) to say the world is 'getting worse'.

I am not suggesting that a 50 per cent non-graduate quota in the House of Commons or US Congress would necessarily improve the quality of national governance. But the lack of representation of the feelings and interests of the less-well-educated, and the gap that has opened up on many issues between the political class and around half the population, has bred political cynicism and created a space in which populist politics has thrived. The case for more cognitive and value diversity in national parliaments seems an overwhelming one.

Some people propose, as an alternative, a bigger role for citizen parliaments and consultations and deliberative forums. They seem to have worked well in Ireland's abortion referendum and elsewhere. It is easy enough to find a representative cross-section of the public; it is harder to be truly neutral in the way that information is presented to such forums.

Bovens and Wille are sceptical about deliberative models, seeing them still heavily biased towards well-educated citizens.

> An important assumption in this model is that citizens are knowledgeable about politics, understand their own interests as individuals and groups, develop thoughtful political opinions, and put these forward by means of political participation. They are expected to be able to read voluminous dossiers, attend lengthy meetings, and to intervene at the right moment and in the right tone of voice. It is only a mild

exaggeration to say that at least a bachelor's degree in political science or public administration is needed to be able to live up to these expectations. Many political reforms are designed by political scientists for political scientists.[42]

But to the extent that such forums do give a voice to the normally voiceless, they are welcome. After all, why should the wisdom of the graduate-only crowd be better than the wisdom of the whole crowd?

LANGUAGE, VALUE AND DESIGN

One of the ways in which cognitive class dominance impinges on mainstream culture is in the language we use and in the ethos of much art and architecture, the latter being the high art form that most directly affects everyday life. Despite all the efforts of the movement for plain English, jargon, management speak and politically motivated euphemism continue to be used by cognitive elites, both consciously and unconsciously, as a badge of distinction and a barrier for entry against the less-well-educated and more plainly spoken. Jargon and bureaucratic obfuscation are forms of professional power. In higher education, too many academics, particularly in the humanities (and what Jordan Peterson has called 'the activist disciplines'), have for more than thirty years allowed their subjects to be rendered almost unintelligible by specialist language; while much of the text produced by public-sector organizations is often hopelessly convoluted and alienating.

Donald Trump understands the power of direct language, bypassing the Head, to speak to the Heart. One of his campaign managers told BBC Radio 4 that the line that won the election for Trump was: 'It used to be that we made cars in Michigan and you couldn't drink the water in Mexico. Now they make cars in Mexico and you can't drink the water in Michigan.' This sort of imagery is very direct and concrete. It cuts through and speaks to how people feel.

An important source of the popularity of Boris Johnson is the belief that he is not afraid to describe things as they are – in his comments, for example, about how a woman in a burkha looks like a letterbox

– and offend against the new rules of discourse. Johnson was also reprimanded for using combative language in the House of Commons in September 2019 after his proroguing of parliament had been declared illegal by the UK's Supreme Court.

There is a danger that violent language used on the national stage can incite people to behave badly. But there is an equal and opposite danger that the gap between the way that people speak to each other in private and the official language of the society grows too wide. One study of American political polarization found that 80 per cent of people thought that 'political correctness is a problem'.[43]

An acquaintance of mine worked on a big regeneration project in Manchester a few years ago and he recalls that they had to run classes for local residents to help them negotiate what they could or could not say in public meetings: people are 'black' not 'coloured', and so on. The residents asked for these sessions with a small group of staff they felt they could trust not to judge them if they said the wrong thing. 'It was bizarre. It was their community, but we had to teach them the words they were allowed to use to talk about it in public,' he says.

But this is a much bigger issue than so-called political correctness, which in mild form is just a form of politeness. The value diversity of modern societies has had the unintended effect of smothering the language of virtue, and ultimate value, for fear of offending those with non-mainstream values. Jonathan Sacks, the UK's former Chief Rabbi, says that this is in part a confusion between judgementalism (you are bad!) and judgement (not all ways are equally good). Sometimes, it seems we have conflated the two and thrown out *both*. This means that the most important questions about how to live a good life are relegated to the private sphere, and too much of our public discussion focuses on technocratic process or economics and becomes dominated by an expert emptiness. It also means that we lack the confidence to praise in the public sphere things that almost everyone values: pro-social behaviour, personal responsibility, respect for nature, sufficiency, working hard, being a good parent, strong marriages. A senior civil servant friend of mine said she had to fight very hard to get some of this language into the relationships education curriculum in the UK as people worried it was too judgemental and old-fashioned. If we cannot praise the successful mastery of the Heart, we shouldn't be surprised that it is less valued.

Charles Murray in his book on the new class divides in the US, *Coming Apart*, blames the new American upper class for not preaching what it practises. The book describes, with a mass of survey evidence to back it up, the diverging way of life of the new upper-class America and working-class America. The new upper class continues to behave in a manner not that different to 1960s America, in terms of marriage, work ethic and religiosity, while all three of those things have partially collapsed in working-class America. (As Daniel Markovits points out, this is driven in part by the desire to transmit their advantages to their children.) In 1963 white people aged thirty to forty-nine were overwhelmingly married (94 per cent of college-educated, 84 per cent of those with just a high-school education); in 2010 the figure was still 84 per cent for the college-educated but had slumped to just 48 per cent for the high-school-educated.[44]

But the new upper class has a code of what Murray calls 'ecumenical niceness'. Children are supposed to share their toys, not hit one another, take turns, and so on. But they are also taught that they should respect everyone else's way of doing things, regardless of gender, race, sexual preference, cultural practices, which leads to the crucial weakness of ecumenical niceness. 'The code of the dominant minority is supposed to set the standard for the society, but ecumenical niceness has a hold only on people whom the dominant minority is willing to judge – namely, one another . . . It has lost self-confidence in the rightness of its own customs and values, and preaches non-judgmentalism instead.'

The blanket of 'ecumenical niceness' makes it harder for us to have the national conversations about value that we need. But surely it is possible to combine the freedom to pursue diverse goals and values with a robust public discussion about the best path to collective well-being and how that should be reflected in our laws and institutions? Perhaps societies shaken by the Covid-19 crisis will find an opening to conduct these more fundamental value discussions.

David Lucas, the children's writer whom I quoted earlier, has been thinking and writing about issues of language and value for many years. Lucas has a wry, outsider's perspective on life and lights up when talking about the ideas that move him. I interviewed him about language and design at his home in Leytonstone, where he lives with his American wife and five-year-old daughter. (Some of the below arises from subsequent exchanges on email.)

He describes how he fell in love with words and writing:

> I found my way into writing through an almost visual appreciation of words – seeing how the short, simple, Anglo-Saxon monosyllables that are the core of English, can be so vivid that it's almost as if the word itself is a picture . . . Anglo-Saxon is an earthy, vulgar language, and there is a *thud thud* rhythm to everyday English that is very different from the fluidity of a language like Italian, where the words seem to blend into one another. By comparison English is inelegant, and the English traditionally have prided themselves on bluntness and honesty: calling a spade a spade. I was born in Middlesbrough, in what was then Yorkshire, and no one is more proud of being plain-speaking than Yorkshiremen.

One of the great treasure troves of modern English, along with Shakespeare, is the King James Bible, which drew heavily on the earlier translation by William Tyndale, who was burned at the stake for his trouble. Lucas lists a few of the vivid phrases that were carried over in the later Authorized Version of the Bible:

> twinkling of an eye
> a moment in time
> seek and ye shall find
> eat, drink and be merry
> ask and it shall be given you
> judge not that you not be judged
> let there be light
> the salt of the earth
> a law unto themselves
> it came to pass
> gave up the ghost
> the signs of the times
> the powers that be
> fight the good fight

'The very familiarity of the phrases,' says Lucas, 'can make it hard to appreciate their beauty. It isn't easy to say things simply, much less to say them with style.'

George Orwell, in his essay 'Politics and the English Language', translated a famous biblical passage from Anglo-Saxon into Latinate English, to show how ugly and unvivid long words can be. This is the original, a famous passage from Ecclesiastes:

> I returned and saw under the sun, that the race is not to the swift,
> nor the battle to the strong, neither yet bread to the wise,
> nor yet riches to men of understanding, nor yet favour to men of skill;
> but time and chance happeneth to them all.

And this was Orwell's translation into management-speak:

> Objective considerations of contemporary phenomena compel the
> conclusion that success or failure in competitive activities exhibits
> no tendency to be commensurate with innate capacity, but that a
> considerable element of the unpredictable must invariably be taken
> into account.[45]

Latinate words are emotionally distancing, which is why they are so favoured by academics, or scientists, or for safety announcements, or when someone is telling you your train is delayed, and so on. They conceal blunt truths, they smooth over rough edges and they sound fancy, as if whoever is speaking is in control.

Lucas sees both verbal storytelling and the visual storytelling of art and architecture as governed more by Heart than Head. He points to the influential British designer Richard Guyatt, who gave his inaugural lecture 'Head, Hand, Heart' at the Royal College of Art in 1951. In art and design, he said, the Head provides the 'how' of something (that is, its function or utility); the Hand describes the 'what' (its physical embodiment); and the Heart reflects the 'why' (its value or meaning). But the culture of high art and architecture has become overwhelmingly Anywhere/Head-dominated. Anywhere architecture is usually faceless and devoid of the ornamentation that was a traditional form of visual storytelling.

As modernism gained momentum in the twentieth century it came to focus mainly on 'how', on function. In architecture, it dispensed with decoration and narrative. Similarly, narrative was downplayed in fine art and highbrow literature.

Lucas is an aesthetic traditionalist and goes back to Hogarth for inspiration:

> In his book *The Analysis of Beauty*, Hogarth praised St Paul's, a new building of his own time, saying its design displays 'the utmost variety without confusion, simplicity without nakedness, richness without tawdriness, distinctness without hardness and quantity without excess. Whence the eye is entertain'd throughout with the charming variety of its parts together . . .'
>
> He thought that a beautiful design, of any sort, is a battle between a host of opposing qualities. A good design sparkles with inner conflict, it is alive with inner tension.

This echoes the idea of the balance of Head, Hand and Heart. Beauty, in all the arts, is a tug of war between mighty forces. Stories work on the same principle: a good book unites all kinds of opposing themes, and a vivid character is alive with conflicting desires.

'There are other parallels between architecture and storytelling,' according to Lucas.

> All traditional architecture (across the globe) has these features in common:
>
> 1. Dramatic vertical asymmetry: i.e. the structure 'builds' to a dramatic climax.
>
> 2. Elaborate horizontal symmetries: like a story which replicates themes and images 'sideways' to create a rich, full world. Characters mirror each other, dilemmas, settings, motifs, etc. all echo one another.
>
> 3. Fractal pattern: so that small elements & details echo the whole.
>
> The driving force of all fiction, of all storytelling, is inner conflict: a good character is torn between what they want and what they need, the conflicting demands of the Heart and the Head. Jane Austen's Emma wants to be in control, not just of herself, but of others around her, but her Heart throws the plans of her Head into disarray. She becomes a more balanced individual as a result: she grows up.

Like a good book, St Paul's works on many levels at once, but for all its variety, it is one coherent story in a commonly understood language: in form and detail and materials, it tells the story of the tribe, reaching back to Christianity's origins in the classical world.

Louis Sullivan, the inventor of the skyscraper in nineteenth-century America, found another union of old and new. He pioneered steel-frame construction, but loved rich ornament. Tradition was losing its grip, but Sullivan never sought to trash his cultural inheritance. He had fun with it, mixing up all kinds of languages of pattern – reflecting the mixed-up-ness of America itself – but underpinned by rigorous classical geometry, just as America was founded on classical ideals. His work is loved and 'the eye is entertain'd' because of that union of opposites in conflict. Sullivan coined the phrase 'form follows function', but he understood that one of the primary functions of architecture is telling the story of the tribe.

A big Victorian railway station such as St Pancras in London is another neat halfway point between old and new: impressive engineering, but still ornamented, with plenty of evidence of the work of the hand, and full of the symbolism of beginnings and endings, like a fabulous gateway.

Europe imploded in the First World War, and in the catastrophe, intellectuals declared a Year Zero. Modernism emerged in this value desert. Le Corbusier said that a house was just 'a machine for living in'. The Seagram building in New York is a black brick, with no curves or diagonals to contrast with the grid of rectangles, with no hierarchy of form, no grand entrance, no sense of what each level might be for, no ornament. The exterior reveals nothing, gives nothing. It is one big 'no', stripped of that energy that comes from 'the union of opposites in conflict' and is impressive only because it is big and uses expensive materials. When you have no other values, those things do impress people. Hierarchy has been abolished in the name of progress, but with it difference and character and distinction. It is architecture of the Head, conceived as a snap-together kit of parts. I asked an architect friend to defend it and all he could praise was its 'purity'. Purity is one-dimensional and inhuman.

A building I love to hate is the Scottish Parliament, which seems to fail in every way. In outline it is fussy and unmemorable, its details clunky and heavy. Attempts at ornament are drab and meaningless. An example is the odd 'water-pistol'-shaped panels. It is actually quite an achievement to find a shape that means nothing whatsoever, and here it is stamped across the face of a building that is meant to be of profound national significance. It's hardly as if Scotland lacks national symbols.

Similarly, the CCTV building in Beijing by Rem Koolhaas, is an eyeless, faceless monster: aggressively random and calculatedly incoherent. All that is left is a sort of desperate showiness, an empty 'look at me!' The truly sad thing is that European civilization has exported its spiritual emptiness worldwide.

A human architecture would not try to remake human nature, or deny the stories and traditions and heritage that give people their identity. It could start by acknowledging that most people like buildings that have a face, buildings with symmetries that mirror the human body, buildings that greet you in welcome. It is human nature to anthropomorphize buildings. Buildings have personalities. They are loved if they are good company, hated if they are bullying monsters, tolerated (just about) if they are boring. And buildings are admired if they have the same qualities we admire in people: self-respect, generosity, authority, warmth, wit, poise, politeness, having something to say, being a bit different, but not being blank, or aloof, or grating, or attention-seeking for its own sake.

The idea of beauty as a union of opposites in conflict goes back to Heraclitus. I see it as a universal truth: a work of art is beautiful in the same way that a good life is beautiful, or that someone's character is beautiful. An integrated person is a 'union of opposites in conflict'. So is a successful life. And a good design. If it was true for thousands of years, did it suddenly stop being true in the early twentieth century?

Modernists experimented on the poor. I grew up in Hackney, in what is now called Victoria Park Village, but the towers of the brutalist Kingshold Estate on King Edwards Road used to overshadow the area, and the estate was like a concrete canyon, a place to avoid, scary, rubbish-strewn and crime-ridden . . . Hackney is lucky in still having lots of beautiful architecture. And Victoria Park Village is now effectively a gated community, house prices keeping out the undesirables. I certainly can't afford to live there. I live now in Leytonstone, and mostly it's a place of modest Victorian terraces, but the larger Victorian buildings have been systematically destroyed, some as recently as last year. Had the same old school buildings and churches been in Hackney or Bethnal Green they would have been turned into flats. The loss of the bigger, grander buildings makes our neighbourhood duller, and harder to love. It is no coincidence that the most crime-ridden street in my area now is the site of two brutalist towers, with comically banal names: Fred Wigg and John Walsh. The people who live in these towers are the poorest in the area. And the architecture makes their lives worse. When I walk past these towers, I stand in awe at their ugliness.

Many of the big arguments of our time are over values and meaning. But what we tend to hear about in the media is the 'how' not the 'why'. Brexit, to most Leave voters, was about values: sovereignty, belonging, identity and so on. David Lucas again: 'Our working-class childminder said of the Remain campaign in 2016: "Why do they think that all we care about is money?" She's an uneducated woman of forty, who lives in a council house and had her first child at seventeen. She was a fount of common sense to us as first-time parents, and a real friend.' Many Remainers assume that Leave voters simply lacked the facts to make the right decision. It is part of the widespread incredulity they feel that people could have voted against what seem to be their own economic interests. This is despite the fact that well-paid members of the centre-left branch of the cognitive class have supported parties of higher taxation for decades, a decision in which values are more important than their economic interests. In politics, the Heart usually trumps the Head.

PART THREE

Hand and Heart

7

Whatever Happened to Hand?

What ordinary people once made, they buy; and what they once fixed for themselves, they replace entirely or hire an expert to repair . . . While manufacturing jobs have certainly left our shores to a disturbing degree, the manual trades have not. If you need a deck built, or your car fixed, the Chinese are of no help. Because they are in China. And in fact there are chronic labour shortages in both construction and auto repair.

Matthew Crawford

When giving talks on my last book, *The Road to Somewhere*, about the value divides that have contributed to recent political upheavals, I would often declare that one of the reasons for the alienation felt by many voters is the *declining status of so much non-graduate employment*. People in the audience would generally nod their heads in agreement. It sounds plausible, especially in the light of the evidence I have presented in earlier chapters of this book on declining relative pay for less-well-qualified workers and the graduatization of so many of the most desirable jobs.

Yet status is a complex, slippery and subjective notion. It is hard to rank people by status in the way that you can by income or social class, though the three do often overlap. Indeed, status is sometimes seen as the lifestyle aspect of class without being completely reducible to it. Where would you place a vicar? A mini-cab driver working on a PhD? Status remains indelibly associated with notions of superiority and inferiority. In pre-democratic Europe status or rank was often overt and expressed in the way an individual dressed or was addressed. In an era of more egalitarian citizenship notions of superiority and inferiority may still be felt but are rarely expressed. Wealth has always been, and remains, an important source of status, but older sources, such as land ownership, have declined while new sources, such as popular celebrity and educational achievement, have emerged in their place.

In an interview from the 1970s in their classic work *The Hidden Injuries of Class*, Richard Sennett and Jonathan Cobb record a house painter saying: 'Whenever I'm with educated people, you know, or people who aren't my own kind . . . I feel like I'm making a fool of myself if I just act natural, you know?' Nearly fifty years on, J. D. Vance's best-selling memoir *Hillbilly Elegy* about his home town in rustbelt Kentucky and his own journey to Yale Law School records many similar moments of feeling exposed before those of higher social and educational status.[1]

Judgements of status can be markedly different depending on where you are standing. So when industrial working-class culture was at its height in the first sixty or seventy years of the twentieth century, manual workers often looked down on white-collar workers or even skilled professionals as people not doing real jobs. In their 1957 study *Family and Kinship in East London*, Michael Young and Peter Willmott, found this: 'A sizeable minority of men in Bethnal Green take a very different view from white-collar people about the status of manual work, placing jobs such as company director and chartered accountant towards the bottom of the scale and manual jobs, like agricultural labourer, coal miner and bricklayer, towards the top.'[2]

At the same time working-class parents were often keen for their own children to escape working-class drudgery and via a decent education move up into Head rather than Hand work. A friend of mine, from a working-class background in eastern England, recalls his childhood just a few years after Young and Willmott's book appeared.

> As an infant before starting school I remember playing with my toys while my mum, gran and aunties were talking, and they all agreed they wanted their children to get an office job and not work with their hands. My dad was a builder and he was my hero, so I was annoyed at this (and still am!). But they meant it. It was partly a gender divide. Male blue-collar culture despised people who worked in offices. My son still does!

There is no longer the same caste rigidity that was once the hallmark of the British class system, as Mike Savage's Great British Class Survey established in 2011.[3] The old three-class structure of upper class, middle class and working class, which still had some meaning in the 1950s, has given way to a much bigger and more fluid middle grouping, with a small, and more meritocratic, elite of around 6 per cent of the population at the top and a larger 'precariat' of around 15 per cent at the bottom.* Two-thirds of the 160,000 participants in the survey said they identified with no social class. This greater fluidity used to be associated with 'classless' America, though, as we saw in Chapter 3, there is some evidence of an emergent hereditary meritocracy in the US.[†]

High educational achievement, which in both the UK and US increasingly means some kind of postgraduate qualification, is now a central source of status, and that working-class resistance of the 1950s on behalf of a useful, masculine Hand culture has largely disappeared. The swot, once a figure of fun, has had the last laugh.

This extends beyond Head achievement representing good employment prospects and secure future income, as Harry, the son of a former colleague of mine, has discovered. My ex-colleague has been professionally successful and sent Harry to a private school, where he did well at GCSE but lost interest when it came to A levels. After a year at university, he followed his Heart and Hand. He dropped out and pursued his ambition to become a car mechanic. He is now an experienced technician in the VW/Audi group and earns more than many of his graduate contemporaries. 'He earns £36k a year, knocks off at 5 p.m. and loves his work and mates. But he is not a graduate, and that makes him feel a bit of a second-class citizen,' says his father.

Harry is a bright, articulate and decent-looking young man, buying his own house and with income to spare, yet he finds that on dating websites being a car mechanic puts him at a significant disadvantage.

---

* When the BBC published the Great British Class Survey they provided a 'class calculator' that 7 million people (more than 10 per cent of the population) used to find out which class they belonged to. Mike Savage says this in itself was evidence of the fact that class membership was no longer obvious.

† In recent years more Americans have begun to identify as working-class instead of middle-class. In 2014 the National Opinion Research Centre found that 47 per cent of people identified as working-class and 42 per cent middle-class.

He shares many interests and opinions with the people he grew up with. He still plays cricket, he is at home in middle-class conversation, but finds that his occupation acts as a filter in making contact with other young people, who are now graduates in junior professional jobs, sometimes earning half of what he does. When he meets old school-friends he is disappointed when they dismiss people like his colleagues (and him), who work in complex, high-tech environments (you cannot service or repair a car these days without it being connected to a laptop) where they get their hands dirty. This is even visible at his work, where smartly suited young service reception employees and technicians exist in an upside-down social pyramid of assumed superiority and income.

Some rare Hand workers – such as a surgeon or artist – are highly respected but because their manual dexterity is usually combined with high levels of knowledge and cognitive ability, they are the exceptions that prove the rule. The cultural bias against ordinary manual occupations, even well-remunerated ones like Harry's that use diagnostic logic not unlike a medical professional, seems to run deep – which helps to explain why it is so hard to fill many well-paid manual positions.

Yet this co-exists with some nostalgia for the jobs of the manufacturing era, especially in the US, even if people would prefer their own children not to be doing them. The American sociologist Mike Hout has found that the social standing of dozens of specific manufacturing jobs scored just as highly in 2012 as they had in 1989 and 1968:[4]

> Less cognitively demanding occupations are as esteemed as ever, though the number of people working in them is a fraction of what it once was. The guy who spent the first twenty years of his working life stressing and straining to manipulate heavy machinery in a factory manufacturing autos, appliances or the steel to make them laments his current circumstances driving a forklift in a big box store – if he is lucky enough to be doing that. A robot does his old job, maybe in the same factory but more likely in Mexico or Brazil. He'd still rather make stuff than move stuff around.[5]

There is, of course, little point being nostalgic for the mass skilled manual labour of the industrial era. The millions of skilled jobs in mining, metal forming, printing and so on are not going to return to rich countries. Nor are those middling secretarial and administrative jobs now done by computers. But equally, we shouldn't underestimate the psychological and political impact of the disappearance of decent Hand employment. There is persuasive survey, and interview, evidence that demonstrates this sense of loss, as I will show later in the chapter.

The middle-income/middle-status jobs represented by skilled manual employment provided social ballast. They also provided the people – mostly men – who performed them with a sense of being valued and useful. The work of a skilled lathe operator in an engineering factory required only moderate cognitive ability, but to do well it required several years' *experience*. This meant that the worker's status was protected; this was part of the point of becoming a so-called 'time-served' skilled worker. He could not easily be replaced by someone with superior academic qualifications.

One should be wary of romanticization, but some skilled jobs – especially skilled trades working with materials such as leather, wood, stone, brick – can also give people a deep sense of meaning and connectedness that goes beyond utility or economic value. Getting intimately involved in any physical process that requires skill, concentration and a deep understanding of a particular material is a way of blurring subject and object, enlarging your sense of self by becoming what you are working with. Winston Churchill meditated by bricklaying. The ancient crafts of Japanese culture are performed as a meditation.

The story of the relative decline in *incomes* for middling and lower-skilled jobs, thanks to more global openness and technological change, is a familiar one (see Chapter 5). The macro picture is captured by Branko Milanovic's famous elephant chart in which he shows the distribution of global income growth from 1988 to 2008.[6] He finds the world's poorest people, the new middle classes in poor countries and the rich in rich countries all benefitting handsomely, while those occupying the seventy-fifth to ninetieth percentiles of world income distribution – essentially the West's working and lower-middle classes – have seen their incomes stagnate.

Typical of this story are the 300 workers at the MG car plant in Oxford in the UK made redundant in 2005. Three academics interviewed them over a period of three years as they sought new jobs, mainly in the service sector, and in some cases retrained. About 90 per cent got new jobs, but very few of them achieved anything like the same earnings level as they had before. In fact, they were earning on average about £6,000 less than they had been at MG Rover. And one-quarter of them admitted to living off their savings or being in financial difficulty.[7]

But this is a story about a whole Hand culture as well as income. In most developed countries there has been a clear decline in the manual and practical competence of the population. It is true that new technologies have produced some new outlets for creativity and commerce – whether being a YouTuber or creating new kinds of games and music – but the overall direction of travel for many people has been away from Hand towards passivity. The disappearance of craft skills in the home, not just at work – playing a musical instrument, knitting, carpentry – has been a big and largely unrecorded story of the past fifty years. And the arrival of ever more sophisticated computers means that there are now many artists who cannot draw and musicians who cannot play an instrument.

A teacher friend reported to me this recent communication with a white working-class boy aged twelve: 'The boy wouldn't engage with my story-writing lesson. I asked him what he was interested in, what he did in his spare time, and all he could talk about was the computer game Fortnite. It's not his fault, it's the impoverishment of his culture, the passivity of being consumers not producers.'

Matthew Crawford, author of *The Case for Working with Your Hands*, has written about the sharp decline of 'shop classes' in US schools in the 1980s and 1990s. These were high-school programmes teaching practical skills such as carpentry and metalworking.[8] Shop class in American schools is now increasingly rare. Writing in *Forbes* magazine in 2012, the American technologist Tara Tiger Brown lamented this decline.

> During my freshman year of high school I was required to take home economics and shop class, where I learned basic skills in sewing, cooking, woodwork and metalwork. Regrettably the cooking never made an impression, but I fondly remember learning along with a class full of boys and girls how to sew a pair of shorts, punch holes into metal to create a hook to hang my bathrobe, cut and bend metal to make a box that still holds my pens to this day and use a rotary saw to make a hot plate that was used on the kitchen table at home.

Twenty years later I can still recall that sense of pride when I finished the blue metal box with only minimal guidance from my shop teacher. I remember him fondly, he wore a dark blue lab coat, coke bottle glasses and was missing the tip of one finger . . . I have continued to use those skills throughout my life both professionally and when needed around the house.

Shop classes are being eliminated from California schools due to the University of California/California State 'a-g' requirements . . . Shop class is not included in the requirements, thereby not valued and schools consider the class a burden to support.

The UC/CA State system focuses on theory and not applied skills; a belief that learning how to swing a hammer or understand the difference between a good joint and a bad joint is part of a bygone era, and as a society these skills are not something to strive for, something people resort to when they are out of options. Looking at shop class in this light is short-sighted and detrimental to America's future.[9]

Brown goes on to argue that it is often through learning practical skills that people can more easily grasp abstract scientific and mathematical ideas, learning 'that' through learning 'how'.

Paul Corby agrees with Brown that it is often the practical that is an avenue to grasping the theoretical. He is a lively and plain-speaking sixty-eight-year-old Yorkshireman from Huddersfield who rose to become a senior trade union leader and construction industry training official.

Like most working-class children in the 1950s and 1960s I failed my eleven-plus and ended up at a lousy secondary modern that taught me very little, and I was completely unable to grasp algebra and geometry. Many of us were dismissed as thick, but most of us weren't. We often flourished in the world of work. I left school at fifteen and did a five-year construction apprenticeship with the Huddersfield company J. Wimpenny. And I was soon using Pythagoras's theorem to work out my angles. In fact, eighteen months after I finished my apprenticeship I was laying the foundations of multi-million-pound buildings using Pythagoras.[10]

Knowing 'how' and knowing 'that' turn out to be complementary. There's an old story about the medieval scholastic who tried to learn how to swim by reading a book on swimming technique. A friend who is training to be a teacher said this story came to mind when he saw trainee teachers in college grappling with issues of lesson planning and behaviour management in theory. He and some other teacher colleagues had been thrown straight into school and knew about these things from direct experience, and their one day a week in college with the full-time students learning about 'synthetic eclecticism' seemed comically irrelevant.

DECLINE OF THE SKILLED TRADES

Some of the neglect of skill training in manual-technical occupations in the UK and US was described in Chapter 4. Skill shortages have been especially acute in the construction industry in the UK. Over 2 million people work in construction, and it is still easily the largest employer of young men.[11] But as more than 90 per cent of enterprises have fewer than thirteen employees, and nearly half of all employees are self-employed,[12] most firms are not in a position to offer much training. And the cyclicality of the work also tends to discourage both employers and workers from investing in skills that may then not be used for several months of the year. The number of construction apprenticeships in the UK has been in freefall. It dropped from nearly 17,000 to just over 8,000 between 2009 and 2017,[13] and most of those apprenticeships were less than two years.

According to the Construction Industry Training Board the numbers entering full-time college-based training also fell from 47,000 to 16,000 between 2005 and 2017. Moreover, most construction qualifications are now just level 2, the equivalent of GCSEs, compared with construction apprenticeships in Germany, which are at least level 3 and sometimes 4 or 5. The construction industry workforce has always been a mobile one, but it is no wonder that more than one-third of people working in construction in London are foreign born.[14]

More than one-third of vacancies in the UK construction sector were described as 'skill shortage' vacancies in the 2017 Employer Skills Survey.[15] Skill shortages in rich countries today are at least as much concentrated in the middle and at the bottom end of the job market as in higher cognitive domains, where the shortages of, say, engineers, computer scientists or web designers tend to be in very specialist fields.[16] The UK Employer Skills Survey also found that two in every five skilled trades vacancies – chefs, electricians, car mechanics – were proving hard to fill for skill shortage reasons.[17] A CBI/Pearson skills survey in 2018 found that only 54 per cent of companies were confident of filling low-skill roles in the future, and only 42 per cent were confident of filling middle-skill roles.[18]

In the US a combination of low investment in training and baby boomer generation retirement has increased skill shortage pressure, one of the reasons employers tend to be pro-immigration. In recent years employers have found it harder to fill blue-collar positions than college education jobs. Jobs with the highest vacancy levels in 2018 were health-care aides and hotel staff.[19] There is an acute shortage of truck drivers in both the US and UK.[20]

France has a similar deficit of skilled trades workers, and according to Insee, the national statistical institute, the hardest-to-fill jobs are carpenters, manufacturing technicians, roofers and metalworkers.[21] Thanks to its apprenticeship system the German economy is not suffering the same lack of skilled trades workers as many other rich countries, but even Germany is struggling to fill some of the more traditional trades or those that require anti-social hours, such as trainee baker.

Why is it that skilled manual work has become so unpopular? It is partly the lure of higher education and graduate jobs for those who are even semi-successful at school. But it is also a sense that these occupations, with the partial exception of jobs such as coding (which is also suffering shortages), belong to the past not the future and do not offer long-term security. It is true that overall demand for the skilled trades has been falling and will probably continue to fall. The jobs are either being made completely redundant by technological change or are being deskilled: consider the switch from the old London black cab driver who has memorized the 'Knowledge' with an Uber driver who just follows directions from his or her phone.

Skilled trades jobs fell by almost 30 per cent in the UK between 1990 and 2018, from 4.7 million to 3.2 million (despite an increase in the UK population of around 15 per cent in that period). Yet a lot of skilled trades people from central and eastern Europe have been attracted to work in the UK thanks to the declining interest in the skilled trades on the part of young British people, combined with the openness of the UK labour market. So it is estimated that about 14 per cent of the 3.2 million working in the UK skilled trades are foreign born.[22]

The skilled trades have seen similar declines in other rich countries: in France and the US the proportion of people working in this area has fallen to between 8 and 9 per cent from around 12 per cent in the 1990s. Germany is an outlier with more than 12 per cent still working in skilled trades.

Moreover, pay in the skilled trades has not kept up with the increase in median UK pay since 1975 (78 per cent) but it has risen on average by 41 per cent for electricians, 52 per cent for plumbers, 39 per cent for cooks and chefs, 38 per cent for lorry drivers and 27 per cent for bricklayers, though some individuals with specialist skills can often earn very much more than those figures imply. (In the US, where median pay has been static since the mid-1970s, the pay for most skilled trades jobs are in the minus range for that period: electricians minus 8 per cent, plumbers and plasterers minus 9 per cent.)

Thanks to the skill shortages described above, the next few years are likely to see a sharp uplift in pay in many of these skilled trades which will, in turn, attract more people into the jobs so long as there are still the colleges and courses and teachers to train them.

In big cities such as London the culture of the skilled trades has also changed, generally for the worse. I have a nephew, Sam Kershaw, who, rather unusually for someone privately educated from an upper class background, became a plumber in west London – the plummy plumber! Sam, who is dyslexic and did not flourish academically at school, did a two-year apprenticeship with the small plumbing company Staunch and Flow in west London, including one day a week at North West London College in Dollis Hill. (He is scathing about the teaching at the FE college, saying that after six months he knew more than the teachers.) He says that it took him at least another two or three years after the apprenticeship before he became a competent plumber. By that time the five employees had bought the company and changed the business model to escape the misery and pressure of London plumbing life.

Plumbers are usually mending something expensive that is broken, so people are not usually happy to see us! And, if you do your job properly you are almost always late, or indeed can't turn up at all. Imagine a typical day: you have a leaking tap in the morning, you are fitting a dishwasher in the middle of the day and you are fixing a hot-water cylinder in the afternoon. But what if the leaking tap turns out to be a pressure issue and takes you two hours longer to fix than you expected? The whole day is then in crisis.

All the incentives push you into doing the most basic, slapdash work and then moving on in the knowledge that no one will hold you to account and in the anonymity of the big city you will avoid reputational damage. From what I know it is different, and better, in smaller towns and the countryside, because there word of mouth counts for more.

Sam says Staunch and Flow has now turned itself into a complete building company, including plumbing, because in renovating houses or helping to build new ones you have much happier customers and you are more in control of the work. But the company no longer takes on apprentices. The pride and prestige once associated with acquiring a skilled trade has drained away as academic qualifications and professional, office work has become the main route to secure and prestigious employment.

The expectations of apprentices were far too high. They expected to be paid full whack as soon as they were qualified. And some of them behaved very poorly, dragging dogshit into houses, speaking disrespectfully to customers and so on. You need soft skills even as a plumber.

The company now has twenty staff, about half of them from abroad – 'German and Italian skilled trades are usually much better than our people, at least the younger ones.' It wants to employ more, but potential staff usually fail to turn up for interviews, or even on the first day on the job. But, says Sam, good people can earn £80,000 to £100,000 a year. 'We have one guy who earns so well he works one month on and then takes one month holiday, through the year.'

The related story of the decline of the work ethic in Hand work, especially in parts of the UK and US, is a constant refrain of exasperated employers. Toby Baxendale, who built the UK's largest fresh fish processor Direct Seafoods, with an annual turnover of £100 million, said that by the late 1990s half of the skilled staff he needed, especially butchers for his meat subsidiary, were from abroad. Butchering skills were simply dying out in Britain, so he was increasingly employing either Australians or east Europeans. But it is not just about some traditional skills dying out. 'I and my core staff found ourselves discriminating against young Brits who would apply for jobs. Why? Their attitude of entitlement, their complete lack of dependability or work ethic, and if we did employ them they usually didn't stick beyond the first week,' said Baxendale.

The overall standing of the skilled trades has also been diminished by the replacement of the old 'patch and mend' culture with a 'chuck it out and buy a new one' culture. A friend told me a sad story about her washing machine fixer.

> It must have been about 2011 when a washing machine repair man came to the house. He had come maybe once or twice before over the previous twenty years, and each time we had had a conversation. He lived in Essex, had set up a business repairing and reconditioning washing machines.
>
> He was probably in his mid-fifties; he was very knowledgeable and saved me hundreds of pounds with various bits of advice about what machines to get and sold us one of his reconditioned machines for a fraction of the price of a new one. It lasted a ridiculously long time – twelve years or so – and then we bought another one, which also lasted really well. On his last visit, he said he was finding it really hard to keep the business going. First, new machines were so cheap it was hard to compete. Second, machines were now so flimsy that they broke easily and were far harder to recondition.
>
> He was very bitter, all those flimsy machines filling up landfill every two or three years. He was probably not much of an environmentalist type but even he could see it was insane. And of course the system had made all his skill and knowledge pointless. He didn't think the business would last him through to retirement. He was angry. And I felt embarrassed standing on the doorstep . . . his hand skill was irrelevant but it shouldn't have been.

This last story is not just about nostalgia for the past, it is about the alienation that too many people, especially older people raised in a more Hand-friendly era, feel about the fact that there seems to be no place for them in a society focused on academic qualifications and digital technologies. These are the people who often live in second- or third-tier towns in Europe or the US without degrees and, in the UK, are likely to be among the 68 per cent of working-class voters who say that Britain has changed for the worse in the past twenty to thirty years or the 62 per cent who think that their children will not be better off than they are. The numbers are similar in the US.

In most societies, the hardest jobs to fill are the menial but often vital positions towards the bottom of the occupational hierarchy. Because of the educational and social trends described in this book, it's very hard in a country such as Britain to motivate people, especially young men, to take work at the lower end of the jobs hierarchy, or even, as we have noted, middling skilled trades work. Why perform work that is not valued and can be done by 'failures and foreigners' – especially if you can earn similar amounts on the fringes of the black economy. Moreover, even lower-level cognitive work is not only more prestigious and better paid; it usually involves more comfortable circumstances and greater autonomy and control over working time.

What the celebration of education and mobility actually means to a significant proportion of the population is that those who don't have decent academic qualifications, and feel corralled into the bottom half of the labour market must submit to those who do. Many young people would prefer to opt out of the system completely than accept that fate. It is possible that this trend could be partially reversed in the wake of the Covid-19 crisis which, at least temporarily, generated a new respect for people doing basic but vital jobs in the food, pharmaceutical and other supply chains.

MEASURING STATUS

In the last two decades it has sometimes felt as if an enormous social vacuum cleaner has sucked up status from manual occupations, even skilled ones, and reallocated it to the middling and higher cognitive professions and the prosperous metropolitan centres and university towns (in the UK propped up by taxpayer-backed student spending).

Yet, as I said at the start of this chapter, status is a fuzzy and con-tested concept. It is usually focused on occupations and includes both objective and subjective elements. Objective status means a kind of ranking that everyone can agree on – a surgeon or an architect has higher status than a plumber (and note this is not necessarily about pay – a successful plumber may be paid more than an architect). Sub-jective status 'reflects peoples' own feelings about the levels of respect or recognition they receive relative to others in society', as Peter Hall and Noam Gidron define it.[23]

The evidence for declining subjective status turns out to be quite elusive. With one or two notable exceptions (the Hall and Gidron paper being one), social scientists have not been digging into how people in rich countries feel about their relative status over recent decades in the light of the new education-based stratifications and the disappearance of so many middling-skill, middling-status jobs. Or rather, social scientists have produced relatively little mass survey evidence, but there is a library of so-called ethnographic research – meaning accounts based on structured individual interviews – on the feelings of the 'left behind' people, the losers from globalization, especially in the US. Not surprisingly these accounts, mainly linked to an analysis of support for populist politics, describe feelings of loss and what Michele Lamont, the American sociologist, has called a 'recognition gap'.

In her book *The Dignity of Working Men*, in which she interviews 150 blue-collar workers in the US and France, Lamont focuses on 'boundary maintenance' as a source of esteem and how people come to feel like losers when it is no longer enough to be a hard worker to be successful. Some of this analysis is partly focused on race and the perceived lost 'cultural privileges' of white working-class Americans as they have seen other groups rising above them economically or attracting more elite attention.[24] Lamont finds the same in France:

> The workers' feelings of isolation and powerlessness are accentuated
> by the fact that the cultural and religious institutions of immigrants
> are gaining in visibility . . . These feelings of loss are also accentu-
> ated by the perception that France is going downhill (mainly due to
> immigrants) . . . French workers deeply resent this perceived loss of

national status given that their nationality is one of their rare high status characteristics.

Justin Gest, in *The New Minority*, somewhat sweepingly detects similar sentiments right across the West: 'Across the post-industrial regions of Western Europe and North America white working class people sense that they have been demoted from the centre of their country's consciousness to its fringe. Whites feel like victims of discrimination. Their politics motivated by a nostalgia that seeks to reinstate a bygone era.' He quotes a white Londoner called Nancy Pemberton saying: 'It's a fact we are the minority . . . I won't allow myself to feel on the outside of my society. But a lot of other people are scared.'[25] Gest has created a measure of deprivation which measures feelings of economic, social and political 'centrality'. He finds that patterns are similar across the US and UK, though the British tend to feel less central socially and the Americans less central economically.

Arlie Russell Hochschild, in her book *Strangers in Their Own Land*, ventured into the heart of red-state America in Louisiana and over the course of five years befriended pipe fitters, plant operators, truck drivers, telephone repairmen, postal workers and so on, most of whom could no longer take pride in their work.[26] She talked to one man who said that the more you stand on your own two feet and the less you depend on the government, the higher your status, echoing the observation of the nineteenth-century sociologist Thorstein Veblen, who observed (in her words) that our distance from necessity tends to confer honour.

Hochschild writes:

> You are a stranger in your own land. You do not recognize yourself in how others see you. It is a struggle to feel seen and honoured . . . through no fault of your own, and in ways that are hidden, you are slipping backward.
>
> Most people I talked to loved the South, loved Louisiana, loved their town or bayou. But they were sadly aware of its low status: 'Oh we're the flyover state,' one tea party teacher told me. 'We're seen as backward and poor.'

This ethnographic work is of some value, but it is easy for researchers to find what they are looking for, and it is not clear how representative the interview subjects of depressed American and British towns are of the wider society.

But alongside the ethnographic work there is what one might call the physical evidence of the toll of low status in depression, alcoholism, drug addiction and suicide. The increase in the US, and to a lesser extent the UK, in deaths from suicide, drug overdoses and alcohol-related liver disease among middle-aged people – the so-called deaths of despair, referred to already – is concentrated heavily among the white lower-educated population.

There were much lower mortality rates from deaths of despair among US whites than in France, Germany or Sweden in 1990, but while those other countries have now converged on a level of 40 such deaths per 100,000 of the population, white Americans have risen to 80 per 100,000. The UK had an unusually low rate of such deaths in the early 1990s but has risen sharply to around that 40 deaths per 100,000 that is the European norm today, with women increasing from 15 to 26 per 100,000 and men from 30 to 60 per 100,000. According to Angus Deaton and Anne Case, this rise in deaths of despair since the turn of the century, especially for 45–55-year-old whites, has been causing life expectancy for Americans as a whole to decline for the first time since records began. If death rates had continued on the downward trend of the twentieth century between 1999 and 2017, 600,000 more people would be alive today.

Deaton and Case suggest that the deaths are linked to a process of cumulative disadvantage for less-educated people along with the weakening of traditional social structures such as church and family. White Americans with no college degree have gone from having mortality rates 30 per cent lower than African-Americans in 1999 to 30 per cent higher now.

There is also the work of British social scientist Michael Marmot on the so-called social gradient, the idea that, as socio-economic status rises, so do health prospects and life expectancy. He pioneered this understanding with his studies of Whitehall civil servants, in which he discovered a steadily rising gradient in the risk of heart disease as you go down the hierarchy. Men at the bottom were four times more likely to die, and less than a third of the gradient disappeared when factors such as smoking and cholesterol were factored out. This finding, which was also found to hold outside Whitehall, is based on the idea that low status in a hierarchy produces constant stress and anxiety – especially for men, who derive more status from work than women – and this produces higher levels of cortisol, which damages the immune system.

Although there is a commonsense connection between poverty and poorer health, and longevity, Marmot's work has been criticized for his assumptions about status and stress. Many people go to work just to earn a living and derive their status from things outside work; moreover, high stress is also associated with high-status individuals with large responsibilities.

In any case I am interested in the wider phenomenon of how the relatively rapid emergence of educational stratification in recent decades and the growth of a large cognitive class has impinged upon those who have not gained entrance to the class, or even to its higher levels, and whether this has more generally disturbed the status balance in society. I therefore wanted to find broader, more objective, empirical evidence of feelings of status decline, especially among non-graduates. I believe I have found a decent amount of evidence for this trend, as I will describe below.

But the evidence for status loss needs to be set in a broader and rather contradictory picture of occupational and labour market change in rich countries, much of which points to *quite high levels of work satisfaction* even for Hand workers (as already mentioned in Chapter 5). Many current ideas about the job market – how insecure employment is for many people, especially young people, or how middle-income jobs are disappearing – turn out on closer inspection to be rather exaggerated, at least prior to the economic fallout from the Covid-19 crisis.

The proportion of people in conventional full-time employment at 63 per cent has hardly budged at all in the past twenty years in the UK,[27] despite quite a big rise in self-employment, and average job tenure remains around nine years, where it has been for several decades.[28] And the numbers in non-standard, non-permanent employment have also held steady: only 2.4 per cent of the workforce in the UK in 2018 were on zero-hours contracts, and most of them were content with the arrangement.[29] In the US the so-called gig economy, in which short-term freelance work is accessed through online market places, is only about 1 per cent of total employment.[30] In 2018 the employment rate was at record highs in Britain and Germany and twenty-two other OECD countries.[31] And the internet has made job 'matching' easier and cheaper for both employers and employees. High minimum wages in many European countries, which have partly replaced the power of organized labour, are also reducing the number of low-paid workers in some European countries; in the UK the proportion has fallen from 21 per cent to 17 per cent since 2015.[32]

Here is Francis Green, a leading British labour market economist:

> In the affluent economies of the industrialized world, life at work in the early twenty-first century has evolved in a curious and intriguing way. Workers have, with significant exceptions, been taking home increasing wages, exercising more acute mental skills, enjoying safer and more pleasant conditions at work, and spending less time there. Yet they have also been working much more intensely, experiencing greater mental strain . . . In many cases, work has come under increased and unwelcome control from above, leaving individual employees with less influence over their daily work lives and a correspondingly less fulfilling experience than before.[33]

It is true, as described earlier in the chapter, that many of the middle-skilled manual jobs of the industrial era that have been exposed to global competition or technological change, from lathe operators to secretaries, have either disappeared completely or been faced with relatively stagnant incomes. But they have been replaced with a 'new middle' in terms of income, though not necessarily skill or status.

A report by the UK human resources think tank CIPD explains:

> The share of low-paid jobs measured by OECD definitions of hourly full-time earnings has fallen from 22 per cent in 1997 to just under 18 per cent in 2018. The share of high-paid jobs also using OECD definitions has not significantly changed since 1997, at just over 25 per cent of all jobs. It must therefore follow that on these measures the share of 'middle wage' jobs has not fallen over this period . . . The middle has not contracted in terms of the wage distribution because the 'old' middle of skilled trades and administrative jobs has been replaced by a 'new middle' which includes managers in low-pay industries, such as catering, and some professional associate and technical jobs.[34]

And most of the net employment increase in the UK over the past decade has been in relatively higher-paid work: an increase of over 1.2 million professional jobs, over 600,000 associate professional roles and over half a million managerial roles.[35] It is a similar story in the US, with around half of the 10 million new jobs created between 2008 and 2018 described as professional, and an even higher proportion in the EU.[36]

Another challenge to the idea of a dramatic polarization between good, mainly Head jobs, and lousy ones, mainly Hand and Heart, comes from the British Social Attitudes Survey of 2015, which had a special focus on work and jobs. It asked people whether they thought they had a 'good job' based on seven factors – security, income, opportunity for advancement, interest, autonomy, opportunity to help others, use to society – and the proportion who thought they did *rose* to 71 per cent from just 57 per cent in 1989.[37]

It is a similar story in the US. About half of American workers say they are very satisfied with their current job, 30 per cent are somewhat satisfied, and the remainder say they are somewhat dissatisfied (9 per cent) or very dissatisfied (6 per cent). Highly educated workers are the most satisfied and the least-educated the least satisfied.[38]

The same more positive story can be found in general indicators of well-being, which have been holding steady or even rising in many rich countries, including the UK and US, though the highest measures of well-being do tend to be correlated with high levels of education and with professional careers.*

These benign trends probably have something to do with the decline in the number of routine manual occupations and manufacturing operations in Britain and other rich countries. For all the nostalgia about industrial jobs, for most people working in a call centre is preferable to working on a production line.

But the same BSA survey and other workplace data point to less benign data too about the rise in stress levels and reductions in autonomy. In 2015 37 per cent said they found work stressful either always or often, up from 28 per cent in 1989, with a slightly higher proportion saying this in professional and managerial jobs.[39]

---

* The UK statistical authority the ONS has been collecting well-being data since 2012, and the indicators have generally been on the rise, at least prior to the Covid-19 crisis. See https://www.ons.gov.uk/peoplepopulationandcommunity/wellbeing.

But Hand and Heart workers have been hit hardest on the loss of autonomy in recent years. While autonomy rose on most counts for professional and managerial staff, the proportion of people in routine and semi-routine jobs who said they were not free to decide how their daily work was organized rose from 42 per cent to 57 per cent between 2005 and 2015.[40] This is Marx's theory of alienation in modern form. For many people work has had all forms of self-expression and self-determination removed. And, as Daniel Bell predicted in his writing about post-industrial society, the rising status of Head workers has gone hand in hand with routinization and loss of autonomy lower down the occupational hierarchy.

The loss of autonomy also informs the concept of 'precariat', a new insecure stratum of the workforce whose long-term job prospects are unclear and who are therefore unable to develop a consistent work identity. Although analysts of the precariat tend to exaggerate the degree of employment insecurity in rich countries, they are describing the status of those who are unable to move from job to career.

So, even if one accepts that working life in general has been improving for the average employee in many rich countries, this is still compatible with relative status decline for those in non-Head jobs, and especially if one takes account of the wider cultural factors surrounding work.

One such factor is that until quite recently most people went to work for *similar reasons*, whether they were a bank manager or a refuse collector. They went out of duty and to support themselves and serve their families. But increasingly since the 1970s, as Head jobs have grown, the world of work has diverged between a large minority with *careers*, something that used to be the preserve of a small elite, and those who still just have *jobs*. And, according to the 'post-materialism' theories of Ronald Inglehart, those with careers increasingly see work as a form of self-expression or self-actualization in the way that a craftsman once did. Inglehart estimates that in most of Europe and the US this idea of work spread to about half the workforce between 1970 and 2006.[41]

On the other hand, according to the 2015 British Social Attitudes Survey, a tenacious 40 per cent-plus of British employees continue to say that a job is just a way to earn money and nothing more, as they have done now since the 1980s.[42] The so-called work 'instrumentalists' are to be found in almost equal number in the US, where Pew finds that 51 per cent of employed Americans say they get a sense of identity from their job and 47 per cent say their job is just what they do for a living.[43]

This divide is unlikely to precisely follow the distinction between Head on the one hand and Hand and Heart on the other, or even that between graduate and non-graduate, but it is just common sense to assume that the majority of graduate Head jobs are careers which provide an important aspect of meaning and identity to those who hold them. And indeed the Pew data from the US does find that 77 per cent of people with a postgraduate degree say their job gives them a sense of identity; 60 per cent of those with a bachelor's degree, 48 per cent of those with some college education and 38 per cent of those with a school diploma or less say the same.[44] Similarly, employed adults with a bachelor's degree or more are nearly twice as likely as those with less education to say their job is a career.[45]

Meaning in work may also be harder to achieve in some of the 'new middle' of routinized white-collar work compared with either upper-professional careers or being a welder in a shipyard, where the purpose and value of your work was obvious. One-third of British workers told YouGov in 2015 that their jobs made no meaningful contribution to the world.[46]

So with declining relative pay, less meaning and autonomy at work and the realization that as a non-graduate you are denied access to the higher-income, more prestigious jobs above you, the declining status of non-graduate employment is surely a major social fact.

One big international social survey does indeed find that the relative social status of non-college educated men is lower, in some cases sharply lower, than it was twenty-five years ago. The International Social Survey Programme (ISSP), which covers twenty developed countries, with sample sizes averaging 1,500 to 2,000, asks respondents to place themselves on a ten-point social ladder reflecting their position in society. The sharpest declines in status between 1990 and 2014 among non-college educated men are found in the UK, Switzerland, Australia, Sweden and Poland, with less sharp declines in Germany, Austria, the US, Norway. Two countries recorded small rises in status, Hungary and Slovenia. The combination of economic disadvantage and shifting cultural norms has pushed lower-status men towards support for populist parties, argue the authors of the paper.[47]

There is another set of questions in the ISSP which provide further support for the status decline thesis, this time asking working-class and professional-class respondents in France, Germany, the UK and US whether their status is higher or lower than their father's. In almost all countries well over half of professional people say their status is higher than their father's and well below half of working-class people say the same. In the working-class US the proportion had fallen from 57 per cent in 1992 to 46 per cent in 2009; in the working-class UK, from 35 per cent in 1999 to 30 per cent in 2009.[48]

There is a gender aspect to this too, as we saw in Chapter 5. Hand work outside the home has traditionally been male-dominated and continues to be so. But as women have moved into the workforce in much greater numbers, both at the top and the bottom, some men have been pushed down the occupational ladder and have lost relative status. The ISSP data finds that over the past twenty-five years the average social status reported by women has risen relative to that reported by men in nine out of the twelve countries for which researchers have data.[49]

So there is certainly some hard evidence for status decline for those in non-graduate jobs in recent years. Status, rather than class, issues also appear to be relevant in the support for Brexit and similar anti-establishment political preferences.[50]

But given how relatively little data there is on the status question, I also commissioned some original polling on the question for this book. YouGov undertook two nationwide surveys, one in the UK and one in the US. The results confirm the public perception of status decline for non-graduates in the UK and US.

When asked 'Do people who have not been to university find it harder or easier to get good jobs than a generation ago, or is it about the same?' 53 per cent of British respondents who had a view on the matter said it was harder. And 57 per cent of Americans agreed. Shifting to questions around status, as indicated by the term 'respect', shows similar results. The question was: 'Do you think that people doing ordinary jobs – like driving a truck or working in a shop – are given more respect in society, less respect or about the same level of respect as twenty-five years ago?' The response: 53 per cent of Britons and 51 per cent of Americans agreed that they received less respect. Moving to respect for those without degrees, we found that 39 per cent of British respondents and 49 per cent of Americans thought non-graduates had lost respect in society. Few respondents actively *disagreed* with the assumption that non-graduates had less good job opportunities and received less respect, ranging from just 12 per cent to 17 per cent. And there were few partisan differences except on the theme of it being harder for non-graduates to get good jobs. Here left-leaning voters tended to identify this as somewhat more of a problem. Conservatives in Britain were less likely to think that manual workers had lost respect over the past twenty-five years.

This unusual degree of agreement across demographic and political groups suggests that a politics of the Head, Hand, Heart 'triumvirate' could establish deep roots. In the US even the partisan gap between Clinton and Trump voters was negligible. Table 1 shows the results for these three questions in Britain by age, class and Brexit vote. While there are some differences, there is a substantial base of agreement that non-graduates and manual workers have lost status and opportunity in the last generation.

Is this status loss an economic or a cultural phenomenon? It is evidently a combination of the two. There has been a shift to Head and away from Hand both in what society rewards in hard cash and, as this chapter has illustrated, in the less tangible and quantifiable matters of respect and status.

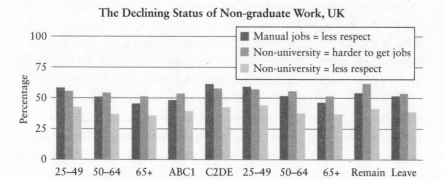

The Declining Status of Non-graduate Work, UK

8

Whatever Happened to Heart?

Modern liberalism is about choice and autonomy. But care
is at an angle to both because it is often about responding to
dependence, human beings after all spend quite a lot of time
at both ends of their life-span dependent.

Madeleine Bunting

Looking at the economic balance sheets of rich countries over the past
few decades, it would be hard to claim that society's Heart – meaning,
in this context, the caring functions once done mainly in the home
and now often done in the public care economy – has been neglected.
In most of those countries health and social spending continues to
rise as a proportion of total spending, and of GDP, and many more
people, still overwhelmingly women, are employed as carers, nurses
and early years teachers than was the case fifty years ago (even allowing for the growth in population). The warfare economy of the 1950s
has given way to the welfare economy of today, especially in Europe.
Moreover, the Covid-19 crisis, and fear of a repeat, is likely to push
up health and social spending even higher.

And pay in the welfare economy is not as low as is often assumed, at
least in the UK. The daughter of a friend of mine is earning £41,000
as a teacher after just five years in the profession, and the daughter
of another friend is earning £36,000 as a National Health Service
(NHS) nurse with just three years' experience (the latter includes
some hefty night shift bonuses, and both include London allowances).

Overall, the pay of jobs in the broadly defined care sector has been
a mixed bag in recent decades, following the general pattern of higher
returns to the more-skilled and lower to the less-skilled. Since 1975

median pay (adjusted for inflation) has risen 78 per cent in the UK; nurses' pay has risen by exactly the same amount, with a 91 per cent rise for midwives and a 79 per cent rise for social workers. The picture is much less favourable for primary-school teachers, who have had just a 19 per cent rise, nursery and creche staff, 13 per cent, and ambulance staff, a miserly 6 per cent. It is a similarly mixed picture in the US, with nurses seeing a 96 per cent rise since 1975 but secondary-school teachers with only a 26 per cent rise.[1]

The pay of most people working in adult social care in the UK has risen by only around 20 per cent in that period – it is particularly low for the domiciliary care workers who care for people living in their own homes – and over the past twenty years the UK has repeatedly failed to follow Germany, Japan and many other rich countries by investing properly in care for the elderly, which suggests that Heart has varying political leverage.

THE PRIVATE REALM AND THE CRISIS OF MEANING

But this is to take a too economistic, Head, view of Heart. There is another way of looking at modern life in rich countries and seeing an emerging crisis of values and meaning, *a crisis of Heart*. The historian and futurist Yuval Noah Harari, who I quoted in Chapter One, has characterized liberal modernity as a Faustian exchange in which meaning (the Heart) has been exchanged for power (the Head). 'Modernity is a deal,' Harari writes. 'The entire contract can be summarised in a single phrase: humans agree to give up meaning in exchange for power.'[2]

That power over the environment means that in many ways there has never been a better time to be alive both in rich and poor countries, notwithstanding the environmental damage to the planet and now, perhaps, the hovering pandemic threat. Over the past 200 years in rich countries each generation has been around 50 per cent better off economically than its predecessor, lifespans have doubled, and recently global poverty has been plummeting too. Harari writes in *Homo Deus*:

At the dawn of the third millennium, humanity wakes up to an amazing realization. Most people rarely think about it, but in the last few decades, we have managed to rein in famine, plague, and war. Of course, these problems have not been completely solved, but they have been transformed from incomprehensible and uncontrollable forces of nature into manageable challenges. We don't need to pray to any God or saint to rescue us from them.[3]

There is, however, a price to be paid for this power, and the price is disenchantment. He predicts that the moral and cosmic certainties of religion will be replaced by 'Dataism', a universal faith in the power of algorithms.

The US, which for some decades defied the general secularization trends of other rich countries, is now catching up, and the European caricature of the Bible-basher, working-class American is wide of the mark. In 1976 81 per cent of the US population identified as white Christian; that is now down to 43 per cent, with only 17 per cent identifying as white evangelical Protestants and poorer white Americans less likely to be observant Christians than richer ones.[4] Overall, 70 per cent of Americans do still self-identify as Christian,[5] but that number has fallen quite sharply in recent years, and only 56 per cent believe in the God described by the Bible.[6]

Europe is still more secular. In the UK the 2018 British Social Attitudes Survey found that 52 per cent of adults did not have any religious affiliation.[7] But that may have been an outlier: other recent surveys have found 55 per cent describing themselves as non-practising Christians, slightly higher than 49 per cent of Germans and 46 per cent of the French. The same survey found the actively non-religious highest in France at 28 per cent, with Germany on 24 per cent and the UK on 23 per cent, though France and Germany also had a higher number of active believers.[8] This European secularization will be slowed, but is unlikely to be reversed, by the higher religiosity of growing ethnic-minority populations and by the revival of religion in some eastern European countries after the end of communism. Harari predicts a secular future of extreme inequality, in which extra longevity and super-human qualities are likely to be the preserve of the techno super-rich, the masters of the data universe.

What about everyone else? Harari writes:

The Russian, Chinese and Cuban revolutions were made by people who were vital to the economy but who lacked political power; in 2016, Trump and Brexit were supported by many people who still enjoyed political power but who feared they were losing their economic worth. Perhaps in the twenty-first century populist revolts will be staged not against an economic elite that exploits people but against an economic elite that does not need them anymore. This may well be a losing battle. It is much harder to struggle against irrelevance than against exploitation.[9]

Are not those deaths of despair in the US people who are dying of broken hearts, people who have become socially, economically and personally irrelevant? Angus Deaton says this about those deaths: 'There is a rising sea of pain and poor mental health in the US among whites with less than a college degree . . . And what surprised us is how *little* material deprivation seems to matter with this story.'[10] Similarly, the new discipline of happiness research finds relationships, work and community hugely more important than income in promoting well-being.[11]

In the US family breakdown is, according to Deaton, one of the key causes of the deaths of despair. The median non-graduate white woman has at least one child out of marriage in the US, and cohabitation tends to be more short-term than in Europe. Many men at the bottom of the pile do not know their children and lack the family support structures that previous generations took for granted. As noted in Chapter 6, in the mid-1960s among white people in the US aged thirty to forty-nine almost everyone was married; in 2010 the figure was still 84 per cent for the college-educated but had slumped to just 48 per cent for the high-school-educated. Similarly, in 2005 85 per cent of children born to upper-middle-class families were living with both biological parents when the mother was forty; among working class parents the figure was only 40 per cent.[12]

There has also been that big decline in religious observance in America among the less-well-educated, and two-thirds of them are utterly cynical about the public realm, believing that elections are rigged by the rich and large corporations.[13]

There is a surprising consensus about the importance of these eroding social norms in the US among both conservative analysts such as Charles Murray and liberals such as Robert Putnam. Putnam describes the country as being beset by 'purple problems', meaning a combination of blue-state concerns over economic opportunity and inequality of all kinds and red-state concerns over status, order and tradition.

Many of today's most pressing social problems in Europe – from the lack of affordable housing to the state of elderly care, mental stress and loneliness – can also be traced back, at least in part, to the weakening of family ties. In Britain today, almost 40 per cent of all fifteen-year-olds do not live with both their natural parents (the number is similar in the US),[14] and family breakdown doubles the likelihood of children failing at school.[15]

Statistics about mental illness are somewhat unreliable as they are often based on self-assessment surveys and are not adjusted for changing attitudes and destigmatization. An official ONS/NHS health survey in the UK in 2016 indicated that 19 per cent of adults had a degree of mental ill health, and it was markedly higher among those in the lowest income quartile.[16] The dispensing of anti-depressants has doubled between 2006 and 2016.[17]

The data relating to actual contact with health services has been rising only gently in the UK: in 2017 around 2.5 million people, about 4.5 per cent of the population, had contact with the NHS over learning disabilities, autism or so-called secondary mental health issues (meaning more serious psychiatric disorders, such as anxiety disorder, severe depression or psychosis).[18] Simon Wessely, one of Britain's leading psychiatrists, is critical of some of the alarmist analyses about an 'epidemic' of mental illness but does point to the Adult Psychiatric Morbidity Survey, a large survey conducted every seven years, which found so-called common mental disorders – depression, anxiety, panic attacks – to have increased sharply for one group in recent years from 19 per cent to 26 per cent: that group is young women aged eighteen to twenty-four.[19]

In the US mental illness is now the second most common cause of a disability claim on the social security system after musculoskeletal disorders,[20] and the Mental Health in America report found 18 per cent of adults to have some kind of mental health condition.[21] Stephen

Ilardi, a clinical psychologist at Kansas University, says that 23 per cent of Americans will experience a bout of depressive illness before the age of seventy-five, and the incidence is rising among younger cohorts. He also says that one in nine Americans over the age of twelve are currently taking some form of anti-depressant.[22] And, as we saw in the last chapter, thanks to the sharp increase in those deaths of despair among the middle-aged – an extreme form of mental stress – life expectancy in the US is now falling.

Loneliness is a significant issue in the US, especially among the baby boomer generation, one in six of whom live on their own. According to the US's General Social Survey, American social networks shrank by one-third between 1985 and 2009 judging by the number of close confidants people say they have.[23]

Loneliness levels are somewhat lower in Europe, according to a NORC University of Chicago study, presumably because family life remains stronger: just 8 per cent of people in Germany and the Netherlands admit to being lonely most or all of the time, and 10 per cent in Sweden, though, surprisingly, the number was higher in less individualistic, more family-orientated southern Europe. The US figure was 16 per cent, though other surveys have put the figure much higher.[24] A British Red Cross survey in 2016 found that 18 per cent of adults in the UK felt lonely always or often.[25]

One should be wary of 'golden-ageism' about the family, and it is certainly true that there is no recent tradition of elderly people living with their adult children in northwest Europe or America, as there is Japan and India. Nevertheless, with the number of intact couples in decline, especially in the US and the UK, the private networks for delivering care to the young and the old have become weaker, particularly at the lower end of the income spectrum, and big majorities in opinion surveys regret this development – 72 per cent in a recent one in the UK said they felt family breakdown was a serious problem.[26] (There is some evidence in the US of a return of the multi-generational, extended family especially among poorer and non-conventional families who cannot afford to buy-in extended family services in the manner of affluent families.)[27]

Married or cohabiting couples with children will not, of course, be persuaded to stay together if a relationship has irrevocably broken down; people can make mistakes when choosing a partner. But family charities argue that plenty of breakdowns could be avoided, or at least delayed until children are older, if there was less economic stress on young couples: half of family breakdown in the UK happens before a child is three with less-committed, unmarried couples counting for the lion's share.[28]

Big, multi-generational families are rare, and the singleton life is increasingly the norm throughout the West. More than one-third of households in some countries now consist of someone living alone; in some Nordic countries it is closer to 40 per cent.[29]

The cognitive-class worldview in Europe and North America, especially what one might call the 'creative-class' wing, leans towards the secular, open, mobile, autonomous and novel; it is often suspicious of national and group attachments and tends towards the androgynous in male–female relations; and while community and belonging are recognized as important, the dominant cultural narrative is that of the unencumbered individual breaking free of tradition and authority.[*30]

Societies that place a high value on freedom and individual achievement are bound to value less the constraints and obligations of long-term partnership, family commitments and community – this is one of the central tensions of liberal modernity. And an inevitable consequence is the weakening of the care economy and the family – the private domain of obligation, unconditional recognition, and submitting to the needs of others. The art and habit of caring is in long-term decline.

Every day, even in rich countries, there are still more hours spent caring, in its many forms, than in any other activity. Carers UK estimate that 9 million people care for others part- or full-time; it is roughly the same proportion in the US. And caring work – in both the private realm of the family and the public economy – is some of the most emotionally, physically and even intellectually demanding

---

* The size, influence and definition of the creative class is contested, but the connection with both liberal attitudes and economic inequality is not. Here is Richard Florida, the author of the concept, himself: 'Across the United States, inequality is not just a little higher, but substantially higher, in liberal areas than in more conservative ones. All of the twenty-five congressional districts with the highest levels of income inequality were represented by Democrats, according to a 2014 analysis.'

labour of all. Yet most economists disregard child-rearing or elderly care work done in the private realm because it is unpaid and so doesn't directly contribute to GDP; some feminists characterize it as a place of entrapment and oppressive burdens for women; while for promoters of the achievement society, it's often seen as a place of wasted cognitive ability. Traditional roles such as male breadwinner and female home-maker have been partially delegitimized and replaced with a far more fluid ideal of family relations.

Freer societies have unavoidably weakened many of the cultural forces that historically legitimized and honoured care and service to others: large families with many economic and social functions performed in the private realm, usually managed by women; religious observance and the idea of acting in the eyes of God; the traditional notion of women as naturally nurturing and altruistic; stable societies with clear gender roles and strong mutual obligations. Care now faces a crisis of identity in achievement societies that are utilitarian, problem-solving and goal-orientated. The writer Madeleine Bunting, author of *Labours of Love*,[31] sees care in tension with modern liberalism's twin priorities of choice and autonomy: 'And good care is about what one might call self-effacement, which is not a virtue that is celebrated in modern culture. It is also *embodied* work in a culture dominated by the abstract and analytical.'[32]

The result of this cultural undervaluing of Heart is plain to see. Most rich countries with ageing populations will see a big increase in demand for face-to-face caring jobs of various kinds, and caring remains partly immunized from automation, yet there is a long-standing crisis of recruitment in these sectors, and few signs that the status or rewards associated with them are rising in response.

There are at the time of writing 41,000 nursing vacancies in the UK's NHS, out of a total nursing workforce of around 300,000, and 24 per cent of trainee nurses failed to complete their three-year degree course in 2017, probably after discovering how demanding it is, especially on clinical placements. In adult social care the situation is even worse, with 130,000 vacancies out of a total workforce of 1.4 million.[33] And almost *one-third* of the workforce leaves every year for better-paying and less-demanding work – that can sometimes mean working as a shop assistant.[34] Germany needs to double its social care workforce in the next twenty years yet is already facing recruitment difficulties.[35] It is a similar story in most rich countries.

The manner in which the Covid-19 crisis tore through care homes for the elderly in several European countries, including the UK, exposed a sector that was unloved, undervalued and underfunded in many places.

WOMEN AND CARE

There is one benign reason for the crisis of recruitment in care jobs, especially nursing: women have many more career options today than they did fifty years ago and, on average, are better educated. Nurse recruitment has undoubtedly suffered from the breaking of glass ceilings. In the decades after the Second World War some of the most capable women in rich countries were working as ward sisters or primary-school heads. Their daughters are partners in City law firms, management consultants or, indeed, medical consultants. Society as a whole has benefitted from this greater freedom for women, but many parts of the care economy, including teaching, have suffered.

My late mother-in-law, Deborah Kellaway, illustrates the generational shift. She had two degrees, including one from Oxford, but partly because of her family commitments chose to become a secondary-school teacher when her three children (two girls and one boy) were of school age. She was an inspirational English teacher at a north London grammar school, but her own children all chose better-paid and more glamorous careers in journalism and financial services.

Hardly anybody wants to return to the family norms of the 1950s,* to overwhelming female dependence on male earnings, high levels of domestic abuse and the stigmatization of single parenthood. But surely it is possible to find ways of valuing care work more in the family and the public economy, both by women *and* men, without abandoning the greater choice and freedom that have been achieved

---

* According to the 2012 British Social Attitudes Survey, only 13 per cent of people agree that 'A man's job is to earn money; a woman's job is to look after home and family', with little difference between the genders. In the mid-1980s the figure was 49 per cent. Surveys in the US show somewhat more traditional attitudes.

by recent generations of women. Yet it now often feels as if we have reached an unsatisfactory compromise, especially in the UK and US. The obligations of the private realm are seen as a constraint on freedom, especially for women, and the state does little to support the family, pushing mothers back into the labour market as soon as possible. Yet women, often by choice, still carry most responsibility for the private realm, leaving many struggling to compete fairly with men in the public realm – thanks in part to that 'double shift'. The proportion of working-age mothers in work in the UK has increased from 50 per cent in 1975 to 72 per cent in 2017,[36] and while men have on average increased their share of domestic work in the home to sixteen hours a week, women still do twenty-six hours.[37]

Although many of the professions are now more or less evenly split between men and women the middle and lower ends of the job market remain highly gender segregated. The proportion of male registered nurses in the UK is about 12 per cent, an increase of only one percentage point from the turn of the century (it is much higher in mental health nursing, which has different historical origins). In the US it is even lower.

'Many women today are less socialized into caring roles, and some women have just given up on care, but men have not, in general, taken up the slack,' says Bunting.[38] Men are, in fact, doing a larger share of domestic labour than in previous generations, and elderly care is shared more equally than child care. But, says Bunting, many women are still doing more care than ever, especially in that corridor from mid-forties to early-sixties, when, thanks to children spending longer in education and the greater longevity of older people, women sometimes have primary responsibility for looking after teenage children still living at home *and* their parents.

Joanna Williams, a former colleague of mine who was raised in a working-class home in Middlesbrough, has an interesting perspective on changing attitudes to care and the family. Her own mother was a carer who later qualified as a social worker, and as the eldest child Joanna had to spend a lot of her childhood looking after her siblings. (Her father did an unusual amount of domestic work for a man of his generation but always made sure that the neighbours could not see him when he was hanging up the washing.)

'I rebelled against the idea of care as destiny for a woman and when I had my first child aged twenty-four, I was back at work, as a teacher, within three months. Me and my husband split most of the domestic work fifty-fifty.' She had a second child at twenty-six partly to escape a job that she had come to dislike and took two years out as a full-time mother. She found that didn't suit her either. 'I was a very controlling mother and needed another outlet for my energy.'

Williams is a successful writer and academic who has not wanted to follow the path of more family-focused women but she thinks that their choices should be respected too. 'Whether it is nature or nurture who knows, but lots of young women want to work with children or look after their own and they derive pride and status from that,' says Williams.

I was growing up in Middlesbrough at the time of the Cleveland child abuse scandal. The abuse proved unfounded, but it cast a cloud of suspicion over the domestic realm. Home was no longer seen as a haven in a heartless world but something you needed to escape from. Rather than taking pride in your home and family you had to look outside the home for validation and respect.

And one consequence of the declining solidarity of working-class communities is that domestic work, and paid care work, are experienced far more as individual burdens to be managed rather than the collective responsibility of one generation to another.

She thinks that some feminists are ambivalent about the idea of raising the status of care, in the family or public economy.

They just don't consider caring to be the big issue. In part this is because feminism is such a middle-class preoccupation – concerned with the proportion of women in parliament, or on company boards. Yet survey after survey suggests only a minority of women identify as feminists in that sense.

Ironically, it is the education revolution that has brought about this class/gender divide in relation to the experiences of women. Back in the sixties/early seventies, when feminism first took off, there was a common experience of being a woman – motherhood, domestic work, limited opportunities in the labour market – that women shared irrespective of class background. When more women gained entry to higher education and entry to the professions, that shared gendered experience disappeared, and class differences were reinforced.

Some feminists seem to fear that even in a world that values care more highly, women will continue doing most of it, that the woman-equals-carer equation will be reinforced – even if it is with a higher level of pay and respect – and the goal of a more gender-neutral society will be pushed back. The evidence in countries like Sweden lends some support to this view: women's status in Sweden is high, and the care economy has higher levels of status and pay than almost anywhere else in the world, and yet occupational gender segregation is higher, not lower, with women overwhelmingly concentrated in the care economy and the public sector.[39]

The preferred alternative of many feminist writers is for more men to take up traditionally female caring roles both in the private realm and the public economy, and this is happening to some extent, but rather slowly, as I have just noted. But if women *are* going to continue doing most care in both the home and the public economy, then surely raising its pay and status – and, in the case of England, finally sorting out the funding of adult social care – ought to be a central concern of all mainstream politicians, but especially of those who prioritize women's issues. The fact that has not been such a central concern seems to reinforce the analysis of Alison Wolf, Joanna Williams and others who argue that family and gender politics have been captured by cognitive-class, professional women whose interests are not always the same as those of other women.

Ever since the failure of the Wages for Housework movement in the 1970s the main concern of women's politics has been equality at work *outside* the home and, in more recent decades, above all equality with professional men in the world of careers. This goal has been substantially achieved, according to Wolf, with women, as already noted, now accounting for half of all members of the top, professional and managerial, social class in the UK, even if they are still largely absent from the very pinnacle of the professional and business tree. There is only a small *gender* pay gap, as such, rather there remains a *motherhood* penalty caused by women with children working part-time or not at all and, for professional women, breaking their careers and so losing out on top positions.

Much policy effort has been expended trying to ensure that the careers of professional women are held back as little as possible by motherhood. But child-care subsidies to make a swift return to work possible are not always the priority of more traditionally minded women or women in lower socio-economic groups. They would often prefer more support to stay at home for a few years when children are very young rather than having to leave them in the care of a stranger and return to low-paid work.

Surveys in the UK show that a modified form of the male bread-winner-support role is still wanted by most women when they have young children, and they also show that most women would stay at home longer when children are of pre-school age if they could afford it. The UK government's Childcare Early Years survey of 2019 found 37 per cent of working mothers with children under four would give up work completely to look after their children if they could afford to, and 65 per cent would like to work fewer hours. Indeed, more generally, opinion surveys find support for gender equality *sitting happily alongside* support for a modern version of domesticity. A British Social Attitudes Survey in 2012 asked how much people agreed with the statement 'most mothers with young children prefer having a male partner who is the main family earner rather than working full-time themselves'. Only 15 per cent of respondents disagreed (and only 1.6 per cent strongly). And the proportion of people thinking the role of housewife is just as fulfilling as the role of worker actually rose slightly from 41 per cent in 1989 to 45 per cent in 2012. 'Watching children grow up is life's greatest joy' has remained at more than 80 per cent agreement for more than three decades.

Yet in the UK, and to a lesser extent the US, the tax system prevents the full transfer of tax allowances from one partner to the other and so punishes the single-earner household and fails to recognize or reward the role of the domestic parenthood *partnership*. 'The demands made by vocal, elite women, and the preoccupations of politicians seeking the "female vote" have become extraordinarily divorced from majority concerns . . . Different women have very different lives and interests, like men, and policy-makers should not just listen to the voices from the female summit,' writes Wolf.[40]

Care and gender equality should not be in conflict. Yet one of the unintended consequences of the priorities of that 'summit' is that equality in the public domain of work, professions and politics seems to have been pitted *against* the private domain of care and nurture. But if the Heart is to take its place as an equal partner with Head and Hand in the future this must be seen as a false divide.

The American philosopher Virginia Held puts it like this in her book *The Ethics of Care*:

> For those previously engaged in care to become more and more like the free and equal, rational and unencumbered individuals of theories of justice will leave no one to nurture the relations of family and friendship, and to cultivate the ties of caring . . . if women, in their justifiable quest for equality, pursue justice at the expense of care, morality will suffer.[41]

Is a more family-friendly, pluralistic form of feminism likely to emerge that acknowledges the large variety of female (and male) preferences from wholly career-orientated to wholly family- and care-focused? When Anne-Marie Slaughter gave up her dream job working for Hillary Clinton at the State Department in 2009 because of family demands, she was dismayed to be portrayed as betraying the cause of female achievement. She wrote a book, *Unfinished Business*, arguing for higher status for child-rearing so that choosing it over paid work is not seen as a defeat. Effective child-rearing, she points out, requires many talents, including good organization, patience and imagination. And there are some younger British feminist writers like Nina Power who are reviving the more idealistic strand of the movement which was not shy about talking of feminine characteristics, and seeing them as strengths, and feminizing society rather than just competing equally with men in professional life.

So how can the priorities of the Heart be better embedded in our societies and job markets? It is true that many of us, male and female, do not have the sensibility or skills to care for our own relatives, let alone anyone else. Adult care responsibilities require expertise, the willing amateur can only go so far and may not be able to sustain care month in month out. But the public care economy faces a double problem. For some of the cultural reasons described above there are fewer people attracted to work in the care economy. And those who do want to work in these sectors often find, after a while, that the care has been squeezed out of them, and too many leave disenchanted. There are 690,000 registered nurses in the UK, and only 350,000 working (300,000 in the NHS and the rest in adult social care and the private sector).[42]

Some economists argue that care is undersupplied because it generates positive externalities, positive benefits for society, that can never be properly captured by the carer.[43] This problem used to be solved by restricting women's opportunity to do anything else. Having relaxed those restrictions, we have not worked out an alternative solution and are today living with the consequences. But why cannot carers, both in the public and private realms, capture more of the honour and reward that is their due? Market signals, corporate business plans and social priorities are not set in stone. In democratic societies they respond, sometimes swiftly, sometimes more slowly, to the mysterious fusion of elite and popular sentiment. And the Covid-19 crisis could be shifting that sentiment with reports, in the UK, of an uptick in applications for nursing courses.

THE FUTURE OF NURSING

It is uncontroversial to state that the historic undervaluing of work in catering, cleaning and caring, at least economically, is because it is overwhelmingly done by women: 88 per cent of NHS nurses, 82 per cent of people working in adult social care, 85 per cent of primary-school teachers are female.[44] The numbers are similar in most rich countries. Patterns of reward were set decades ago, when women were more likely to work part-time, were seldom the main household breadwinner and, if married, had their main focus of concern on the family.

Nursing and teaching have been better protected in pay because they usually involve work in large units and are heavily unionized, with national pay review bodies in the UK. But although nursing is decently paid at the start, it has a flat pay structure and mid-career pay, given the levels of stress and responsibility, is often insufficient to lure back women who have left to start families. Pay levels in nursery care and adult social care remain very low.

Patterns of esteem, too, have been heavily 'gendered'. Care has historically been regarded as an intuitive ability which comes more naturally to women. It was a given and so needed little special attention or compensation compared with the high rewards attached to cognitive achievement. If one asks an economist why people in social care homes are paid so little, they would probably say, 'Because almost anyone can do it.' We all know that is not true. Anyone who spends half an hour in a care home, or indeed a hospital, knows that there are, as in most occupations, good carers, middling ones and poor ones. But the economist is in fact correctly describing a low qualification threshold – many care home jobs require minimal or no qualifications for the most basic roles, even though you may be changing a catheter on your second week on the job. Care jobs end up being judged by cognitive standards, or the lack of them, because there is no alternative 'care' criterion.

Many care jobs are highly demanding along both a traditional cognitive dimension – requiring, in the case of nurses, increasing medical knowledge enabling them to prescribe drugs, evaluate medical conditions and even perform minor surgery – and along a distinctive caring dimension too. 'One of the most physically skilful and emotionally demanding things I ever have to do is to help a severely injured person to undress and wash,' one nurse at St George's Hospital in Tooting told me. The necessary emotional intelligence to read a face, respond empathetically and skilfully to someone who is lonely or in pain, can be developed in people, according to Madeleine Bunting. She suggests that it is learned by example, and inspired by a culture. 'It combines intention – the desire to help – imagination, and cognitive ability. It requires Head and Heart.'

One of the predicaments of nursing-type care in an instrumentalist-utilitarian culture is that it is often about containment of pain or distress and its results are elusive and *hard to measure*. Any nurse will tell you that the least prestigious nursing role in a hospital has always been geriatric care. Compared with the technology-dependent acute specialities, it is hard to measure the success of making a very old person's day slightly less miserable or lonely.

The idea of nurse as quasi-doctor which has driven the move to making nursing a graduate profession in many countries sometimes sits uncomfortably alongside the impulse to see professional care as a distinctive skill and tradition in its own right.

There is no reason why, in principle, these two approaches to care should conflict; after all, Florence Nightingale herself was both a caring nurse and a statistician. But the graduatization of nursing in the UK along with various neglect scandals in hospitals and care homes, most notably in the Mid-Staffs hospital trust in 2008, has led to a popular complaint that too many nurses are now 'too posh to wash' and that old-fashioned care has got crowded out of the system.

There are real problems with the diminishment of care, but graduatization of nursing and other care roles is not a big factor, and the evidence shows, to repeat, that health outcomes are better in hospitals and wards where there are more graduate nurses.[45]

When informal family-based care is replaced on such a large scale with more impersonal, paid care, given by people who have little, or at least less, emotional attachment to the toddler or elderly person in their charge, some diminution of care is unavoidable. Other causes are more avoidable and are related to economic and organizational factors that we *can* do something about. When, in the summer of 2019, I spoke to a group of nurses at the giant teaching hospital, St George's, in Tooting, south London, some of them were nostalgic for a time when more time could be devoted to care and building relationships with patients. Most of them had become nurses before 2013, the year when a degree became a condition of becoming a registered nurse, but most of them had acquired degree-equivalent qualifications, and none of them opposed the move to make nursing a graduate profession.

One nurse explained that it is partly the nature of the modern hospital that gives the impression of diminished care. 'When my mother was a ward sister, more patients stayed for weeks, and you got to know them. Now because of more technological medicine there is much quicker throughput, and its harder to build relationships. But I think that does mean we are less patient-centred than we used to be,' she said.

Specialist wards are better, another nurse said, who also felt ambivalent about recent changes. 'It's an odd mix. In the age of the graduate nurse we do have more authority and status and we can do more medical things that we could not do in the past, like prescribing drugs, cannulation, ordering X-rays and blood tests. On the other hand, everything seems more rule-bound and less patient-centred, and we somehow end up with less autonomy.'

As with other occupations that are moving to graduate-only entry, there seemed to be that attitude, among the nurses at St George's, of 'if you can't beat 'em, join 'em'. If deferring to the dominant cognitive motif of the age was the only way to achieve the status that registered nurses feel is their due, then so be it.

Julie Goldie, a senior nurse who is now head of Professional Support and Development at St George's, shares the general ambivalence. She acknowledges that people are living longer and have more complex care needs and that nursing must therefore become more technically and cognitively sophisticated. 'Nursing has never just been about being a nice person, obviously you have to be capable to be a good nurse. But I worry that the soft skills of communication – talking, listening and what many nurses refer to as "basic nursing care" – addressing patients' hygiene and nutritional needs is viewed by some as having less status. The term *basic* denotes a devaluing of these fundamental nursing skills.'

There are other routes into nursing. There is the least skilled health-care assistant role and the intermediate nursing associate role, which Goldie has helped to introduce at St George's, and the latter does provide a ladder up into becoming a full registered nurse. But Goldie also worries about a problem we have seen elsewhere – graduate expectations. 'There is nothing wrong with high expectations. However, it sometimes means that ambitious nurses want to move on into other careers or continue studying straight after graduating.'

The graduate nurse is now typical in the UK, US, France and Scandinavia, but not everywhere in continental Europe (it is not common in Germany or Portugal), though equivalent competence is usually acquired via a non-university training. In the US people queue up to get into the top nursing schools partly because it is possible to earn a very good salary and it is possible to set oneself up as an independent 'nurse practitioner', a nurse equivalent of a medical GP in the UK.

So has graduatization raised the status of nursing in the UK? 'It is not clear that is has, but without graduate status the recruitment problem would probably be even worse,' according to Professor Ian Norman, Dean of the Nursing Faculty at King's College, London.

To Alison Leary, professor of health care at London South Bank University, it is just common sense to think of nursing as a STEM profession and health care as a 'safety critical' knowledge industry. Her work is partly about finding ways to measure the outcomes of nursing care, in the same way that we do with, for example, surgery. Leary locates the perceived decline of care in excessive workload. She has calculated that there are 1 million episodes of care every seventeen hours in the NHS, and nurses are simply being asked to do too much. 'This creates a kind of moral distress for many nurses, and the only way to cope is by becoming more distant from the suffering all around them,' she says.

A writer friend of mine tells a personal anecdote that supports this analysis.

> I experienced a rare complication of c-section after my daughter's birth, and the symptoms of my increasing illness were basically ignored by staff nurses on the post-natal ward despite my family's best efforts to get help. This was not because the nurses were indifferent or negligent, rather because they had something like fifteen mother/baby couples per nurse to keep an eye on, and there was just no time to notice anything. When they finally realized something was very wrong, my daughter and I ended up back on an acute ward, and the difference in care – with sometimes even the same staff delivering it who had just been ignoring me on post-natal – was astonishing. The simple difference was that the staff ratio was three beds to a nurse, not fifteen. You could do a lot to solve the failures of hospital care by just giving nurses more time.

Leary adds that because of staff turnover there is also a big 'rookie' factor in too many hospitals. And pay incentives, as in so many other occupations, tend to encourage people to seek promotion into managerial posts that they may not want or be suited to, rather than just being rewarded for staying put and doing a good job as a ward nurse.

Elaine Maxwell, another health academic, has a different emphasis.

She says that care suffers from lack of a clear definition and that it must be seen as a discipline *distinct from medicine*.

> A nurse must not be just a technical assistant to a doctor. Nursing has been dazzled by the supposed status of becoming a quasi-doctor. But a lot of these things like administering and handing out the right pills can be done by specialists like pharmacy technicians. Nursing must assert its autonomy. It is about helping people adjust to their health conditions. The modern way is to distance yourself from the person and just treat the symptoms, nursing is about keeping the person whole and integrated.

You cannot, to put it another way, put health *into* someone; you can only help them gather the strength to fight off cancer or some other illness.

Maxwell thinks that, paradoxically, being reduced to a second-rank doctor is one of the reasons so many of the 690,000 registered nurses leave the profession. 'I had more autonomy as a nurse in the 1980s, I could decide things such as frequency of observations and timing of medicines that are now decided by doctors.' She agrees with the St George's nurses, and Alison Leary, that the crisis of care arises in part from the way a modern hospital is managed with a big focus on targets and bed management and with caseloads that are too high. She wants to close the status gap between nursing and doctoring and thinks, like Leary, that finding ways of quantifying and then incentivizing relational skills will help in that process, as will acknowledging that caring is teachable, like leadership.

Jonathan Hanbury, a former Associate Director of Nursing at Barts NHS Trust, agrees with Maxwell but has a different focus:

> Nurses now do a lot of things that medics used to do and that is broadly good. But we are under-selling nursing. Nurses essentially run the NHS. The core management of most hospitals is ex-nurses, I think about one-third of NHS trust chief execs have a medical background. Even a ward sister has a budget of millions and forty people under her.
>
> We are not attracting enough highly capable A students. But after you have been on the front line for a few years a huge range of options and disciplines open up for you. There are all sorts of nursing-medical

specialisms, you can manage people, if you have a mathematical bent you can go over to the data side. Indeed, the NHS has a huge shortage of data analysts who also know something about patient care.

These different perspectives, all grappling with how to raise the standing of Heart (combined with Head) in the health-care sector, are not mutually exclusive. Indeed, the challenge may be to attract into nursing both those who want to be quasi-doctors and those who want to care in a more holistic way. There are, for example, many different types of law and engineering, yet we tend to place nursing into one undifferentiated, albeit poorly defined, category.

A more holistic approach is being tried in primary care – in the UK that means the local doctor or General Practitioner (GP). A campaigning doctor, Sir Sam Everington, has pioneered something called 'social prescribing' by GPs among the mainly low-income patients of Tower Hamlets in east London which considers the much broader social and psychological context of illness. 'About 70 per cent of illness has a raft of other factors behind it,' says Everington. The results of social prescribing have been impressive, and the practice is spreading.

Jonathan Hanbury is also an innovator. He has now left the NHS and set up his own social enterprise, Atlas Respite and Therapy, to help individuals and families living with dementia. Dementia has been rising almost everywhere because of rising life expectancy. The Alzheimer's Society says there are some 850,000 dementia patients in the UK, rising to over 1 million by 2025 (although in the UK it has actually been falling recently among males in the 65–75 age group). But mild to severe dementia is estimated to impact nearly half of all 75–85-year-olds and three-quarters of all those over eighty-five in the UK in the coming years.[46]

Hanbury complains that one of the problems with the underfunding of adult social care in England (Scotland and Northern Ireland have merged it into the NHS) is that there is very little innovation. 'Innovation tends to follow the money, and a sector that consists of lots of small companies and lots of charities and volunteers tends to stick with what it knows.'

In Japan, in part because of a social insurance levy for elderly care paid by those over forty (in Germany everyone pays), there is plenty of innovation, from 'happiness centres' for elderly people and their families to villages for the elderly which allow old people to retain more autonomy than in a home, and novel uses of digital technology to monitor people remotely. The Dutch also have model villages for the elderly and the so-called Buurtzorg system of self-managed community nurses, which gives the nurses far more autonomy and makes the work far less bleak and pressured than it usually is in the UK (Buurtzorg is now being trialled in the UK).

Jenny, the sixty-year-old cousin of a friend of mine, experienced that bleakness first hand working as a domiciliary care worker in Warwickshire visiting people in their homes for a range of tasks from administering drugs, cooking for them, dressing and bathing them, changing incontinence pads, and so on. The training was basic. Jenny, like any such care worker, has abundant stories of having to respond to extreme situations of distress and misery. 'It was probably the toughest job I have ever done,' she says. The visits were usually anything between fifteen minutes and one hour – it was reported in 2013 that 500,000 care visits a day are less than five minutes – and if anything went wrong with one of the 'service users' it could make the whole day a frantic catch-up. And all this for something around the minimum wage, or even less if the petrol allowance was inadequate.

This does not make for good or consistent care. Camilla Cavendish, author of the 2013 Cavendish Review into the training of junior health and social care staff who are not registered nurses, tells the story of one elderly man who noted the names of all the carers who visited him in the course of the year so he could greet them by name – at the end of the year he listed 102 different names. Cavendish complains that people doing the most close-up care in hospitals, care homes or home-visit care are often looked down upon by colleagues or described as unskilled because they have talents which are not academic.

> The phrase 'basic care' dramatically understates the work of this group. Helping an elderly person to eat and swallow, bathing someone with dignity and without hurting them, communicating with someone with early onset dementia; doing these things with intelligent kindness, dignity, care and respect requires skill. Doing so alone in the home of a stranger, when the district nurse has left no notes, and you are only being paid to be there for 30 minutes, requires considerable maturity and resilience.[47]

This is care where too often there really is too little time to care. Jenny says: 'I remember the first day on the job overhearing one of the managers say, "She's going to be one that cares too much."' But she says it is not really the fault of the domiciliary care providers, who are usually doing their best with limited resources. What shocked her most was the heartlessness of some families who knew that their elderly relative should have been in a proper care home but did not want to face the cost.

Jenny also worked in a residential care home. She found that slightly less stressful than home visits but could not help noticing that the care home made far more effort with the elderly people who were visited than those who weren't.

Even before the Covid-19 crisis right-wing think tanks in England were proposing that funding for the adult care system should be socialized, and what is seen as the arbitrary and unfair means-tested payment system, for both domiciliary care and care home support, should be swept away and merged into the tax-funded NHS, as it has been in Scotland and Northern Ireland. The English system currently costs taxpayers about £22 billion a year, with another £10 billion paid by users, and employs 1.4 million people to look after around 400,000 people in homes and 500,000 in their own home. Socializing the costs would add an extra 1 per cent to UK public spending.[48]

But whatever happens to the funding of the system, the status of the people who work in it will also remain an issue if the UK and US and other rich societies are going to avoid an even more intense recruitment crisis in these jobs. The longer-term response to the Covid-19 crisis will surely require us not only to build more emergency capacity into our health services but also to improve the career structure and pay of the Cinderella parts of the care economy.

All reputable surveys of future skill requirements in rich countries focus on what Adair Turner calls the 'Hi-Tech, Hi-Touch' combination, meaning higher-order cognitive and technical skills on the one hand and interpersonal skills in education and health on the other – sometimes shortened to 'coders and carers'. The latter skills will generate many more jobs than the former thanks above all to the fitness, care and health needs of ageing populations – health-care workers, home carers and physical therapists of many kinds.

The latest data on pre-crisis job creation in the UK bears out this assumption, with one-quarter of the twenty fastest-growing occupations since 2011 being caring jobs, but the single biggest rise (160,000) coming in the category 'programmers and software development professionals'.[49] And, as we have seen repeatedly, many of the caring jobs are currently low-paid and low-status. The US Bureau of Labor Statistics forecast for job creation up to 2024 finds that eight out of ten of the fastest-growing job categories pay far below the average wage, and one-third of them are care-related – personal care aides (top of the list) and nursing assistants among them.[50]

Some fields of care in the UK have in fact been professionalized in recent years, notably child care. Everyone who works in a nursery school or child-care centre must now have relevant qualifications, and each establishment must have the right mix of qualified staff, including someone with a paediatric first-aid qualification. And, unlike care homes for adults, there is a minimum child/staff ratio. Both qualifications and staffing levels are subject to regular inspection, and this seems to have raised the status of early years work.

Jill Manthorpe, director of the Health and Social Care Workforce Research Unit at King's College, London, says the professionalization of child care should be a model for elderly care. 'Is it too much to ask that these levers of change could apply to other carers? Staff need proper training and professional pride,' she says, 'and care needs its own Royal College or equivalent to oversee standards.' There are many medical colleges, including the Royal College of Physicians and Royal College of Nursing and even a Royal College of Paediatrics and Child Health, but no Royal College of Child and Adult *Care*.

Camilla Cavendish's Review into the 1.3 million frontline NHS health-care assistants and adult social care staff, many of whom have little or no formal training, proposed new common training standards across health and social care. And one of the problems with elderly care in the UK is that, because the system is so fragmented, it does not have a proper national career structure, at least below the higher management level.

WHAT ABOUT MEN?

And what role is there for men in an upward revaluation of caring roles? According to the Centre for Time Use Research in the UK, men's share of all unpaid work in the home has risen from 27 per cent to 38 per cent since the 1970s.[51] That partly reflects the fact that women on average actually spend *less* time on cooking, cleaning and clothes care than they did in earlier decades, presumably because of a big increase in work outside the home plus domestic appliances of various kinds.

But both men and women have spent more time on child care since the 1990s, when ideals of intensive parenting and involved fathering spread widely, especially among the highly educated. Nearly two-thirds of all fathers in most developed countries are now classified as *involved fathers*, spending an average of almost two hours a day on child care. The highly educated often focus on activities that improve the cognitive skills of their children – so-called neuroparenting – and highly educated fathers are more likely to share the ideal of equal sharing of domestic labour. The picture is not so clear for less-educated men. The breadwinner role has historically provided status and was itself a form of care: wage-earning as service to the family. As men are seldom today the sole earner and sometimes not even the main earner in the household, the breadwinner role has been weakened.

But the old idea that family commitments help to make men more caring people and better citizens is still borne out by the statistics, which show men with partners and children are far less likely to be jobless, and prisoners who are visited by families are 40 per cent less likely to reoffend.[52] Conversely, men cope much less well than women after divorce: some men just go into a spiral of decline.

Much writing about men, Grayson Perry's for example, assumes that masculinity is in crisis because men are clinging to an old model of domination that doesn't work any longer and that they need to become more feminine and emotionally attuned. That may be part of the story, but it may also be because men, particularly lower-status men, have lost male caring roles that gave them some dignity as breadwinner and protector and they have not been replaced with anything that men feel comfortable with.

The rise of 'safetyism' and the banishing of risk and physical challenge from modern life can also have a corrosive effect on some men. They may take up an extreme sport or take ridiculous risks in their work or relationships to fill that gap. And one reason for the persistence of a low-level ridiculing of health and safety culture is it seems to deny to men the capacity to judge risk for themselves and the opportunity to be praised and valued for their courage and initiative. A shoot-'em-up video game is designed to scratch that primal itch of heroism, but of course there is no risk involved, and young men are further distanced from any sense of the dangerous reality of physical courage.

A new model of manhood has yet to emerge for a world in which some traditional male virtues – strength, physical courage, emotional stoicism – are less valued. The feminist model which remakes men along more feminine lines has gained little traction, and the conservative idea of a return to a world of restraint, chivalry and protection is even more implausible.

A disproportionate number of jobs that are out of the reach of automation are those traditionally done by women. But if the past is a guide to the future, a big move by men into nursing and other traditionally female occupations seems unlikely – one UK survey found that 85 per cent of men would not consider a career in social care.[53] And Daniel Susskind, in his book *A World Without Work*, reports that most adult men in the US displaced from manufacturing roles prefer not to work at all than take up 'pink collar' work.[54]

In recent years the care sector has become more, not less, female as women have moved into medical roles (a majority of GPs in the UK are now women). The gender imbalance in adult care is less extreme than in nursing – about 18 per cent of staff are men[55] – and there are some corners of care such as mental health nurses and paramedics and ambulance staff that are mainly male. And if men can increase their share of labour in the home relatively swiftly, the same might be possible in the public care economy.

Jamie, a twenty-five-year-old nurse at a London teaching hospital, was one of just thirteen men out of 460 trainee nurses on the degree course at Nottingham University. Three years into the job he finds the work rewarding and challenging, but it still sometimes feels a bit odd being a man in a very female profession, no doubt a feeling many women experience in male-dominated professions. 'Some of the older nurses clearly feel a bit ambivalent about male nurses,' he says.

There are historic precedents for the male nurse to draw upon, such as the Knights Hospitaller order that became a Catholic military organization but started life providing medical care to Christian pilgrims to the Holy Land. And change can happen rapidly. In the 1960s, for example, IT was seen as a female, secretarial function, but as it became more technical and better paid men muscled in. The same could be true of parts of nursing and adult care. But that then raises the so-called 'glass escalator' issue for men that some female nurses resent – the fact that men are disproportionately found in the most prestigious nursing disciplines like intensive care and in the higher ranks of nursing management. The nurses I spoke to at St George's pointed out that three out of the top four nursing positions there are occupied by men, though it was also recognized that women have entered traditionally male-dominated senior medical positions in large numbers. A planned NHS recruitment campaign for male nurses stressing how quickly they could rise to senior positions had to be dropped after senior female nurses objected.

Jamie's ambition is to be an advanced clinical practitioner, a form of nurse that is quite close to being a doctor. He wants to do it because of the autonomy it grants. It is not clear whether he is a model for a future with less of a gender bias in nursing and caring jobs but if all those jobs are to be filled in the future, he might have to be.

COUNTING CARE

It is not unreasonable to assume, in conclusion, that an ageing society that values gender equality will inexorably edge towards placing a higher value on the work of carers, paid and unpaid. And this will require some change in culture and behaviour from people and governments. A change that the fall-out from the Covid-19 crisis might promote.

One way to honour dedicated caring work in the UK is through the official honours system. The kind of self-effacement that is often characteristic of care is, as Madeleine Bunting points out, not generally admired in mainstream culture. And in 2012 the British Empire Medal (BEM) was reinstated specifically to recognize people, often volunteers, away from the public eye in places such as hospices.

But there is some disgruntlement in the voluntary and charity world that the BEM is a second-class honour which is not personally awarded by the Queen or the Prince of Wales and gets nothing like the same attention as OBEs and MBEs. One person who advises on honours for people working in the NHS says this: 'The problem is that conventional honours are meant to be for outstanding contributions or exceptional service. But what about some of the people who do extraordinary service every day as a matter of routine at the sharp end of our care services?'

If the honours system is about signalling what society values, then it should be used more overtly to reward the things that really matter. So should our system of measuring the economy. The economist Paul Ormerod says, 'We could easily put a value on unpaid domestic labour and put the numbers into GDP; there are already a lot of non-market transactions in GDP figures.' Thanks to the existence of time-use data we now have good measures of the hours devoted to market work and non-market work. The Centre for Time Use Research calculates that including domestic labour would add nearly £500 billion a year to GDP.[56] (The ONS estimated the value of *all* unpaid work in the UK in 2014 at £1.01 trillion.)[57] It would not, of course, change living standards at all or the status of care roles in the short term but it would give a more accurate account of what is happening in society and help people to see and value the productive, Heart, work, going on in the unpaid private realm. It might also help to connect GDP more closely to well-being. For one reason that people often sense a disconnect between rising measures of GDP wealth and their own levels of contentment or stress is that economic growth is sometimes directly linked with *reductions* in caring work in the home.

Jooyeoun Suh and Christopher Payne, researchers at the Centre for Time Use Research, explain:

Fifty-three per cent of women aged 16 to 64 in the UK engaged in paid work in 1971, but this figure had risen to 74 per cent by 2014. As women increased their average hours of paid work, they also decreased their average hours of unpaid work. While men were doing a bit more unpaid work over the same period, this increase has not been sufficient to fully take up the slack created by women's decrease in unpaid work.[58]

The authors conclude that improvements in families' living standards as measured through GDP may have been overestimated. Though it is surely more accurate to say that their economic living standards will indeed have risen as a result of a higher second income, but their standard of life and well-being may have declined because of the loss of the productive care labour that is no longer taking place.

This overestimation is the product of an economistic-measurement bias that does not value whatever cannot be measured for GDP purposes and regards care as simply unpaid work. It also reflects a collective amnesia about the contribution of the stay-at-home wife and mother of past decades. She was not sitting at home twiddling her thumbs. She was undertaking productive labour in caring for children and the elderly and also often playing a vital role in community organizations. The decline of such labour has not been cost-free to families or society at large (between 2005 and 2015 alone there was a 15 per cent drop in the number of hours dedicated to volunteer work in the UK).[59]

Family care work in the home can be experienced as crushingly dull and limiting – 'a comfortable concentration camp', as Betty Friedan put it – and many women have eagerly swapped it for paid employment. This is Marilyn French in her 1977 feminist classic *The Women's Room*:

> Years of scraping shit out of diapers with a kitchen knife, finding places where string beans are two cents less a pound, intelligence in figuring the most efficient, least time-consuming way to iron men's white shirts and wax the kitchen floor . . . these not only take energy and courage and mind, but they may constitute the very essence of a life . . . I hate these grimy details as much as you do.[60]

In recent decades this has generally been the dominant narrative underpinning the shift of female labour from the home into the public economy. But domestic and care work is also experienced by others as meaningful. In the US about one in seven adults provide unpaid care of some kind to another person and, according to Pew, the US polling organization, the vast majority regard it as very meaningful.[61]

And educated young mothers raised in a gender-egalitarian culture are often shocked at the raw, inescapable gender-differentiation of motherhood. Here is Mary Harrington, the British political blogger, writing for the magazine *UnHerd*:

> A breastfeeding mother needs to stay physically close to her baby, and runs on the baby's timetable for months . . . The other partner can support the mother in practical ways but is more free to maintain a normal daily schedule or return to work, as most fathers typically do following the legally-allotted two weeks . . . Reports lament the poor uptake of shared parental leave, but given that males cannot breastfeed, it should not come as a surprise . . . This in turn shapes how housework is divided.
>
> There is no doubt that socialisation plays some role in a distribution of housework between men and women, but the rubber really hits the road when children arrive, and this is to no small degree because of a mother's desire to be close to her baby. It will feel logical for a mother to take on the lion's share of house and child management during maternity leave. By the time she returns to work – and over three-quarters of mothers with dependent children in the UK now work – it is highly likely that a pattern will have emerged in which this is normalised, and the mother has become more oriented toward managing the household while her partner is more focused on work.[62]

Every woman, like every man, is different, and, given greater choice, an enormously varied balance of work and family would be chosen. But according to Catherine Hakim, adult women in Britain can be loosely divided into three broad groups: 20 per cent are overwhelmingly work-focused, 20 per cent overwhelmingly family focused, and 60 per cent are adaptive, meaning they want to combine the two in varying ways.[63] The happiest group of people in the UK according to well-being data from the end of the twentieth century are women with young children who work part-time.[64]

I recently met a senior official from the UK's Department for Health and asked her, if she was granted one wish to improve the functioning of the NHS, what would it be? Her reply was more challenging than I expected: 'I would want people to have the same moral and legal responsibilities for looking after their elderly relatives that they have for their children.'

Better-funded adult care from the state *combined with* more moral stigma, and possibly even some financial sanction, directed at people who do not care for their elderly parents, is perfectly imaginable in the coming years. This could be reinforced by the potentially benign influence on western societies of South Asian minorities with stronger family obligations (though the cultural influence can also flow the other way). Add to that the evolution of a new form of feminism that honours women's caring role in the private domain as well as success in the public one; an increased movement of younger men into caring jobs at all levels, including more stay-at-home fathers; plus a less dominant role for higher cognitive aptitudes in the labour market of the future, and a better Head, Hand, Heart balance becomes not just possible but probable.

Often what we really value becomes clear only when it is too late, and we are regretting on our deathbed. People seldom wish they had done more paid work or got more promotions at work. Social psychologists have actually measured this, researching what people say when close to death, and found that the regrets of the dying are overwhelmingly linked to our sense of belonging, to love and to family, and hardly at all to work or achievement in the public realm.[65] A woman I know who runs a hospice told me that men, in particular, invariably ask for forgiveness from those close to them for not being a more loving or caring husband or father.

PART FOUR

The Future

9

The Fall of the Knowledge Worker

The urban, educated people who voted against populism will
have a whole new attitude when globalization and automation
get up close and personal.

Richard Baldwin

There are two fundamental reasons why cognitive ability has become
so central to status and reward in modern societies. First, the industrial
and then post-industrial economy and society has simply demanded
more highly qualified professional people with above-average levels
of cognitive ability. Second, appointing, promoting and rewarding
people according to their cognitive ability seems fair. This fairness, it
is true, is qualified by the fact that cognitive ability is partly inherited,
and the IQ tests and exams we use to measure it may not be fully
measuring what we want them to measure, as discussed in Chapter 3.

Ken Charman knows this landscape. He is an Oxford postgrad
who conducted undergraduate admissions interviews at Oxford and is
the CEO of a subsidiary in a big multinational. He is often involved in
recruitment and promotion decisions and says that all the gatekeepers
are looking for is 'fair enough': 'Everyone likes to think that they can
spot the very best people, but, in reality, so long as you fill graduate
positions with people who you can prove are in the top X per cent
of IQ or degree class, you are in the clear. You have an objective
yardstick that avoids disaster and is above criticism of bias.' He himself is a highly capable and successful businessman from an ordinary
background and points out that he left school with no maths, science
or language O levels and at senior school only got As in PE, art and
metalwork (he failed maths repeatedly and was not allowed to take

a science or language O level). 'Under the grade-based *must be seen to be fair* selection criteria we use these days . . . with my O levels? I wouldn't get close to an interview,' he says. In 1968 he went to the then brand-new Abbs Cross Country Technical High School in east London, with smart engineering and science labs from which you could see the Ford factory at Dagenham. It now specializes in the performing arts.

'Even people with weak grades like me were pushed into the professions in those days. But it seems that getting an X *Factor* audition, or having your own YouTube channel, is now the main career aspiration, especially for the white kids who don't come from aspirational families,' he comments. He also has strong views about fairness and social mobility.

> Putting the best people in the most important and difficult jobs is just common sense, but, so far as we are able to do that, that is the easy part. The bigger problem comes when they get rewards and status that place them too far above everyone else. Then the people in the top jobs fear that their children will drop down and they do everything possible to help them, I know because I have done it myself.
>
> But that has the effect of blocking off other peoples' perhaps more deserving children. If the differences in reward and status in the hierarchy were less dramatic, then perhaps people would relax more and not try to game the system.
>
> I know this sounds egalitarian and Scandinavian but I'm not talking so much about income as status, and I say this because I know so many good people who don't want to strive and don't want to have to join the middle class in order to have a decent life. I don't myself! I don't like art, opera, middle-class dinner parties. I never did parents' socials at the private schools my children went to. I never felt comfortable there.
>
> Becoming middle-class enabled me to lead a safer, more comfortable life and provide security for my children. But those seem like things that everyone should have without having to go to university or change class. Why shouldn't people who clean offices or drive lorries experience that too?
>
> When I meet my friends from my time at Bradford university, many of whom have done very well from a working-class background, we

turn to this subject often. In the safety of each other's company we prefer working-class warmth, wit, cynicism, pragmatism, stoicism, wryness, rude honesty, crude humour, lack of pretention, dryness, simplicity, humanity, flaws, vulgarity . . . Obviously, it doesn't make us inferior or superior. These are just social manners. And I don't want to give them up as the price of being respectable and worthy of my place where the big decisions are made.

And his desire for a less jagged distribution of status may now have history, and economics, on its side. For that first fundamental reason that cognitive ability has been so central to status and reward in recent decades – economies and companies have simply demanded more and more cognitively trained staff – is drawing to a close.

Consider, again, the bigger picture of Head, Hand and Heart. Andy Haldane, chief economist at the Bank of England, put it like this when I visited him at the Bank: 'During the first three industrial revolutions the skills workers needed to keep one step ahead of the machine were largely cognitive. So institutions emerged to nurture thinking skills, in children and young adults, to increase the chances of successful transition to the cognitively-intensive future world of work.' Hence mass primary, then secondary, then higher education.

The so-called fourth industrial revolution, meaning robots and artificial intelligence, will mean, as Haldane puts it, 'humans will no longer have the cognitive playing field to themselves'. Thinking and other non-routine tasks will increasingly be taken over by machines. They will be able to process more quickly, more cheaply and with fewer errors than their human counterpart, at least in some activities.

Two big shifts in working life are imminent. The first is a demographic one. Someone born today can be expected to live to 100. That means multiple changes of career, not just job, are likely during a lifetime. The second shift is in the demand for skills. In the past, this skill-shift has been all one way. Demand for skills of the Head have dominated demand for skills of the Hand and, to lesser extent, of the Heart. 'This may be about to go into reverse,' says Haldane.

The thin, intense Haldane was born in Sunderland and educated at a Leeds comprehensive school and speaks with a mild Yorkshire

accent. He is one of the most creative and respected economic thinkers in the country. To the extent that the Bank of England has tried
to listen to the concerns expressed in the Brexit vote, he is the man
responsible. He seems a bit out of place in the mandarin splendour
of the Bank of England, where I talked to him. But, warming to his
theme, he explained to me the future role for humans:

> My guess is that there are three areas where humans will preserve some
> comparative advantage over robots for the foreseeable future. The first
> is cognitive tasks requiring creativity and intuition. These might be
> tasks or problems whose solutions require great logical leaps of imagi-
> nation rather than step-by-step hill-climbing . . . And even in a world
> of super-intelligent machine learning, there will still be a demand for
> people with the skills to programme, test and oversee these machines.
> Some human judgemental overlay of these automated processes is still
> likely to be needed.

The second area of prospective demand for human skills, says Haldane, is bespoke design and manufacture. Routine technical tasks
are relatively simple to automate and are already well on their way to
disappearing. But the same is not true of non-routine technical tasks
– for example, the creation of goods and services that are distinctive
in their design, manufacture or delivery.

> A rise in global income is likely to create an increasing demand for lux-
> ury goods and services of this type, whose characteristics are unique
> and supply constrained. Indeed, this can be seen already in the rising
> demand and price of rare art and artefacts and independently pro-
> duced foodstuffs and beverages. To meet this demand, Mark Carney
> [Governor of the Bank of England] has spoken about the re-emergence
> of a new artisan class.

The third, and perhaps the biggest, potential growth area of all,
argues Haldane, is social skills, Heart jobs, that is, tasks requiring
emotional intelligence (sympathy and empathy, relationship-building
and negotiation skills, resilience and character) rather than cognitive
intelligence alone. These are skills robots are likely to find it hard to
replicate. And even if they could replicate them, humans might still
prefer humans to carry them out.

The future could see a world of work in which EQ rivals IQ for supremacy, he continues. Professions involving high degrees of personal and social interaction – such as health, caring, education and leisure – will see demand rise. Indeed, it is possible the balance between cognitive and social skills might alter significantly even in jobs which traditionally have been cognitively intense.

> Take medicine. The doctors of the future might be valued far less for their clinical competence in diagnosing illness and prescribing solutions. In a world of individual medical records and data-hungry diagnostic algorithms, much of the process of diagnosis and pre-scription might fall to a machine rather than a human. But that is unlikely by itself to eradicate the need for doctors. Patients are still likely to want to discuss their diagnosis and prescription. And they will want this advice delivered personally and empathetically. In surveys of patient satisfaction it is a doctor's bedside manner, rather than clinical competence, that matters most. In future, that balance between social and clinical skills may shift further. And, most likely, those social skills will be demanded from flesh-and-blood rather than robo-doctors.

Haldane sees that the future requires a better balance between the cognitive, technical and social – Head, Hand and Heart. He is not alone. In fact Paul Krugman, whom I quoted in Chapter 1, spotted back in 1996 (pretending to look back from the end of the twenty-first century) that high returns to education might not last long.

> In the 1990s everyone believed that education was key to economic success, for both individuals and nations. A college degree, maybe even a postgraduate degree, was essential for anyone who wanted a good job as one of those 'symbolic analysts'. But computers are very good at analysing symbols; it's the messiness of the real world that they have trouble with . . . So, over the course of the 21st century many of the jobs that used to require a college degree have been eliminated.[1]

Richard Baldwin, author of *The Globotics Upheaval* and one of lead-ing experts on the impact of robotics, also agrees with Haldane about a future in creativity, craft and caring.

Machines have not been very successful at acquiring social intelligence, emotional intelligence, creativity, innovativeness, or the ability to deal with unknown situations. Experts estimate it will take something like fifty years for AI to attain top-level human performance in social skills that are useful in the workplace.

The sheltered sectors of the future will be those where people actually have to be together doing things for which humanity is an edge. This will mean that our work lives will be filled with far more caring, sharing, understanding, creating, empathising, innovating, and managing people who are actually in the same room.[2]

So the knowledge economy is likely to need fewer knowledge workers in the future. Indeed, according to Phil Brown and Hugh Lauder, that future is already here. In their book *The Global Auction* they argue that the notion that western societies will be the global Head and developing countries will be content to remain the global Hand is now just a historical curiosity. Thanks to improvements in technology and education it is now much easier for people in poorer countries to do the knowledge work that was once the preserve of western graduates.

> Since the late 1990s, we've been investigating the changing contours of the global economy, talking to corporate managers and executives, along with national policy advisers, in several countries including the United States, Germany, China and India. The compelling conclusion to emerge from over 250 face to face interviews with these leaders, public and private, is that the relationship between education, jobs and incomes is being transformed in ways that cast doubt on the traditional rhetoric that 'learning equals earning' and the crucial role education plays in creating middle-class jobs.[3]

German car-makers, who as recently as the late 1990s thought it would be impossible to make top-end cars outside Baden-Württemberg, let alone Germany, are now building their entire product range in emerging economies. German car-makers were among the last to succumb to the globalization of industry, which is now an old story. But now in *services* it is increasingly the same story: emerging economies are no longer restricted to data-entry and call-centre functions. Brown and Lauder cite a global law firm headquartered in New York that has moved some of the work previously given to newly qualified lawyers in London or New York with annual salaries of around $100,000 to law graduates in the Philippines, where the same work is done for less than $15,000.[4]

The barriers to higher education that previously protected the western middle class are falling. 'China and India are "leap-frogging" decades of technological development in the West to compete for high-skilled, high-value work, including research and development,' according to Brown and Lauder. China is heading towards 200 million graduates in its workforce and is currently graduating three times more students every year than the US.[5]

This is not just about more global trade in services, following in the footsteps of manufacturing. Both of these trends could in theory be reversed by protectionism, maybe driven by fear of future pandemics. But the same technology that is helping to create a single global market in services is undermining the western knowledge worker at home too via so-called Digital Taylorism.

'If the twentieth century brought mechanical Taylorism – mass production where the knowledge of craft workers is captured, codified and re-engineered in the shape of the moving assembly line – the twenty-first century is the age of Digital Taylorism. This involves codifying, standardising and digitising knowledge into software prescripts, platforms and packages that can be used by others regardless of location,' write Brown and Lauder.[6]

New technologies, they point out, have increased the potential to translate knowledge work into *working knowledge*, leading to the standardization of an increasing proportion of technical, managerial and professional jobs. Managerial jobs look likely to be increasingly deprived of discretion and analytical content by new technology. The classic example is the local bank manager, who used to use his judgement and knowledge of local businesses to decide whether to lend the bank's money. In many banks a software package now automatically assesses a loan application according to standard criteria. Only if there is an appeal against the software's judgement does the manager have a role. Another example is the travel agent who made a decent living getting you nifty special deals, who has been replaced by Expedia and online booking of flights.

Brown and Lauder show that many big corporations have adopted a narrow view of talent management, severely limiting the numbers of employees recognized for their cognitive or problem-solving ability, leaving many other employees with a graduate education performing increasingly routinized tasks. As mentioned earlier, they break down service jobs into three categories – overlapping to some extent with the modern multinational's three layers of core, periphery and contingent, that we met in Chapter 5 – which they label Developers, Demonstrators and Drones.

Developer roles, which are no more than 10 to 15 per cent of a typical organization's workforce, are given 'permission to think' and include senior researchers, managers and professionals. Demonstrator roles are the second-level, partially deskilled professionals who are invariably graduates but whose main job is to execute or implement existing knowledge. Communicating well is usually their main function. Drone employees are involved in monotonous work and not expected to think. (As noted in Chapter 5, this implies that western business has not learned the lesson of Japanese Total Quality Management, which draw on the brains and initiative of *all* workers.)

The swift decline of the professions has also been predicted in an influential book by father and son Richard and Daniel Susskind, *The Future of the Professions*. They write: 'Our focus is on doctors, lawyers, teachers, accountants, tax advisers, management consultants, architects and journalists (amongst others) . . . Our main claim is that we are on the brink of fundamental and irreversible change in the way that the expertise of these specialists is made available to society.'[7]

They give some examples of what they mean. There are more unique visits each month to the WebMD network, a collection of health websites, than to all the doctors working in the US. In the legal world three times as many disagreements each year amongst eBay traders are resolved using 'online dispute resolution' than there are lawsuits filed in the entire US court system.

The key question, as they see it, is how do we share expertise in society?

In what we term a 'print-based industrial society', the professions have played a central role in the sharing of expertise. They have been the main channel through which individuals and organisations have gained access to certain kinds of knowledge and experience. However in a 'technology-based Internet society' we predict that increasingly capable machines . . . will take on many of the tasks that have been the historic preserve of the professions.[8]

One of the main objections to this argument is that people will still want the reassurance of an empathetic human expert. Their response: 'We do not deny for a second that great comfort can be given from one person to another. Indeed we identify the "empathizer" as an important future role. However, our experience suggests that many of the recipients of professional advice are in fact seeking a reliable solution or outcome rather than a trusted adviser *per se*.'[9]

Like Haldane and Baldwin, they advise young people either to look for jobs that favour human capabilities over artificial intelligence – above all creativity and empathy – or to be directly involved in the design and delivery of these increasingly capable systems as a data scientist or knowledge engineer.

LESS ROOM AT THE TOP

There is plenty of plausible scepticism about how swiftly AI is going to advance. But even if some of the predictions do turn out to be over-enthusiastic, there is other evidence for the *decline and fall of the knowledge worker* all around us: the decline in the graduate pay premium especially in the UK, the increasing number of graduates in non-graduate jobs and even the shrinkage, or at least slower growth, of the top managerial and professional social class.

It is obvious that as the number of graduates has increased dramatically over recent decades the prestige and economic returns associated with going to university would dip. A recent OECD report found that, on average across OECD countries, the earnings premium associated with higher education for 55–64-year-olds was 70 per cent, twice that of younger adults, at just 35 per cent. And the same report found the decline to be accelerating.[10]

Looking more closely at the story in the UK in 2018, at age twenty-nine the average man who attended university earns around 25 per cent more than the average man with five good GCSEs, who did not. For women the gap is more than 50 per cent (thanks to the fact that non-graduate women are more likely to be working part-time or in lower-paying, often care-related, sectors). However, once you control for differences in pre-university characteristics (by, for example, comparing the earnings of someone who got similar A level results to an undergraduate but did not go to university), the average impact of attending university on earnings at age twenty-nine is much less – 28 per cent for women and just 8 per cent for men. Moreover, with that adjustment, as many as one-third of male British graduates get effectively no higher return from going to university.[11]

Anna Vignoles, one of the leading researchers in this field, shows that the median earnings of men from the bottom twenty-three universities were *less* than the median earnings for non-graduates.[12] And there are twelve institutions for which she estimates *statistically significant* negative returns for men at age twenty-nine.*

There is a brutal hierarchy among universities which partly determines the size of the premium – with Oxbridge, the top London colleges and the Russell Group all linked with much higher returns and most of the former polytechnics producing significantly lower or non-existent premiums. In fact, fully half of students now attend a UK university with an average income uplift of less than 10 per cent.[13] Male Russell Group graduates earn over 40 per cent more than those who attended the former polytechnics (35 per cent more for women). When controlling for pre-university factors, a Russell Group university degree still confers a 10–13 per cent increase in earnings over non-Russell Group universities.[14]

Subject choice has a big impact on the premium too. Medicine and economics degrees have the highest returns, around 20 per cent higher than the average degree (and 25 per cent more than English or history),[15] and business, computing and architecture degrees all offer relative earnings uplift.[16] Creative arts, which enrols more than 10 per

* They are University College Falmouth, Goldsmiths, Glamorgan, Bath Spa, Leeds City, Middlesex, Bolton, University of the Arts London, West London, Ravensbourne, Wolverhampton, Bangor. (Some of these are colleges of art and design, which for most graduates is a precarious and low-paid sector.)

cent of all students, has very low returns: around 15 per cent less than the average degree.[17] Other low scorers, partly reflecting pay levels in their sectors, include: social care, sports science, communications, English, sociology, psychology and education.[18]

Social class also plays a role in graduate premium outcomes. After controlling for all other characteristics, degree subject and institution, graduates from private schools earn around 7 per cent to 9 per cent more than those graduates from the lowest socio-economic backgrounds.[19] In the US attending the most selective state university causes earnings to be about 30 per cent higher than the white male average. The Ivy League graduate earns on average twice as much as graduates of other colleges.

In some ways it is remarkable how the so-called graduate premium has held up to the extent that it has. That is partly because, at least until recently, the economy has been generating more graduate-level jobs. But it is also because of occupational 'filtering down'. As Ken Mayhew, professor of education at Oxford, explains:

> Imagine a hierarchy of jobs. Top of the hierarchy is the best-paying job and as we move down the hierarchy pay gets lower and lower. Graduates occupy the jobs at the top of the pay hierarchy but as more and more of them enter the labour market some of them occupy jobs further and further down the hierarchy. Thus the average pay of graduates falls. But so does the average pay of *non-graduates*. So, the average graduate wage premium can remain unchanged despite the fact that lots of young people have been to university only to enter jobs once occupied, as it were, by their non-graduate mothers and fathers.
>
> From an individual's economic point of view it makes sense for them to attend university given the current structure of the education and training system and the incentives presented to young people. However that does not mean that it makes sense for society, which has to ask whether, for many people, higher education is the most cost effective way of preparing them for the labour market.[20]

This describes exactly what has been happening in the US in recent years. In the last two decades male earnings between the fiftieth and eightieth deciles (so just below the top 20 per cent) have been static. But the graduate premium over those with just a high-school diploma remains significant (averaging over $30,000 a year), albeit flattening out in recent years, so it still makes economic sense to go to college if you can.[21]

The premise on which the whole expansion of higher education (and social mobility policy) has been based – more and more well-paid, professional, middle-class jobs with a high cognitive content – no longer holds. This is beginning to filter through into the choices that young people make, as more people share either their negative experience of university and their disappointing post-university careers or, alternatively, the positive experience of even middle-class young people who decided not to take the expected path to higher education, thereby avoiding the double blow of significant debt followed by disappointment in the job market.

In the UK all the incentives still push young people down the university path, as I spelt out in Chapter 4, but politicians and newspaper columnists are also starting to think and talk more positively about non-university post-school paths such as high-level apprenticeships. In the UK the returns to a sub-degree STEM qualification (level 4 or 5 in the jargon of international education) are higher than the returns to most degrees outside Russell Group universities.[22] Stefan Speckesser of the National Institute of Economic and Social Research in London has established that the average income for those who obtained a degree from a non-Russell institution is 11 per cent lower by the age of thirty than it would have been had those same individuals achieved higher-technical qualifications instead.

A big part of the fall of the knowledge worker story is just how many graduates *are now doing non-graduate jobs*. Looking at the bigger picture for rich countries the OECD Skills Survey (which asks people whether they have 'more skills to cope with more demanding duties') finds that around one-third of *all* workers think that they have under-utilized skills. Looking just at graduates, the figure was also around 40 per cent for the UK and averaged around 35 per cent for graduates across all OECD countries.[23] A 2015 Linkedin survey of users found 37 per cent of mainly professional people said their current job did not fully use their skills.

Relying on workers' own perceptions of their skill potential is maybe too subjective, but the UK's statistical body, the ONS, which uses a more objective job-classification methodology, reports similar numbers. In 2017 it noted that the number of recent graduates working in non-graduate jobs had risen from 37 per cent in 2001 to 47 per cent in 2013 and 49 per cent in 2017. The percentage of non-recent graduates (more than five years) working in non-graduate jobs is 35 per cent.[24] As one might expect, the proportions tend to be highest in poorer regions of the country, where there are fewer graduate jobs. The labour economist Peter Elias has gone even further and declared that *over half* of graduates were in jobs unlikely to be requiring, using or rewarding their investment in higher education.[25]

The ONS also uses the concept of 'overeducation', meaning having more education than required to do the job. In 2017 around 16 per cent of all those in employment aged sixteen to sixty-four years were overeducated; the corresponding figure for graduates (with first degree or equivalent) was around 31 per cent.[26] Those with postgraduate qualifications are not immune. About half (51 per cent) worked in a job that required such a qualification, another quarter (26 per cent) worked in a job for which a first degree would have sufficed, and the rest were in positions that required no higher education, according to the UK Skills and Employment Survey of 2017.[27]

Ken Mayhew and Craig Holmes have also looked at jobs categorized as graduate jobs but where the skills people acquired doing their degrees are largely irrelevant. They examined twenty-nine occupations, which account for almost a third of total employment. The report concludes that while for many of these jobs the number of graduates has increased sharply over the last thirty years, *the skills required for the job have not appreciably changed.*[28] Examples of this include managers in manufacturing, transport and communication, health associate professionals, nursery nurses and a number of examples from clerical work; also technicians in manufacturing, managers and senior administrators in the public services, and sports coaches and fitness instructors.[29] Graduates who drop down the job hierarchy often end up doing jobs that they are not suited to and become bored with very quickly – recall in Chapter 4 the graduates whose expectations make them poor at relatively routine technician-type jobs.

Ken Mayhew, whose name has cropped up frequently in the preceding paragraphs, is a reassuring guide through this corner of the maze.

Not only is he a professor of education at Oxford University but he has worked in government and gives the impression that he has seen everything come round at least three times. He is the son of a tailor who went on a full scholarship to Manchester Grammar School, from his home in Ashton-under-Lyne, and for a high-ranking academic has an attractively vivid way of talking about labour markets, often drawn from his own life or extended family. I am sitting with him in a Café Rouge restaurant in north London, picking his brain about the rise of the graduate in a non-graduate job. He looks around to illustrate his point and says: 'A junior purchasing manager working for a restaurant chain like Café Rouge will now be required to have a degree, but this is mainly a screening/signalling effect – they are very unlikely to use anything they have learned doing a three year bachelor's degree.'

All in all, many of today's graduates are entering occupations which at least by their title, are, as Mayhew puts it, just the same as the ones entered by their non-graduate mothers and fathers: 41 per cent of new recruits to property, housing and estate management are now graduates, compared with just 3.6 per cent in 1979, and 35 per cent of new bank and post office clerks are now graduates, compared with 1979 when just 3.5 per cent were. The increase in the graduate mix within financial services (from the 1990s) has had little effect on skills upgrading for the roles: it has been estimated that 45 per cent of recently employed graduates in finance were working in jobs suitable for school leavers, which had not been upgraded at all.[30] Studies of estate agents, press officers, software engineers, financial analysts and laboratory technicians have suggested only limited use of specifically graduate skills in jobs that have recently become dominated by, or exclusive to, those with degrees.[31]

The fall of the knowledge worker can also be glimpsed in non-repayment of student loans. After all, if graduates are mainly going into decent graduate jobs, why are so many struggling to repay those loans? Under current repayment terms the majority of UK graduates will never earn enough to fully repay their debts – with the IFS estimating that 77 per cent will have some of their debt written off after the end of the thirty-year repayment period.[32]

How does this picture compare with the US and France and Germany? Although graduate filtering down is common across Europe, it is rather less so in France and Germany, and both countries have fewer graduates who believe they aren't using their skills.[33] According to one academic paper the figure for the US of graduates in non-graduate jobs is a little bit below the UK at 32 per cent; France stands at 28 per cent, and Germany at 16 per cent.[34] Daniel Susskind, in *A World Without Work*, says that one-third of Americans working in the fast food industry have some college education and one-third of Americans with degrees in STEM subjects are now in roles that don't require those qualifications.[35]

The result of all the trends discussed above is that the increase in the number of people in the top occupational classes is starting to slow down and even stop, at least in the UK. After continuous expansion since the categories were first invented, it appears that, according to the leading social mobility researcher John Goldthorpe, there has been 'less room at the top' in recent years.[36]

As noted, education policy and social mobility policy in most rich countries have been premised on the assumption of an ever-growing cognitive class of people in professional jobs. This has, indeed, been a big part of the story over recent decades. Even now, taking the top three occupational classes (in the ONS nine-class schema) in the UK, there appears to be some continuing growth. The proportion of people in those top three groups – managers, directors and senior officials; professional occupations; and associate professional and technical occupations – has risen from 39 per cent to 45 per cent between 2001 and 2018.[37]

The government classifies these top three groups as graduate-level jobs. But if you look more closely at the classification system it turns out that the third group, associate professional and technical occupations, has many occupations that are explicitly non-graduate, requiring only higher-level vocational qualifications. They include: police community support officers, fitness instructors, marketing associates, managers in retail and property and estate managers. According to Anna Vignoles, there are genuine classification problems here: 'Is a web designer the equivalent of a managing director or a binman?' But she agrees with Goldthorpe that there has been a slowdown or even a complete halt to the increase in the number of well-paid, higher-professional jobs, which means that downward mobility has become greater than upward mobility at the top of the occupational hierarchy.

All of this suggests that the rather simple human capital theory notion of higher returns to individuals and higher productivity for economies flowing from more higher education is no longer working. The idea has been very popular among politicians as well as economists, as it seemed to solve both the economic problem and the fairness problem by placing educational meritocracy at the centre of progressive politics, both for centre-left and centre-right. It was given a further boost at the end of the 1980s with the invention of the idea of the knowledge economy (a term that seems to have gone out of fashion in recent years).

Forecasts about the jobs of the future provide more support for the idea of the decline and fall of the knowledge worker, especially at the middling and lower level. The demand for Head jobs will still be there, but it will focus on the most able and creative, and the sharpest rise in demand will be for Heart and certain kinds, of technological jobs that combine Hand and Head.

A cottage industry has emerged over recent years estimating gross job loss from automation as anything between 10 and 50 per cent. Most analysts agree that many jobs will go, but few whole occupations. Some of the potentially powerful effects of automation on jobs and wages are already apparent. According to McKinsey, 18 per cent of all hours worked in the US are devoted to 'predictable physical activities', and half of these hours could be automated away even with current technology. That McKinsey report looked at the prospects for twenty-five different skills across five broad categories in the US: physical and manual, basic cognitive, higher cognitive, social and emotional, and technological skills. The conclusion is that between 2016 and 2030 the hours worked on old-school *physical and manual* skills will decline 11 per cent (though at 26 per cent of hours worked in the economy it will remain the largest sector in 2030), hours worked on *basic cognitive* skills will fall 14 per cent, *higher cognitive* skills will increase by 9 per cent (but not increase its overall share in 2030, which will remain at 22 per cent), *social and emotional* skills will rise by 26 per cent, and *technological* skills by a whopping 60 per cent (though still only 16 per cent of total hours in 2030). A similar trend is expected in western Europe.[38]

It is not all bad news for the knowledge worker, even though there will be fewer of them.

> The growing need for creativity is seen in many activities, including developing high-quality marketing strategies. Other types of higher cognitive skills – such as advanced literacy and writing, and quantitative and statistical skills – will not see a similar increase in demand, and indeed our analysis suggests the need for them could remain stable or even decline to 2030. In writing and editing, computer programs already produce basic news stories about sporting results and stock market movements for many newspaper chains. Of course, the decline in this skill does not imply that there will be no authors, writers, or editors in the future – but as in many other occupations, some of the more basic aspects of the work will shift to machines.

And that bank manager whose judgement has been replaced with a loan approval algorithm is emblematic of a broader shift in lower-level financial service jobs which is likely to have a big impact on heavily financialized economies such as the US and UK. As the report says: 'A range of back-office functions to be automated, include financial reporting, accounting, actuarial sciences, insurance claims processing, credit scoring, loan approval, and tax calculation. Computer algorithms and "robotic process automation" can drastically reduce the time and manpower devoted to these activities.'[39]

CAPITALISM IN THE AGE OF ROBOTS

So what does all this mean? The knowledge economy needs fewer knowledge workers than expected. The recent expansion of higher education in much of the West will stop or even go into reverse as the demand for the middling- and lower-rung jobs of the knowledge economy will decline, a process that the Covid-19 crisis will accelerate. And companies, partly out of bitter experience, will place less confidence in the signalling effect of a degree, even from a good university, and revert to offering more apprenticeships, including degree apprenticeships, to capable school leavers. This is already happening in several big employers and appears to be more than a fad.

The big consultancy firm EY made a splash in the UK in 2015 with the announcement that it would drop degree classification from the entry criteria for their hiring programmes; you would not need to be a graduate to apply for even their top entry-level training programme.[40] The firm said it would focus on a 'strengths-based assessment', looking for people who are 'strong communicators, team players, adaptable, analytical, numbers savvy, in the know'.[41] Other big UK consultancies such as KPMG and Deloitte and banks, including Barclays, have made similar announcements.

Opening up different routes into high-status cognitive-analytical jobs is not in itself tilting the balance away from Head, though it could weaken the grip of degree credentialism. But the indications are that the pendulum of prestige will gradually swing, at least somewhat, away from the cognitive-analytical and towards the 'high-touch' jobs, often face to face, in care and education and fitness, and to some higher Hand niches too, both technical and artisanal.

There will also be a renewed interest in the old generalist tradition, often seen as an English gentlemanly deformation in the nineteenth and early twentieth centuries compared with continental specialization, though now it will be celebrated as 'cross-domain' competence. The model for this is something like the website designer who requires both technical know-how and some aesthetic/design ability too.

But hanging over this potentially benign evolution hangs the spectre of inequality. The knowledge economy will lose many of its rank-and-file soldiers but it will still have an officer corps of highly skilled individuals, both those managing the machines of the fourth industrial revolution and the superstar professionals of the winner-takes-all markets. Soaring corporate pay packages in recent decades have already led to chief executives of the top 500 US companies earning on average 379 times more than their average employee; the figure is 149 times for the top 100 companies in the UK.[42]

My friend who described the new multinational corporate structures in Chapter 5 also had this to say about what is happening.

People like me, who are successful meritocrats at the top of big corporates and with contingent skills that command a high market price, are open to the criticism that we think the rest of the world is like us. We need to remember we are not representative. People like us have been blessed with the genes to constantly learn, adapt and compete. I know we go on about how hard we work and how much we have sacrificed, but we are mainly just the lucky minority who were born with a bigger share of advantages. Most people do not possess our advantages, and many will struggle to maintain their income and status in a Future of Work strategy that sets them in constant competition with each other and a global labour market without borders.

My job is to supply crucial data to decision-makers in large companies. My hope is that the power of data will convince the very bright people who run financial institutions, global business and governments that we have to spread the gains from increasing productivity across a much wider cross-section of local and global society.

Some very sober mainstream commentators, such as Adair Turner, former chairman of the Financial Services Authority in London, agree with my friend and worry a great deal about the further deep inequality they see built into the economic trends. At the top end of the income distribution returns to high skill will be very big and very concentrated.

Here is Turner from his 2018 paper 'Capitalism in the Age of Robots':

In a world of ever increasing automation possibilities, we only need a very small number of very clever IT literate people to write all the code we need for all the robots, all the apps, and all the computer games, and we need only a minuscule fraction of the global population to drive inexorable progress towards ever more profound artificial intelligence and super intelligence.

Three decades or more since we first began to talk of living in a computer age, the total number of workers employed in the development and production of computer hardware, software and applications is still only 4 per cent of the total workforce in the US, and the US Bureau of Labor Statistics predicts just 135,000 new jobs in software development over 2014 to 2024, versus 458,000 additional personal care aides, and 348,000 home health aides. Total employment in the giant mobile phone, software and Internet companies which dominate global equity values is a minute drop in the global labour market. Facebook, with a market capitalisation of $500 billion, employs just 25,000 people.[43]

Turner takes issue with Tyler Cowen's book *Average Is Over* in which he argues that rising income inequality is inevitable but will not lead to social revolt because low earners will still enjoy adequate living standards, as long as housing costs are kept low.

Cowen imagines a future in which 'say 10 to 15 per cent of the citizenry is extremely wealthy and has fantastically comfortable and stimulating lives', while 'much of the rest of the country will have stagnant or maybe falling wages in dollar terms, but a lot more opportunities for cheap fun and cheap education' because of the free or new-free services which the internet makes available.[44] The average citizen will not be able to afford to live well in the successful big cities, where the top 10 to 15 per cent congregate, but will migrate to those parts of the US, such as Texas, where plentiful land and easy zoning rules make housing affordable. Meanwhile, talented bohemians who want nothing to do with the rat race competition of the top 10–15 per cent will tend to congregate in those cities (such as Berlin or Detroit) where past economic changes have left surplus housing and where fulfilled and less stressful lives can be financed from modest incomes derived from artistic or craft activities. The future may therefore be highly unequal, but cheap houses, clothes, food, video entertainment and computer games will ensure that there is no social revolt. As a result, Cowen says, 'We shouldn't really expect rising income and wealth inequality to lead to revolution and revolt . . . the long term picture will be fairly calm and indeed downright orderly.'[45]

Turner does not like this view of the future but thinks Cowen is probably right that inequality in the future could be combined with a reasonably high floor and need not be coupled with widespread poverty; he also agrees that the cost of housing and transport will drive most low earners out of big, successful, cosmopolitan cities; and the consequence of that will be increasing spatial segregation between the top 15 per cent and the rest. This segregation is less likely to happen on a significant scale in more densely populated Europe, but in both the US and Europe we are already starting to see economic-cum-cultural residential divisions, partly to do with the movement of graduates.

The Cowen prophecy is avoidable if the current Head–Hand–Heart balance can be reformed. Yet we are still promoting and subsidizing cognitive-analytic aptitudes in ever-expanding university sectors in the false belief that feeding more graduates to the economic machine will miraculously create more comfortable, high-status, professional jobs.

Raising the rewards and prestige attached to Hand and Heart will happen only slowly over generational time, and some of the policies required – chipping away at concentrations of Head wealth, raising wages for care services, celebrating craft skills, education for life – I will consider in the final chapter.

IO

Cognitive Diversity and the Future
of Everything

> Not everything that counts can be counted, and not every-
> thing that can be counted counts.
>
> *Albert Einstein*

The title of this book is misleading. It implies that Head, Hand and
Heart, or thought, craft and feeling, are distinct domains. They are
not, of course, and too rigid a division between the three is one of the
pathologies of the cognitive era.

Many Hand occupations require a great deal of Head. Matthew
Crawford, the American philosopher whom I have cited several times,
left a think tank to set up a motorcycle repair shop and says he found
skilled Hand work more mentally engaging than working on policy
questions. He lovingly describes the kind of reasoning he uses to
locate the fault in the engine of a vintage Italian motorbike – requiring logic, experience and, sometimes, imagination.

Similarly, with the Head and Heart. As we saw in Chapter 8, many
of the Heart caring and nursing jobs in modern societies also require
significant degrees of Head. Conversely an over-reliance on just one of
the triumvirate – a narrow Head utilitarianism, devoid of Heart – is
one of the abiding weaknesses of modern liberal politics.

Politics is an argument about what we value, and public life, just
like private lives, can get things out of balance. In recent decades
public life has been too dominated by a cognitive class who have
been trained to value the cognitively complex and quantifiable, and
too often this has led to a narrow rationalism and economism. The
New York Times columnist David Brooks reports that, according to
Google, over the last thirty years there has been a sharp increase in

the use of economic words and a decline in the use of moral words: gratitude down 49 per cent, humility down 52 per cent, and kindness down 56 per cent.[1]

In the summer of 2019 I heard David Miliband, the former British Foreign Secretary, talking about Brexit, and when asked whether Labour in power (1997–2010) might have contributed to the alienation expressed in that vote, all he could talk about was economic growth and inequality. Nothing about identity or immigration, nothing about national sovereignty, nothing about the rapid change that makes many people feel that the past was better than the present. This exceptionally talented man seemed to have learned nothing about emotions in politics in the three years since the Brexit vote.

Privileged or highly successful people often have less incentive to ask big questions about value; there can be a blandness and invulnerability about them. But loss and failure are important teachers. James Stewart in *It's a Wonderful Life* only sees the true value of his life and his family when he's at his lowest point.

In the course of writing this book I had a lesson in loss when a love affair ended unexpectedly. Someone with whom I had felt a deep connection decided to end the relationship after a few months. It knocked me back for a time and was compounded by a back injury that made me physically lame. Before this happened, I had recently established a contented new life for myself. I had moved into a new flat after an amicable separation from my wife of twenty-five years and had published a successful book a couple of years before. I was healthy and had no financial worries, I felt in a good place and was perhaps a bit *too* sure of myself.

Crashing back down to earth made me think about why I had invested so much in this one person. All of us are on a journey to finding a kind of wholeness, especially as we get older. Was my life a bit out of kilter? Was it too dominated by professional success and the invulnerable ways of the Head? Had this prevented me from paying attention to the other things that matter: close friendships, meaningful conversations with my children, an absorbing hobby, volunteering in my community, making more effort to see myself as others see me?

At the same time that I was thrown off balance emotionally I happened to be reading Iain McGilchrist's remarkable book *The Master and His Emissary: The Divided Brain and the Making of the Western World* about the radically different worldviews of the left and right brain hemispheres.[2] 'The hidden story of western culture, as told by the author, is about how the abstract, instrumental, articulate and assured left hemisphere has gradually usurped the more contextual, humane, systemic, holistic but relatively tentative and inarticulate right hemisphere,' as the philosopher Jonathan Rowson sums it up.[3]

We live in a left-brain, Head world. The way that McGilchrist talks about the abstraction, instrumentalism and utilitarianism of the left hemisphere, its love of certainty and its inflated sense of its own autonomy and cleverness, seems a perfect metaphor for the pathologies of the Anywhere cognitive class. The right hemisphere, by contrast, is the domain of a sense of wholeness and mystery with a religious tolerance for what can't be said or understood – 'It is what it is says love' in the words of Erich Fried's famous poem.

The two hemispheres need each other, just as Head and Heart need each other. But, as this book has been arguing, we also need a better balance between them. To some readers this little detour might be a rather unwelcome lurch into personal anecdote and mysticism. But McGilchrist is an accomplished psychiatrist whose arguments are certainly contested yet are rooted in hard science.

And I have become more convinced in the course of writing this book that a better Head–Hand–Heart balance is an unsentimental political requirement, even more so after the Covid-19 crisis. When I started writing at the beginning of 2019, I saw a better balance as a desirable ambition but a somewhat 'new age' one, reinforced by learning that Head, Hand and Heart is the motto of that most new age of schools, the progressive English private school Bedales! As I have read and researched I have increasingly concluded that the rebalancing is not just desirable but necessary, and probably inevitable, not just because of the economic trends that will eat into much cognitive employment, as described in the last chapter, but also because of the fundamental questions of meaning, value and human flourishing that national and global politics requires us to address.

Western society has been dominated in the past two generations by *centrifugal* forces that have extended individual freedom but weakened collective bonds and the power of tradition, and in the process allowed cognitive ability to claim undue economic and political rewards. The cognitively blessed have become more powerful, but many others feel they have lost place and meaning. The end of the Cold War and the emergence of post-industrial societies has weakened collective national and class identities; ethnic and value diversity has reduced trust and common social norms; while social media has created conditions of 'connected isolation', promoting narrow tribal allegiances and individualistic identity politics. And all the while, depression and mental illness has increased.

Recent political trends, surely reinforced by the pandemic, suggest we are moving into a more *centripetal* phase, in which the nation state will be consolidated and economic and cultural openness will be a little more constrained. This phase will place more stress on social stability and respect for the wisdom ingrained in institutions, it will be more sceptical of the claims of the Head and more sensitive to the humiliations and mass resentment built into modern, achievement societies.

The American historian Christopher Lasch argued many years ago that a democratic society should not aim to create a framework for competition, where the most able succeed and the others fail. Yet this is precisely what we have achieved in recent decades as the ideology of meritocracy and social mobility, endorsed by the rise of the university-educated cognitive classes, has swept all before it. Competition is a vital force in inspiring innovation and challenging entrenched economic and political power. But too much competition and comparison at the individual level can generate a permanent state of anxiety and make it harder for people to align their expectations with their actual capacities – perhaps the best route to personal happiness. There will always be hierarchies of competence in all domains of human aptitude, and we need to preserve meritocratic selection procedures for important jobs, from running the country to captaining the local football team, while, at the same time, exploring ways of spreading respect and status more evenly.

The centripetal push-back against twenty-five years of centrifugal opening is democracy working, not failing. But Brexit, Trump and European populism are in part *value* challenges to the previous political mainstream and, as the Brexit impasse showed, we have not been very good at negotiating fundamental questions of value (as discussed in Chapter 6). Modern liberalism is supposed to support value pluralism, but many modern liberals struggled to do so when their own values were challenged. And it turned out that several decades of pushing back the boundaries of individual freedom, of encouraging a generous diversity of goals and gods and ultimate ends, had left us in the UK – in the long Brexit argument – without the psychological and institutional capacity to come together and compromise over some version of the common good.

As the British philosopher John Gray has argued, value pluralism is now a permanent feature of liberal democracies, but to function well it turns out that we also need a bedrock of shared norms, rules of the road, that everyone can stand on – peaceful and respectful disagreement, the rule of law, accepting majority decisions tempered by minority rights, and so on. The more solid that bedrock, the easier it will be to conduct robust public arguments about value *differences* – arguments that have been suppressed by Charles Murray's 'ecumenical niceness' – and negotiate some other big challenges that are looming.

The most obvious one is climate change and the future of the planet. The left hemisphere/Head worldview treats the body as a machine and the natural world as a heap of resources to be exploited. This has had inevitable consequences, and if technology cannot come to our aid it is going to require some very hard conversations within and between countries about burden-sharing. We are not yet in a position to have these discussions. There has been some shift in awareness about the heaviness of the human footprint. David Attenborough's *Blue Planet* changed the way that many of us think about plastic. But the pious consensus in most rich countries about the threat of climate change is not at all reflected in our behaviour as citizens (either economically or politically), and is unlikely to be so until the threat to us is very much more immediate.

And even if there was an authority we could all trust which was able to spell out the relative risks of different courses of action, there is every likelihood that there would be fundamental disagreements between people of differing temperaments and values – high/low risk-takers, those ready to sacrifice for future generations and those not

– as to which course to take, as there was at the height of the Covid-19 crisis. The same applies to how much we should invest now to minimize the threat from future pandemics and the threat of antibiotic resistance.

Another imminent value challenge concerns human enhancement and 'playing God'. Already there are many pharmacological ways of temporarily enhancing brain functioning and in the future we might be able to manipulate our own DNA to improve cognitive ability or select the embryos of our babies to favour only those with the highest innate ability.* The more optimistic accounts see cognitive improvement technology as narrowing the current cognitive divides in the way that glasses level out the optical playing field for those with good and poor eyesight. There are also many dystopian accounts of rising cognitive and income inequality and how cognitive manipulation might open the way to a caste society divided between the normals and the super-intelligent who are able to afford the expensive treatments.

The regulation of social media ought to be a more manageable challenge. The institution of social media is still in its infancy and will surely emerge from the 'wild west' period both in terms of the spiteful culture it has bred and in the neurotic anxieties it generates thanks to the culture of mass comparison (as described by Jean Twenge and others). It is increasingly hard to make the argument that there should be one law for old media and another for new media. But it will take time to work out how to suppress the damaging aspects of this new technology without undermining the beneficial. As Richard Layard has pointed out, in 1930 the car killed 7,300 people in Britain; by 2016 that had been reduced to 1,700 – despite a huge increase in car ownership – largely thanks to regulation.[4] But individuals will also need to develop healthier habits for using the technology.

We have succeeded in tackling big problems in the past both nationally and internationally – from smallpox eradication to ozone layer

---

* Some people think the Rubicon has already been crossed when the Chinese biophysicist He Jiankui announced that he had edited an immune system gene in early embryos leading to the birth of twin girls resistant to HIV. This so-called germ-line editing lasts indefinitely into the future, unlike the ordinary manipulation of an individual's genes for some medical purpose, and has therefore been almost universally condemned. But it is hard to see how it will be prevented.

depletion and chemical weapons treaties. But the negotiation of *value* differences – for example over how open a society should be – is harder than dealing with the *interest* clashes of the socio-economic politics that dominated the postwar world. And it is harder to split the difference on value questions than it is on, say, the desired level of public spending or taxation.

For this reason we need a far greater appreciation of *cognitive* diversity. The idea that the top 15 per cent of the IQ bell curve should dominate all top jobs and run society was never a good one, as I argued in Chapter 3. Meritocracy of various kinds has a central place on the sports field, in the concert hall, in the science lab, maybe even in the higher ranks of officials in government departments, but the super-bright should be our servants, not our masters. This is not an argument for stupid politicians, but where the big decisions are made, a breadth of human perspectives is required.

It has taken its time, but after several decades of debating the virtues of race and gender diversity we are finally talking about cognitive diversity too. Matthew Syed, the influential British commentator, now argues in his latest book *Rebel Ideas* that the shared training of the higher end of the cognitive class in abstract reasoning and analytical intelligence is not sufficient to tackle the complex problems heading our way. Syed defines cognitive diversity as 'about differences in perspectives . . . and the models and heuristics we deploy to make sense of the world . . . and also perhaps differences in thinking styles . . . some of us are analytical thinkers and other more holistic and contextual thinkers'. He quotes countless papers on how cognitive diversity produces better outcomes in business, government and research.[5]

One paper on diverse thinking styles by researchers at Carnegie Mellon University in the US defines three different cognitive styles: 'Verbalizers, spatial visualizers, and object visualizers . . . Journalists and lawyers tend to be verbalizers; engineers and people in other math-driven professions are spatial visualizers, who think analytically; and artists are object visualizers, who tend to think about the bigger picture.'[6]

A lot of the attention on cognitive diversity is linked to Collective Intelligence. Collective Intelligence is a much-debated concept but is essentially about how people 'pool' their different intelligences so that something emerges that is more than the sum of the parts of individual intelligences. The jury system at its best acts as a kind of collective intelligence. A friend of mine recalls the very different styles of thinking at work on a jury he served on a few years ago, on the way to making the right decision. 'Some people used their intuition and ability to judge character. Others were happier with a more sceptical, evidence-based approach. Together we ended up balancing Heads and Hearts all round, it was a lesson in trusting people to do the right thing.'

Diversity must also apply to ideology and political values, as highlighted by the Heterodox Academy in the US, founded by social psychologist and author Jonathan Haidt as a counter to the dominance of secular, leftist ideas on US campuses. Writing on the Heterodox Academy website, the sociologist Musa al-Gharbi puts it like this: 'If we care about demographic diversity and inclusion . . . we also must care about *ideological* (political, religious, etc.) diversity and inclusion. To the extent that we attempt to pursue one to the exclusion, or at the expense, of the other – we are setting ourselves up for failure.'

He also makes the point that white liberals are often unaware of how culturally specific is the idea of 'making the best of yourself' and how off-putting that can sometimes be to the very people they claim to be looking out for:

> US institutions of higher learning are dominated by white, Protestant, bourgeois norms of independence, meritocracy, and a focus on the self. First-gen and minority students often struggle to adapt, flourish or feel they 'belong' in these spaces in part because their own cultures, values and priorities tend to stress duties to others, mutual aid and interdependence – and are generally less self oriented (perspectives strongly associated with conservativism and religion).[7]

These initiatives and new forms of thinking all sound like variations on a theme of bringing McGilchrist's left and right hemispheres into a more harmonious working relationship. They also overlap with a new interest in the concept of *wisdom*, about which more below, and expanding that base of shared assumptions on which pluralism can more comfortably rest.

Robin Wales, the former Labour mayor of the London Borough of Newham, a super-diverse east London borough of more than 300,000 people, is an enthusiastic supporter of cognitive diversity based on his experience of running a large bureaucracy. 'I have done a lot of work looking at different ways to manage large organizations,' he says. 'Our Newham small business initiative encouraged entrepreneurialism and generated substantial savings, and it was partly based on an analysis of the failings of large organizations run by the highly educated people you are writing about.' A crucial aspect of the failure of management in large organizations, argues Wales, is that more educated people are effectively trained in the ability to explain away evidence which contradicts their view – rationalization versus rationality (as discussed in Chapters 3 and 6). Or, to put it more simply, people who have achieved academic success tend to acquire a lot of confidence in their own ability and then tend to assume that they are always right.

The transparency requirements of modern institutions also encourage a performative, virtue-signalling political culture which makes it harder for people to identify as insiders and come to reasonable compromises. We live in low-trust societies with declining respect for professional judgement yet we have, rightly, high requirements for accountability and measurable impact. The result is a dramatic increase in the volume of legal regulations and instruments governing everyday activities, a mark of the disappearance of the implicit understandings found in more cohesive cultures. It all makes work for the cognitive class to do.

One good example is the comparison between the Glass-Steagall Act of 1933 in the US, which prevented banks from undertaking risky and speculative activities, and the Dodd-Frank Act of 2010, which was similarly designed to prevent future banking crises. Glass-Steagall was thirty-seven pages long and written in relatively comprehensible English; Dodd-Frank was 848 pages supplemented with 398 pieces of rule-making, running to some 30,000 pages. It is estimated that altogether Dodd-Frank was about 1,000 times longer than Glass-Steagall.[8]

ACHIEVING A BETTER BALANCE

This is more of a diagnosis than a policy book, but a book suggesting a somewhat different direction for society should provide at least a few thoughts on how to get there. So in this final section I want to pull together a few threads and policy ideas on how the better balance between aptitudes associated with Head, Hand and Heart – the human triumvirate – can be achieved.

There is a substantial body of cross-society support for raising the status of Hand and Heart, as the opinion poll in the Chapter 7, indicated. There are also, to underline again, some deep trends that are already nudging rich countries in this direction: technology's elimination of so many middling cognitive jobs and the end of the golden age of mass higher education; the ageing of society and the rising visibility of care functions of many kinds, especially after the Covid-19 crisis; the greater concern for place, ecology and belonging – thanks to those odd bedfellows the green movement and the populist revolt. Moreover, countries in the developed world with relatively low inequality and so-called 'inclusive growth', with stakeholder rather than shareholder forms of capitalism, seem to have weathered the Covid-19 crisis most successfully.

And we also know just how swiftly social norms can change. As Cass Sunstein has pointed out, neither the French nor the Russian nor the Iranian revolutions were expected. Norms and expectations can shift very fast when people discover that many others share their views. If new norms on gender and race equality, homosexuality, smoking, animal rights (and even voting Conservative in former Labour constituencies) can be established in relatively short periods of time, then why not new assumptions about Head, Hand and Heart?

So here are some ideas in five domains: inequality and the cognitive meritocracy; place and mobility; upgrading care; celebrating craft; and education for life.

Inequality and the Cognitive Meritocracy

Market forces are starting to adjust some of the inflated returns to Head of recent decades as the graduate premium shrinks and the shortage of both skilled and unskilled manual workers pushes up Hand wages, at least in some sectors. At the very top there remains an inequality issue thanks to the 'war for talent', the gaming of executive pay incentive systems, winner-takes-all markets and the way that first-mover advantage, especially in digital markets, can confer enormous rewards on people without them having to go through the sweat of decades building a business. Many commentators, from Yuval Noah Harari to a legion of economists, believe that the default setting for modern liberal societies is ever-higher levels of inequality and the emergence of a class of the meritocratic super-rich who may even, with the help of the latest science, evolve into some new strand of humanity.

I think this danger is somewhat exaggerated, partly because this super-class needs to live somewhere and will be subject to old-fashioned social democratic tax and regulation in most places (including of their medical experiments in extending lifespan), certainly in the UK and Europe. But as Adair Turner argues, 'In a world where much new wealth derives from uncreated increases in the relative price of land, and where without intervention differential inheritance will have a huge influence on life chances, there is a strong case for increasing the effective taxation of property wealth, capital gains, and inheritance.'[9]

Restrictions on the breadth of application of intellectual property rights and for shortening the length of copyright protection to reduce the super-rents enjoyed by some first movers in the digital and other marketplaces are also feasible. The economist Mariana Mazzucato has pointed to how much apparently private innovation builds upon public support for basic research.[10]

As I argued in Chapter 3, very clever people obviously remain of great value to society, even if the cognitive class as a whole – including those of merely average ability – has taken too much reward and prestige for itself in recent decades. More big brains make technical problems easier to fix, especially with the connectivity of the internet, as we saw with the scientific collaborations at the height of the Covid-19 crisis.

In pre-modern agrarian societies, the community needed warriors to protect them against other warriors. Hence monarchy and aristocracy. In those societies, strength and bravery were esteemed, and the Head played only a minor role. As societies became more sophisticated and required more intricate management, Head started to come into its own and develop its own centres of training, above all the universities. Henry I had no need for them; Henry VIII could not have managed without them. If there is a post-apocalyptic dystopia and we revert to the Dark Ages, the strongman will replace the nerd again at the apex of the hierarchy and would have to be bribed into protecting rather than plundering the community by some combination of tribute and flattery. In a science- and commerce-based post-industrial society there is a similarly utilitarian argument for rewarding the very able to ensure they are socially useful. But how they are rewarded, and how much they are rewarded, is of course where the argument begins.

How much money does a smart CEO need to do a good job? Must it be money? Why not honour? Public honour can work up to a point in parts of the public sector. It is why, in the UK, we have an honours system, and some very clever people remain in the civil service, awaiting their knighthoods, on middle-management salaries way below what they could earn in the private sector. Could this also work in the private sector? It seems unlikely, but a negative version: naming and shaming overpaid business people by shareholder activists and others does seem to have had some impact. Public dishonour might be a surprisingly powerful weapon in constraining the super-rich. The very public distribution of their fortunes to charity by some of the digital billionaires shows how seriously some of them take their public standing. From 2020 all UK public companies with more than 250 employees will have to reveal the ratio between the pay of the CEO and the average employee, which is a step in the right direction.

Another idea for regulating the very pinnacle of the cognitive meritocracy is to make the jobs as temporary as possible and strictly rewarded according to performance. In these circumstances, as Nicholas Lemann puts it, there would be as little lifelong tenure on the basis of youthful promise as possible. 'Successful people would have less serene careers than they have now, and this would give them more empathy for people whose lives don't go smoothly.'[11]

Place and Mobility

The Brexit vote was, among other things, a vote for localism on an international scale. In the UK context it was a vote against London as well as Brussels, as Boris Johnson acknowledged in a speech in Manchester on his second day as Prime Minister. But most rich countries are ambivalent about community. We want security, familiarity and belonging, all the warm things we associate with settled communities, but we also want freedom, individual autonomy, ambition and social mobility, which weaken settled communities by encouraging people to leave them – particularly the most able.

As noted many times, just as America has divided between red states and blue states, France between 'France Périphérique' and 'France d'En Haut',[12] and Germany between west and east, so the UK is increasingly divided between London (plus the other metropolitan centres and university towns) and the rest. In some places this is not just a wealth divide but a cultural, worldview and even ethnic one.

The double goal is clear enough: to invest sufficiently in the expensive metropolitan centres to allow poorer people to stay put with a reasonable quality of life, and, at the same time, to prevent people from the smaller towns and suburbs feeling like resentful second-class citizens.

Adair Turner argues that for even the low-paid to enjoy a reasonable standard of life in the metropolitan centres the provision of good public services – health, education, public transport, public spaces – and, as important, affordable housing, is a higher priority than Universal Basic Income (UBI). UBI potentially disconnects people from work, which for many is an important source of meaning and companionship. Indeed, happiness researchers, such as the British economist Richard Layard, argue that the state guarantee of a minimum-wage job for anyone unemployed for more than six months – even accompanied with the stick of having benefits withdrawn for those who reject the offer – is a better safety net for generating well-being. That is especially true for jobs that have an obviously beneficial purpose such as insulating homes or installing solar panels.

A less ugly built environment has belatedly become a political issue in some countries partly in response to the brutalist postwar developments in both Europe and America, which usually ran completely counter to mainstream aesthetic feelings. Nicholas Boys Smith, who is co-chair of the UK government's Building Better, Building Beautiful Commission, says that there are still too many shocking examples of ugly town planning from recent years in the UK

> there was the malign Pathfinder Programme which tried to revive northern cities by knocking down Victorian homes, or the investment in out of town shopping centres which promptly drained the life out of the town centre . . . Many of the proudest structures in England's towns and cities are 19th century civic buildings, such as Rochdale Town Hall or St George's Hall in Liverpool. Somehow, somewhere, we have lost not just the ability but even the desire to create public buildings of beauty and moral worth. We need to rediscover that confidence and ability.[13]

Boys Smith was struck by the evidence one architect gave to the Building Beautiful Commission in 2019, recounting how, working on a hospital project, he was 'told by the contractor to put in a more expensive material that looked cheaper because there was real sensitivity about anything in the NHS looking expensive'.

Hospitals should be our new cathedrals. Noble buildings, built for a noble cause. In many towns they are the biggest and most important building for miles around, and it is a great sadness that they so often look shoddy and disposable. I am lucky enough to live in Hampstead in north London and as I write this I am looking out on the Royal Free Hospital, an ugly blot in one of the most architecturally precious corners of London.

And what about the smaller towns and suburbs and country areas that so often feel unloved and left behind by the centre? This happens in all rich countries but is a particular problem in England, because so many young people move away to residential universities, plus that London magnet factor.

The obvious answers – but far easier said than done – include: better post-school education options that allow people to stay at home, or at least in their home town; a more even spread of decent jobs, or the transport infrastructure to commute to them in a reasonable time; and town centres and local civic life, and media, that help instil some local pride. Many places have these things already; too many don't and can enter a spiral of decline that is hard to break. Around 70 per cent of the German population live in towns of less than 100,000. It contributes to a sense of a more settled society than in the UK.

Mobility is not, of course, a vice. And it is very different today than in the nineteenth century. Then you seldom saw or spoke to your family again. Now you can phone, email, Skype, WhatsApp and maybe return home from London at the weekend, moving doesn't seem as daunting. And a successful, London-based journalist I know who comes from Bury, near Manchester, likes to challenge people who talk too passionately about communitarian values by asking 'So, do you think I should have stayed in Bury, then?'

The technology of connection that makes it easier for leavers to stay in touch should also make it easier for stayers to feel they do not need to leave to avoid feeling marginalized. The internet has opened up many new possibilities for small-town and rural businesses to transcend distance and to build local networks in more remote places, so long as broadband connections are good enough. It also makes the local barter economy of the so-called 'time bank', in which people trade their skills and time, far easier to organize.

A recent *New Yorker* report entitled 'The one traffic-light town with some of the fastest internet in the US' underscored this point. Keith Gabbard, the man behind the fast internet in the town of McKee, is quoted thus:

> I don't think having broadband is necessarily going to make a 500-job factory move in, but it certainly can make people's lives better and keep them from having to drive 100 miles a day, back and forth, to work . . . It can help education, it can help entertainment, it can help the economy, it can help health care. And I even think that people's mind-set can be improved.[14]

In recent decades we have subsidized (via higher education and higher incomes in metropolitan centres) and applauded leavers; perhaps it's time we subsidized and applauded stayers. Of course, not everything can stay the same, some communities are not sustainable, the story moves on. But many people in rich countries feel that change has been happening too fast in recent decades, from national politics to their local neighbourhoods.

Is it too much to ask that if a popular local pub that acts as a focus for community is having to close – like one I went to recently in Swindon – it receives support from some national community fund or receives a refund from the high duties it has to charge or a lower business rate? After all, in the 1990s huge sums were channelled from middle- and lower-income people via the lottery into creating new museums, many of which subsequently closed. The only way for many pubs to survive is to diversify, but in practice that means being reinvented for prosperous middle-class young people. Local newspapers, which are a focus for local identity, are often dying too. They are sometimes replaced by lively local bloggers who help to keep local politicians accountable but in many places they are replaced by nothing.

Upgrading Care

The slow upward revaluation of Heart jobs will happen as politics redirects more resources to health, social care and education. Just as hospitals are often the most imposing building for miles around, health care is a central industry in many parts of the country. It is decentralized by its nature: unlike global banks or factories, people need hospitals in all regions. It employs lots of people of all classes and ability levels and generates local economic development. And it is a fiscal equalizer, redistributing income from the metropolitan centres with their cognitive elites to the rest of the country.

But caring more about caring is not only about spending more money – though in the UK adult care and adult care workers' pay certainly needs investment. Returning to nursing some of its autonomy and giving care itself a more central role in our technocratic health systems is part of the answer to the crisis of nurse recruitment. Technology is not itself the problem, indeed, when used properly, it releases doctors and nurses to listen to the whole patient, not just a bundle of symptoms.

The training for nurses and indeed all medical professionals needs to change. There needs to be more focus on emotional and human interactions with patients alongside the traditional practical and cognitive skills needed for qualifications. If health systems are to deliver patient-centred care and equip staff to manage complex patient and family interactions it requires a rethink of the balance of the curriculum and how grades and outcomes are judged.

In a society that runs on quantifying everything of value, care has suffered both in the hospital and the home because it has not been adequately measured. It is high time that unpaid labour in the home was included in GDP figures (or parallel GDP figures) – it is estimated that it would add about £500 billion a year in the UK. It would not make us any richer but it would give a more accurate account of what is happening in everyday life and help people to value more the productive work going on in the private realm.

Some progress has been made in the UK in building subjective well-being into economic analysis and statistics, and the so-called Green Book, which describes how policy proposals should be judged, has social well-being as its objective. But it is time that we regularly published, alongside conventional GDP measurements, broader measurements of well-being and quality of life that would include data on life expectancy, crime, state of the family, drug use, teenage pregnancy, mental health, environmental quality and so on.

One cause of the pressure on adult care services and the NHS is weaker family ties and fewer intact couples to look after each other or elderly parents. Helping more families to stay together and rewarding partnership and care in the home is just common sense. Yet state support for young families is very sketchy in the UK and US. (And marriage as an institution is dramatically weaker in lower-income households in both countries: in the UK 90 per cent of parents with young children in the top income quintile are married, compared with just 25 per cent in the lowest quintile.) Why not make relationship counselling free? Even if it only helped 10 per cent of couples stay together, it would be a big win for the state and society. More important, why not ease the economic pressure on couples through making it easier for one parent to stay at home when children are very young? If going to work is supported with subsidized child care, why not support staying at home too? Is that not also useful work? Allowing the stay-at-home parent to transfer their tax allowance to the working parent, thus recognizing *partnership* in the tax system, is considered normal in much of continental

Europe. Indeed, the idea of a transferable tax allowance for stay-at-home carers *of all kinds*, not just carers of young children, would further support partnerships and encourage more care to remain in the home. The Carer's Allowance in the UK for looking after an old or disabled person (who might or might not be a relative) is just £66 a week, for at least thirty-five hours' care. That works out at less than £2 an hour, yet it costs many hundreds of pounds to look after someone for one night in a hospital.

Rebooting domesticity for an age of gender equality might also mean changing planning rules to encourage the return of 'cottage industry', small enterprises run from the home that make it easier to combine care and work, as Mary Harrington has suggested. Writers, child-minders, therapists, beauticians and many others have traditionally worked from home, and decent broadband connections open the possibility to many more occupations. Many people experienced the potential of more home-working during the Covid-19 crisis and became more adept at managing the technology.

The public care economy is more than 85 per cent female. Men are doing more domestic labour than in the past, nearly two-thirds of all fathers are now classified as 'involved fathers', but there has been little gender desegregation of nursing, adult social care or primary-school teaching. Indeed as more women have moved into medical roles, hospitals are becoming more, not less, female. Some *positive discrimination* towards young men in some of these jobs could help create a critical mass of male employment where it remains largely absent. (And maybe we need some new words to think about a typical carer. The word nurse inevitably conjures up the image of a woman.)

A limited degree of automation in adult care might help increase pay and status in the care home and thus attract more men. Ageing Japan is experimenting with robots which can perform social care functions such as lifting an elderly person into a bath. One of the key social care roles of the future may be a male technician in charge of twenty robots.

Volunteering cannot fully make up for weaker families but it has as yet unrealized potential when combined with the convening power of the internet. The appetite for volunteering was underlined in many countries during the Covid-19 crisis. Why not build on that experience and establish a version of the Territorial Army for health and adult care systems, a reserve army of people with some basic training who can step in to help during a crisis. This could even be extended to some non-crisis situations to help out in vital social services so long as the volunteer roles do not undermine proper paid employment. Corporate Social Responsibility programmes could also usefully focus more on local volunteering by encouraging staff to simply visit old people, read to them, shop for them, take them out on trips.

Teaching, especially at primary level, is at least as much a Heart as a Head job. I am often struck by how many teachers I know talk about loving their kids (and sometimes finding them intolerable too). A friend who has become a primary-school teacher in middle age says this: 'The best part of primary teaching is just building real relationships with the children. To do the job properly you have to love them, you have to become emotionally involved.' The latest research on good teaching confirms this. Andreas Schleicher, head of the OECD's influential PISA programme of cross-country educational assessment, says that more important than curriculum content is the relationship between pupil and teacher. The child learns anything, everything, better when they think the teacher knows and cares about them. One of those things our grandmothers could have told us for nothing, and something our schools should try to reflect!

Care, like craft, is what many people do in their spare time, both as duty and pleasure. It can be a chore doing the shopping for Granny, or taking a child to a playground, but most people know that the time spent with dependent family members is part of the real, valuable stuff of life. If I was bored or distracted or talking on my mobile phone when taking one of my children to the park, as I often was, that was my failing, my inability to be fully in the moment. Parents then often end up lamenting how quickly children grow up. Where does all the time go?

Caring and craft are linked to one another in that both depend on paying attention, deeply, to what is there in front of you, to the needs of the moment. In the case of craft, it is paying attention to the needs of the material, and in care, to the needs of the person. The feeling that a Head-dominated world does not pay sufficient attention to many of the things that really matter is one reason for the growing interest in mindfulness and meditation (the number of yoga teachers in the US has been growing at more than 10 per cent a year for several years). Paying attention is the essence of mindfulness and meditation, trying to see what is really of value. Living slow rather than fast.

Celebrating Craft

One of the things that might prevent open, semi-meritocratic societies degenerating into genetic caste societies is that with the reduction of economic insecurity for most people, more highly able people will choose to do more rewarding things than work as a high-flying lawyer or banker. There will increasingly be no single hierarchy of wealth and status. Perhaps we are beginning to see this in privileged families where at least one of the children becomes a chef or takes up an artisanal calling of some kind.

Jobs that have a high level of satisfaction but not necessarily a high level of pay, such as working as a National Trust ranger, are already highly sought after. And in the countryside, as conventional farming is increasingly replaced by organic farming, with its more labour-intensive concern for nature and animal welfare, new agricultural Heart jobs will be created. Public policy, so far as possible, should have a bias towards work that produces high job satisfaction: that often means working in a team solving problems together against a common adversary.

Similarly with craft jobs. Every year in the UK the Heritage Crafts Association produces a list of crafts which have become extinct and those that are endangered (including now the making of cricket balls). It would not be a waste of public resources to keep that list as short as possible. Some of the craft jobs that almost disappeared over the course of the twentieth century, such as stonemason or thatcher, are now making a comeback. Beautiful old buildings require a skilled workforce to keep them standing. The art of weaving was showcased for the first time at the Frieze London art show in 2019. Over the coming century more people are likely to find satisfying jobs as artists, gardeners, surfboard designers, cooks, small organic farmers and beekeepers than as software developers or AI technicians.[15]

The UK organic food market is now said to stand at £2.5 billion a year. Craft breweries are growing fast – there are now 5,000 in the

US, 2,000 in the UK and a comparable growth in much of Europe. Today there are more than 300 independent British cheese-makers, up from just sixty-two in the mid-1970s.[16] (There is also some evidence that people are now cooking from scratch more often, and sales of raw ingredients are rising.)[17]

As noted in Chapter 1, when people retire they usually take up something embodied and rooted, a sporting or musical or 'making' hobby of some kind. And with retirements stretching longer, the young-old and their Hand/Heart concerns will loom ever larger in our culture.

Also, assuming we take at least some of the benefits of the next stage of automation in the form of increased leisure, everyone will have more time to develop sporting, musical and craft skills, which is why it is so important that the arts and music are taught as rigorously as possible to as many children as possible in school.

It is true that many non-academic, 'creative' subjects such as design and art have been very poorly taught in the past and seen as soft options. Such subjects have been explicitly downgraded by the UK's Department for Education. But some of the most successful schools academically, such as the very traditional Michaela state school in inner-city London, also have the most impressive art and music departments.

And why not require everyone in school by the age of eighteen to have learned at least one manual/technical skill to a basic level, from carpentry to coding? And there is a good case for teaching these skills away from school at special youth skill centres, which would also provide an opportunity for social and ethnic mixing – a mini-version of National Service.

Education for Life

It sometimes feels that we are more schooled, but less educated, than ever before, as the writer Joanna Williams puts it. And it is absurd that so much higher education is focused on those aged eighteen to twenty-two. The conveyor belt that has been sending millions of young people into three or four years of higher education at the age of eighteen or nineteen should be slowed down. Many of them have acquired useful life experience and grown into young adults away from home for an extended period for the first time. Many have also acquired useful professional skills or pursued intellectual interests for the sheer joy of it. But far too many have learned little of value, and what they have learned they have quickly forgotten, their degree acting primarily as a signal to a future employer that they have the right personal characteristics to enter the bloated cognitive class. Many of them would do better to follow the advice a friend of mine gave to his nephew who was wondering whether to continue a social science degree having failed his second-year exams:

> Rather than ploughing on with something you are either not very good at or not very interested in, and acquiring at least £50,000 of debt, you would do far better to borrow £15,000 to spend on a six-month coding course that guarantees a reasonably well-paid job in a tech company. If in five or ten years' time you get a hunger to go deeper into computer science or just want to understand Byzantium, you will get far more out of it then.

The American venture capitalist Peter Thiel has been offering money to would-be entrepreneurs to leave university and focus on web-based start-ups instead, and some British private schools are encouraging pupils to take vocational qualification in business, hospitality and so on, with a view to going straight into jobs. Northeastern University in Boston has pioneered a hybrid form of learning somewhere between an apprenticeship and a conventional degree, with students signing up for three six-month internships as part of their degree course.[18]

In Israel young people tend to go to university later because of National Service and they are more mature and often get more out of it. One way to encourage people to go to university later would be to charge older students lower tuition fees.

Part of my critique of the expansion of higher education in Chapter 4 was that it was driven by a cultural bias towards academic forms of knowledge that is often economically dysfunctional, when what business wants is shorter, more practical courses. This is going to become even more the case as AI eats into cognitive occupations. 'Colleges are continuing to generate twentieth-century professionals . . . to undertake tasks for which machines are now better suited,' as Richard and Daniel Susskind put it.

But looking to the future of the university, and of education at all levels, we need more hard thinking about education for life and lifelong learning. This has become a cliché. We talk endlessly about lifelong learning but do very little about it; indeed in the UK in recent years we have been going backwards, thanks to the current financial incentives, with fewer mature students or people returning part-time to college to reskill (there was a sharp drop in part-time study after England's tripling of student fees in 2012).

Rather than the life-cycle model of the past couple of hundred years, with a fixed period of education and a fixed period of work, we need a 'rotation model' in which work and education are rotated over the course of a career. But, as Andy Haldane of the Bank of England points out, existing universities in most countries are not designed for this, and the future university will need to be a very different kind of creature.

> It may need to cater for multiple entry points along the age distribu-
> tion, rather than focussing on the young. And it may need to cater for
> multiple entry points along the skills spectrum, rather than focussing
> on the cognitive. Those skills will be social and technical every bit as
> much as cognitive, with Head, Hand and Heart sharing equal billing.
> It would, in short, need to be plural rather than singular – a 'multiver-
> sity', rather than a university.[19]

Massive Open Online Courses – so called Moocs – have not taken off as some people expected outside niche areas. It seems that people like human contact when learning. But some combination of online and classroom is popular, and one of the home-working success stories of the Covid-19 lockdown was higher education, with many courses moving online.

And the spirit of the old autodidact, who just had an urge to read up everything about, say, botany, has not disappeared, even in a more educated society. There will always be a substantial minority with a thirst for knowledge for its own sake, as can be seen from the reach of intellectual popularizers such as Brian Cox and Martin Rees in the UK, Steven Pinker and Jared Diamond in the US and Yuval Noah Harari across Europe and North America.

Also coming back into its own is the old generalist model of the nineteenth-century educated person. This is now called 'cross-domain knowledge' and often combines both scientific and artistic forms of thinking, as has always been the case with architecture. Subjects such as digital literacy, entrepreneurship and emotional intelligence will become less 'soft' and more relevant.

As this implies, in a world where rapid productivity growth can be driven by a very small number of people who programme the robots and occupy the top layer of the professions, the rest of us will need to nurture aptitudes for caring, craft and creativity, both for the jobs of the future and to fill the countless hours we are no longer at work. The idea of the individual learning account – in which the state invests a fixed sum in every individual that can be drawn down for any kind of post-compulsory education – is an old idea that deserves revisiting.

The focus on raising the academic floor for all young people in secondary education has in some places been at the cost of breadth of education. But, as noted, many forms of creativity can be taught rigorously, just like maths and biology can be.

The same can apply to craft skills. In addition to the youth skill centres proposed above, those sixteen-year-olds not in the academic stream at school should be encouraged to undertake a part-time skill pupilage with a local 'master' (car mechanic, baker, social care manager, hairdresser, local authority clerical officer and so on). The master would get some inexperienced free labour and in return for that, and a tax allowance from the government, would supervise good work habits and the foundations of a useful skill. Where the system works well, the pupil could start work proper from the day they leave school.

And what about education for life and citizenship? Our conversations about education, including in this book, are far too economy-orientated; the intense discussions about education in the nineteenth century were hardly ever about the economy, despite our societies being much poorer then.

There is, in particular, a largely missing conversation about educating people for democracy and for mental and physical well-being. The American educationalist E. D. Hirsch says a democratic republic can't exist without an educated citizenry who are equipped to distinguish fact from fiction, to respect other people's arguments and to understand the complexity of some of the challenges we face. Studying history, for example, should not just be about the exam result you get. Indeed, it doesn't matter if you get a D in history so long as you leave school knowing more about your country's history than you did when you started.

Recalibrating the balance between Head, Hand and Heart is partly about reimagining what we mean by skill. It also therefore means having a school curriculum that values Hand and Heart alongside Head and is not pushing as many children as possible into middle-ranking cognitive jobs that are evidently in decline. This is starting to happen: School 21, an influential free school in East London founded by Peter Hyman, Oli de Botton and Ed Fidoe (and where my daughter taught for two years), has thought deeply about how to incorporate Heart and Hand into their core curriculum. Not everyone can excel at academic school work but over the years of compulsory schooling every child should be able to find something they enjoy doing and learn how to do it well. Even without UBI most people will be working fewer hours in the robotic future, and a broad education that includes plenty of music, sport, dance, drama and art is more necessary than ever.

To finish, here is an appealing Head, Hand and Heart list from Iain McGilchrist of what he would like children to learn in school on top of the academic basics:

> All children should learn practical embodied skills in the crafts and arts, working not just with machines and ideas, but with actual materials, such as wood, metal and fabric, to make things that are both useful and beautiful. All children should be taught mindfulness and some form of spiritual exercise. They should learn some sort of practical life-skills, such as how to recognize cognitive distortions in oneself and others, and how to mediate in disputes. These are quite practical things that can easily be taught, and transform lives.

TO BOLDLY GO

I have scarcely mentioned religion in this book. I am not a religious man, but in the course of writing it I have become more sympathetic to aspects of the religious worldview. And the notion of spiritual revival certainly flickers around the edge of the Head, Hand, Heart readjustment. The Head world is generally a secular one with little feel for the mysteries of life, which is why so many of us today seek a substitute for it in everything from yoga and meditation to the green movement. Yet it is striking what a disappointing failure humanism has been. It has been an effective critic of religion but has provided no convincing alternative set of ideas on how to live well or provided the consolation that many have drawn from religious belief.

John Maynard Keynes, writing about a world in which economic necessity has been largely overcome in his essay *Economic Possibilities for Our Grandchildren*, sees a return to religious principles.

> I see us free, therefore, to return to some of the most sure and certain principles of religion and traditional virtue . . . We shall once more value ends above means and prefer the good to the useful. We shall honour those who can teach us how to pluck the hour and the day virtuously and well, the delightful people who are capable of taking direct enjoyment in things, the lilies of the field who toil not, neither do they spin.[20]

I recently visited St Edmundsbury Cathedral in Bury St Edmunds, where the tour guide told us about the carved angels looking down, wings spread, upholding the roof. Apparently, the backs of the angels are carved in just as much intricate detail as the front even though no one can ever see the backs (without scaffolding). The medieval craftsmen were doing their work for God. In a self-centred age it is hard not to be impressed. But God can be stripped out of that process: in today's language a craftsman could be working 'to be the best that he can be'.

Many secular people are suspicious of the religious impulse for its dogmatism. Surely in our more divided and tribal age the last thing we need is a more religious sensibility? How do we conduct the more public debates we need to have about ultimate values if the religious people already know the answer? But it has also become a truism to argue that even liberal secularists have not fully escaped religious ways of thinking.[21] Religion is born of the need to face death, and we secular people face death too. Moreover, the still revolutionary idea of the moral equality of all people regardless of talent or wealth – an idea bequeathed by Christianity – is the core inspiration behind the wish to rebalance human value away from Head towards Hand and Heart.

We will need wisdom along the way, and wisdom is at least as much a religious as secular idea. It is due for a comeback. The American author Jonathan Rauch argues in his book *The Happiness Curve* that while wisdom may be struggling in our civic and political culture, it is coming into its own in medicine, psychology and neuroscience. He interviewed one of the pioneers in wisdom research, the US-based Indian psychiatrist Dilip Jeste, who argues that it is a distinct and measurable human quality which has remained surprisingly constant across regions and civilizations. Rauch writes:

> Again and again, modern scholarly definitions mention certain traits: compassion and prosocial attitudes that reflect concern for the common good; pragmatic knowledge of life; the use of one's pragmatic knowledge to resolve personal and social problems; an ability to cope with ambiguity and uncertainty and to see multiple points of view; emotional stability and mastery of one's feelings; a capacity for reflection and for dispassionate self-understanding. You might think that people with the fastest mental processors would bring more cognitive power to bear on reflection and therefore would be wiser; but voluminous research finds that raw intelligence and wisdom simply do not map to one another, at least not reliably. In fact, on some dimensions, such as wise reasoning about intergroup conflicts, cognitive ability and wisdom, seem to be negatively related.[22]

Wisdom expresses itself, often, in counterpoint to ideology. Whereas ideology pushes us towards certainty, purity and adversarialism, wisdom prizes humility, multiplicity and compromise. And it is a package. 'On *Star Trek* . . . a recurrent theme is that the most blazingly intelligent character, the Vulcan Spock, lacks the instinctive empathy of Dr. McCoy and the pragmatic decisiveness of Captain Kirk. None of the three alone is wise. Wisdom arises from the (sometimes tense) interaction of the triumvirate.'

Head, Hand and Heart brought into harmony on the Starship *Enterprise*.

Notes

CHAPTER 1 : PEAK HEAD

1   James Flynn: *Are We Getting Smarter?: Rising IQ in the Twenty-First Century* (Cambridge University Press, 2012).
2   See chart at https://data.oecd.org/chart/5NKF.
3   Nikou Asgari, 'One in Five UK Baby Boomers Are Millionaires', *Financial Times*, 9 January 2019, available at https://www.ft.com/content/c69b49de-1368-11e9-a581-4ff78404524e.
4   See www.davidlucas.org.uk
5   Damian Hinds, Secretary of State for Education, Technical Education speech, Battersea, 6 December 2018, available at https://www.gov.uk/government/speeches/damian-hinds-technical-education-speech.
6   Patrick J. Deneen, *Why Liberalism Failed* (Yale University Press, 2018).
7   Justine Greening, 'Unlocking the Potential of a New Generation', speech to the UK Social Mobility Commission, 30 March 2017, available at https://www.gov.uk/government/speeches/justine-greening-unlocking-the-potential-of-a-new-generation.
8   Michael Lind, *The New Class War* (Atlantic, 2020), p. 16.
9   Foreword to Sutton Trust report *Home and Away*, 27 February 2018, available at https://www.suttontrust.com/our-research/home-and-away-student-mobility/.
10 Abhijit V. Banerjee and Esther Duflo, *Good Economics for Hard Times* (Penguin, 2019).
11 Nicholas Carr, *The Shallows: What the Internet is Doing to Our Brains* (W. W. Norton and Company, 2010).
12 Paul Krugman, 'White Collars Turn Blue', *New York Times Magazine*, 29 September 1996.
13 Conversation with Professor Luciano Floridi of the Oxford Internet Institute.
14 *Economist*, 22 June 2019, p. 65.

15 Hannah Jones, Nancy Kelly and Katariina Rantanen, *British Social Attitudes 36: Women at Work*, NatCen, 2019, available at https://www.bsa.natcen.ac.uk/media/39297/4_bsa36_women-and-work.pdf.

CHAPTER 2: THE RISE OF THE COGNITIVE CLASS

1   Kirby Swales, *Understanding the Leave Vote*, NatCen, December 2016, available at http://natcen.ac.uk/our-research/research/understanding-the-leave-vote/.
2   OECD Family Database, available at http://www.oecd.org/social/family/database.htm.
3   *Populations Past – Atlas of Victorian and Edwardian Population*, available at https://www.populationspast.org/about/.
4   David Brooks, 'The Nuclear Family Was a Mistake', *The Atlantic*, March 2020.
5   Guy Routh and Charles Booth, *Occupations of the People of Great Britain 1801–1981* (Macmillan Press, 1987); French Occupational Census of 1911, *Monthly Review of the U.S. Bureau of Labor Statistics* 5/1 (July 1917); US Census Bureau, *Part II Comparative Occupation Statistics 1870–1930: A Comparable Series of Statistics Presenting a Distribution of the Nation's Labor Force by Occupation, Sex and Age*; *Employment by Occupation – ILO Modelled Estimates*, November 2018.
6   Geoffrey Millerson, *The Qualifying Associations* (Routledge and Keegan Paul, 1964).
7   Alison Wolf, *Does Education Matter?* (Penguin, 2002), p. 51.
8   Millerson, *The Qualifying Associations*.
9   Ibid.
10 G. W. Kekewich, *The Education Department and After* (Forgotten Books, 2019).
11 Michael Sanderson, 'Education and the Economy, 1870–1939', *ReFRESH* 17 (Autumn 1993).
12 Robert Anderson, *British Universities Past and Present* (Bloomsbury, 2006).
13 Matthew Crawford, *The Case for Working with Your Hands* (Penguin, 2010), pp. 161–2.
14 David F. Labaree, *A Perfect Mess: The Unlikely Ascendancy of American Higher Education* (University of Chicago Press, 2017), p. 25.
15 Nicholas Lemann, *The Big Test: The Secret History of the American Meritocracy* (Farrar, Straus and Giroux, 1999), p. 347.

16 Sanderson, 'Education and the Economy'.

17 Ibid.

18 Frederick Jackson Turner, *The Significance of the Frontier in American History* (American Historical Association, 1893).

19 'Charles Murray on *Coming Apart*', interview in *Uncommon Knowledge* (Hoover Institution, 2012), available at https://www.hoover.org/research/charles-murray-coming-apart.

CHAPTER 3: COGNITIVE ABILITY AND THE MERITOCRACY PUZZLE

1 Polly Mackenzie, 'The Myth of Meritocracy', *UnHerd*, 17 April 2019, available at https://unherd.com/2019/04/the-myth-of-meritocracy/.

2 Linda S. Gottfredson: 'Mainstream Science on Intelligence: An Editorial With 52 Signatories, History, and Bibliography', *Intelligence* 24/1 (1997), pp. 13–23.

3 Carol Dweck, *Mindset: The New Psychology of Success* (Ballantine Books, 2007).

4 See, for example, Robert Plomin and Sophie Von Stumm: 'The New Genetics of Intelligence', *National Review of Genetics* 19/3 (2018), pp. 148–59.

5 Lemann, *The Big Test*, p. 23.

6 Tomas Chamorro-Premuzic: 'Ace the Assessment', *Harvard Business Review*, July/August 2015.

7 Christopher Chabris interview with Dr Scott Barry Kaufman, *The Psychology Podcast*, June 2015, available at https://scottbarrykaufman.com/podcast/straight-talk-about-iq-with-christopher-chabris/.

8 Nassim Nicholas Taleb, 'IQ is Largely a Pseudoscientific Swindle', *Medium*, 2 January 2019, available at https://medium.com/incerto/iq-is-largely-a-pseudoscientific-swindle-f131c101ba39.

9 James Flynn: *Are We Getting Smarter?: Rising IQ in the Twenty-first Century* (Cambridge University Press, 2012).

10 James Flynn: 'Massive IQ Gains in 14 Nations: What IQ Tests Really Measure', *Psychological Bulletin* 101/2 (1987), pp. 171–91.

11 James Flynn: 'The Mean IQ of Americans: Massive Gains 1932 to 1978', *Psychological Bulletin* 95/1 (1984), pp. 29–51.

12 Howard Gardner: *Frames of Mind: The Theory of Multiple Intelligences* (Basic Books, 1983).

13 Toby Young, 'The Fall of the Meritocracy', *Quadrant*, 7 September 2015, available at https://quadrant.org.au/magazine/2015/09/fall-meritocracy/.

14 David Robson, *The Intelligence Trap: Why Smart People Do Stupid Things and How to Make Wiser Decisions* (W. W. Norton and Company, 2019).

15 Apenwarr, 'The Curse of Smart People', 1 July 2014, available at https://apenwarr.ca/log/?m=201407.

16 Quoted in Julia Ingram, 'Cardinal Conversations Speaker Charles Murray Stirs Campus Debate', *The Stanford Daily*, 30 January 2018.

17 Robert Plomin, *Blueprint: How DNA Makes Us Who We Are* (Allen Lane, 2018).

18 Niki Erlenmeyer-Kimling and Lissy Jarvik, 'Genetics and Intelligence: A Review', *Science* 142/3590 (1963), pp. 1477–8.

19 Daniel W. Belsky et al., 'Genetic Analysis of Social-class Mobility in Five Longitudinal Studies', *PNAS* 115/31 (2018), pp. 7275–84.

20 James Bloodworth, *The Myth of Meritocracy* (Biteback Publishing, 2016), p. 102.

21 Erzsébet Bukodi and John Goldthorpe, *Social Mobility and Education in Britain* (Cambridge University Press, 2018).

22 Alice Sullivan, 'The Path from Social Origins to Top Jobs: Social Reproduction via Education', *The British Journal of Sociology* 69/3 (2018), pp. 782–4.

23 Jo Blanden, Paul Gregg and Stephen Machin, *Intergenerational Mobility in Europe and North America* (Centre for Economic Performance, London School of Economics/ Sutton Trust, 2005).

24 Peter Saunders, *Social Mobility Myths* (Civitas, 2010), p. 69.

25 Michael Young, *The Rise of the Meritocracy, 1870–2033* (Thames and Hudson, 1958).

26 Charles Murray, *The Bell Curve Explained*, available at https://www.aei.org/society-and-culture/the-bell-curve-explained-part-1-the-emergence-of-a-cognitive-elite/.

27 For summary see Young: 'The Fall of the Meritocracy'.

28 'The Rise and Rise of the Cognitive Elite: Brains Bring Ever Larger Rewards', *The Economist*, 20 January 2011.

29 'Modern Women Marrying Men of the Same or Lower Social Class', *IPPR*, 5 April 2012.

30 David Willetts, *The Pinch: How the Baby Boomers Took Their Children's Future – and Why They Should Give It Back* (Atlantic Books, 2011).

31 Charles Murray, *Coming Apart: The State of White America, 1960–2010* (Random House, 2012), p. 59.

32 Richard Reeves, *Dream Hoarders: How the American Upper Middle Class Is Leaving Everyone Else in the Dust, Why That Is a Problem, and What to Do About It* (The Brookings Institute, 2017).

33 Daniel Markovits, *The Meritocracy Trap* (Allen Lane, 2019).

34 Bloodworth, *Myth of Meritocracy*, p. 67.

35 Richard Breen, *Social Mobility in Europe* (Oxford University Press, 2004).

36 Andrew Hacker, 'The White Plight', *The New York Review of Books*, 10 May 2012.

37 Robson, *The Intelligence Trap*.

38 Dalton Conley, Jason Fletcher, *The Genome Factor: What the Social Genomics Revolution Reveals about Ourselves, Our History, and the Future* (Princeton University Press, 2017).

39 Kwame Anthony Appiah, 'The Myth of Meritocracy: Who Really Gets What They Deserve?', *Guardian*, 19 October 2018.

40 Young, *The Rise of the Meritocracy*, pp. 135–6.

41 Kwame Anthony Appiah, *The Lies That Bind: Rethinking Identity* (Profile Books, 2018), p. 178.

CHAPTER 4: THE ERA OF EDUCATIONAL SELECTION

1 Mark Bovens and Anchrit Willie, *Diploma Democracy* (Oxford University Press, 2017), p. 21.

2 Terry Wrigley, 'The Rise and Fall of the GCSE: A Class History', *History Workshop Online*, 1 December 2012.

3 Mike Hicks, 'The Recruitment and Selection of Young Managers by British Business 1930–2000', D.Phil. dissertation, St Johns College, Oxford, 2004, p. 109.

4 US National Center for Education Statistics, available at https://nces.ed.gov/programs/digest/d19/tables/dt19_103.20.asp?current=yes.

5 Nick Hillman, 'Why Do Students Study So Far Away from Home?', *The Times Higher Education Supplement*, 23 July 2015.

6 David Willetts, 'Abolishing private schools is not the education fight we need', *Financial Times*, 27 September 2019.

7 David Soskice and Torben Iversen, *Democracy and Prosperity* (Princeton University Press, 2019).

8 Nicola Woolcock, 'Vocational Courses Get a Makeover', *The Times*, 8 July 2019.

9   Michael Shattock, *Making Policy in British Higher Education* (Open University Press/McGraw-Hill Education, 2012).

10 *The Robbins Report/ Report of The Committee on Higher Education*, 1963, para. 26.

11 John Pratt, *The Polytechnic Experiment 1965–1992* (Taylor and Francis, 1997).

12 Chris Belfield, Christine Farquharson and Luke Sibieta, *2018 Annual Report on Education Spending in England*, IFS, September 2018, p. 10.

13 Based on data from Robert C. Feenstra et al., 'The Next Generation of the Penn World Table', *American Economic Review*, 105/10 (2015), pp. 3150–318.

14 BBC News, 'Tuition Fees Changes "to Save Students £15,700"', 3 October, 2017.

15 The Augar Review, *Post-18 Review of Education and Funding: Independent Panel Report*, 30 May 2019, available at https://assets. publishing.service.gov.uk/government/uploads/system/uploads/attach ment_data/file/805127/Review_of_post_18_education_and_funding. pdf.

16 Ibid.

17 Alison Wolf, 'We Must End "The One Degree and You're Out" Education System', *Financial Times*, 1 June 2019.

18 https://www.ukonward.com/wp-content/uploads/2019/10/Politics-of-Belonging-FINAL.pdf.

19 Paul Lewis, 'The Missing Middle: How to Get More Young People to Level 3–5', paper delivered at a Policy Exchange seminar, London, 6 June 2019.

20 Damian Hinds, Secretary of State for Education, Technical Education speech, Battersea Power Station, London, 6 December 2018.

21 Augar Review, *Post-18 Review of Education and Funding*.

22 Office for National Statistics, *Earnings and Hours Worked, Occupation by Four-digit SOC: ASHE Table 14*, available at https:www.ons.gov. uk/employmentandlabourmarket/peopleinwork/earningsandworking hoursdatasets/occupation4digitsoc2010ashetable14.

23 BBC News report, Brian Wheeler from the Liberal Democrat conference, 6 October 2014.

24 Francis Green et al., 'What Has Been Happening to the Training of Workers in Britain?', LLAKES research paper 43, 2013.

25 Hinds, Technical Education Speech.

26 Paul Johnson, 'My Son Taught Me a Lesson about University', *The Times*, 5 January 2018.

27 YouGov, 'Many Recent Graduates Are Unconvinced that University Was Worth the Cost', 23 June 2017.

28 Hinds, Technical Education Speech.

29 Richard Reeves, 'Yes, Capitalism Is Broken. To Recover, Liberals Must Eat Humble Pie', *Guardian*, 25 September 2019.

30 Markovits, *The Meritocracy Trap*.

31 *Demos Quarterly*, Winter 2014/15.

32 Crawford, *The Case for Working with Your Hands*, p. 19.

33 Ibid., p. 20.

34 Daniel Bell, *The Coming of Post-Industrial Society*, new edn (Basic Books, 1976).

35 Laura Bridgestock, 'How Much Does It Cost to Study in the US?', *Top Universities*, 17 May 2019.

36 Erin Duffin, 'Community Colleges in the United States – Statistics and Facts', *Statista*, 29 April 2019.

37 Ibid.

38 Nat Malkus, 'The Evolution of Career and Technical Education', *American Enterprise Institute*, May 2019.

39 Claudia Goldin and Lawrence F. Katz, 'The Race Between Education and Technology', Harvard University paper, July 2007.

40 Lemann, *The Big Test*, p. 351.

41 Apprenticeship Toolbox, Higher Education and Research in France Facts and Figures, Euroeducation.net.

42 John Lichfield, 'French Universities Crisis: Low Fees and Selection Lotteries Create Headaches in Higher Education', *Independent*, 25 September 2015.

43 'Higher Education and Research in France Facts and Figures', in Isabelle Kabla-Langlois (ed.), *Higher Education and Research in France, Facts and Figures – 49 Indicators*, 10th edn (Paris: Ministère de l'Éducation nationale, de l'Enseignement supérieur et de la Recherche, 2017), available at https://publication.enseignementsup-recherche.gouv.fr/eesr/10EN/EESR10EN_RESUME-higher_education_and_research_in_france_facts_and_figures_summary.php.

44 See https://www.hochschulkompass.de/hochschulen/hochschulsuche.html.

45 Most of the information about the German apprenticeship system comes from an interview with Dr Michael Meister of the German Federal Ministry for Education and Research in Berlin, September 2019.

46 Alison Wolf, 'Falling Productivity and Slowing Growth: Do Our Post-2008 Problems Have Anything to Do with Universities?', The King's

Lectures: Making Higher Education Policy, Lecture 3, King's College, London, 25 March 2019.

47 See this analysis of the negative correlation between more graduates and increased productivity from the German economic research institute DIW, https://www.diw.de/sixcms/detail.php?id=diw_01.c.672546. de.

48 Peter Walker, 'Rising Number of Postgraduates "Could Become Barrier to Social Mobility"', *Guardian*, 7 February 2013, https://www.theguardian. com/education/2013/feb/07/rising-number-postgraduates-social-mobility.

49 Bryan Caplan, *The Case Against Education: Why the Education System Is a Waste of Time and Money* (Princeton University Press, 2018).

50 Richard Arum and Josipa Roksa, *Academically Adrift: Limited Learning on College Campuses* (University of Chicago Press, 2011), p. 2.

51 Jean Twenge et al. 'Declines in Vocabulary Among American Adults Within Levels of Educational Attainment, 1974–2016', *Intelligence* 76 (September 2019).

52 Jonathan Neves and Nick Hillman, *Student Academic Experience Survey 2019*, Higher Education Policy Institute, 13 June 2019, available at https://www.hepi.ac.uk/2019/06/13/student-academic-experience-survey-2019/.

53 Harry Lambert, 'The Great University Con: How the British Degree Lost Its Value', *New Statesman*, 21 August 2019.

54 *Demos Quarterly*, Winter 2014/15.

55 Wolf, *Does Education Matter?*.

56 Andrew Hindmoor, *What's Left Now: The History and Future of Social Democracy* (Oxford University Press, 2018).

57 Fraser Nelson, '"I'll eat you alive" – Angela Rayner Interview', *Spectator*, 6 January 2018.

58 Paul Swinney and Maire Williams, 'The Great British Brain Drain', 21 November 2016, https://www.centreforcities.org/reader/great-british-brain-drain/migration-students-graduates/.

59 *Daily Telegraph*, 22 October 2019, reporting on a paper in the journal *Nature Human Behaviour*.

60 Andy Haldane speech at St James's Park, Newcastle, 24 September 2019, cited by David Smith, *The Times*, 4 December 2019, p. 43.

61 Ken Mayhew and Craig Holmes, 'Over-qualification and Skills Mismatch in the Graduate Labour Market', CIPD Policy Report, 2015, p. 3.

62 Sally Weale, 'Levels of Distress and Illness among Students in UK "Alarmingly high"', *Guardian*, 5 March 2019.

63 William Whyte, 'Somewhere to Live: Why British Students Study Away from Home – and Why It Matters', Higher Education Policy Institute Report 121, November 2019, p. 9.

64 Ibid.

65 Caplan, *The Case Against Education*.

66 Noah Carl, 'Lackademia: Why Do Academics Lean Left?', Adam Smith Institute Briefing Paper, March 2017.

67 Pew Research Center, 'Republicans Skeptical of Colleges' Impact on U.S., but Most See Benefits for Workforce Preparation', 20 July 2017.

68 Crawford, *The Case for Working with Your Hands*.

CHAPTER 5: RISE OF THE KNOWLEDGE WORKER

1   See, for example, Claudia Goldin and Robert A. Margo. 'The Great Compression: The Wage Structure in the United States at Mid-Century', *Quarterly Journal of Economics* 107 (1992).

2   Richard Baldwin, *The Globotics Upheaval: Robotics and the Future of Work* (Weidenfeld and Nicolson, 2019), p. 33.

3   Ibid.

4   David Autor, 'Work of the Past, Work of the Future', Richard T. Ely Lecture delivered to the Annual Meeting of the American Economic Association (2019).

5   Ibid.

6   Ibid.

7   Ibid.

8   Angus Deaton, 'Why Is Democratic Capitalism Failing So Many?', keynote address, Tri-Nuffield Conference, 6 May 2019, available at https://www.youtube.com/watch?v=ref8y99ewHQ.

9   Gary S. Becker, 'Investment in Human Capital: A Theoretical Analysis', *Journal of Political Economy,* 70/5 (1962).

10 John Burton, *Leading Good Care* (Jessica Kingsley, 2015), p. 13.

11 Office for National Statistics, *New Earnings Survey and Annual Survey of Hours and Earnings*, available at https://www.ons.gov.uk employmentandlabourmarket/peopleinwork/earningsandworkinghours/adhocs/006332newearningssurveynesandannualsurveyofhoursandearningsashe publicandprivategrossweeklytimeseries; United States Census Bureau, *Statistical Abstract of the United States 1976*, available at https://www.census.gov/library/publications/1976/compendia/statab/97ed.html; US Bureau of Labor Statistics, *May 2017 National Occupational Employment*

and Wage Estimates United States, available at https://www.bls.gov/
oes/2017/may/oes_nat.htm.

12 Autor, 'Work of the Past, Work of the Future'.

13 Robert J. Samuelson, 'Where Did Our Raises Go? To Healthcare',
Washington Post, 2 September 2018.

14 Guy Michaels, Ashwini Natraj and John Van Reenen, 'Has ICT Polarized Skill Demand? Evidence from Eleven Countries over Twenty-Five
Years', *Review of Economics and Statistics* 96/1 (2014), pp. 60–77.

15 Office for National Statistics, *UK Labour Market: December 2018*,
available at https://www.ons.gov.uk/releases/uklabourmarketstatistics
dec2018.

16 International Labour Organization, *Employment by Occupation –
ILO Modelled Estimates, November 2018*, available at https://bit.
ly/34gR6VB.

17 Center for Economic and Policy Research, *The Decline of Blue Collar
Jobs, in Graphs*, 22 February 2017, available at https://cepr.net/
the-decline-of-blue-collar-jobs-in-graphs/.

18 Stephen Clarke and Nye Cominetti, *Setting the Record Straight: How
Record Employment Has Changed the UK*, Resolution Foundation
Report, 2019, p. 35.

19 Department for Business, Energy and Industrial Strategy, *Trade Union
Statistics 2018*.

20 Clarke and Cominetti, *Setting the Record Straight*, p. 6.

21 Stephen McKay and Ian Simpson, *British Social Attitudes 33: Work*,
NatCen, 2016, available at https://www.bsa.natcen.ac.uk/media/39061/
bsa33_work.pdf.

22 Golo Henseke, Alan Felstead, Duncan Gallie and Francis Green, *Skills
Trends at Work in Britain: First Findings from the Skills and Employment Survey 2017*, Economic and Social Research Council, Cardiff
University and the Department for Education Mini-Report, 2018, Section 5.

23 Mike Hicks, 'The Recruitment and Selection of Young Managers by
British Business 1930–2000', D.Phil. dissertation, St Johns College,
Oxford, 2004, p. 112.

24 Calculated by Mark Williams using Office for National Statistics, *New
Earnings Survey and Annual Survey of Hours and Earnings*; United
States Census Bureau, *Statistical Abstract of the United States 1976*;
US Bureau of Labor Statistics, *May 2017 National Occupational
Employment and Wage Estimates United States*.

25 OECD, *Education at a Glance 2018* (OECD Publishing, 2019).

26 Dr Gavan Conlon and Pietro Patrignani, *The Returns to Higher Education Qualifications: BIS Research Paper 45* (London Economics on behalf of the Department for Business, Innovation and Skills, 2011), p. 16.

27 Michael Hout, 'Social and Economic Returns to College Education in the United States', *Annual Review of Sociology*, 38 (2012).

28 Anna Vignoles et al., *The Impact of Undergraduate Degrees on Early-career Earnings* (Institute for Fiscal Studies, 2018), p. 5.

29 Hugh Hayward, Emily Hunt and Anthony Lord, *The Economic Value of Key Intermediate Qualifications: Estimating the Returns and Lifetime Productivity Gains to GCSEs, A Levels and Apprenticeships* (Department for Education, 2014).

30 OECD, *Education at a Glance 2018* (OECD Publishing, 2019).

31 Philip J. Cook and Robert H. Frank, *The Winner-Take-All Society: Why the Few at the Top Get So Much More Than the Rest of Us* (Virgin Books, 2010).

32 Robert Frank and Philip Cook, *UK Employment Policy Institute Report*, January 1997.

33 Philip Brown, Hugh Lauder and David Ashton, *The Global Auction: The Broken Promises of Education, Jobs, and Incomes* (Oxford University Press, 2012).

34 Henseke et al., *Skills Trends at Work in Britain*, Section 3.

35 Mayhew and Holmes, 'Over-qualification and Skills Mismatch'.

36 Ibid., p. 3.

37 Ibid.

38 Willis Commission, *Quality with Compassion: The Future of Nursing Education: Report of the Willis Commission* (Royal College of Nursing, 2012), available at https://www.macmillan.org.uk/documents/newsletter/willis-commission-report-macmail-dec2012.pdf.

39 Linda H. Aiken et al., 'Nurse Staffing and Education and Hospital Mortality in Nine European Countries: A Retrospective Observational Study', *Lancet* 383/9931 (2014), pp. 1824–30.

40 BBC News, 'Nursing to Become Graduate Entry', 12 November 2009.

41 Willis Commission, *Quality with Compassion*.

42 Ken Mayhew and Craig Holmes, *Alternative Pathways into the Labour Market*, CIPD Policy Report, October 2016, p. 25.

43 UK Department for Education, *Graduate Labour Market Statistics 2018*, available at https://assets.publishing.service.gov.uk/government/uploads/system/uploads/attachment_data/file/797308/GLMS_2018_publication_main_text.pdf.

44 Mayhew and Holmes, 'Alternative Pathways', p. 11.

45 BBC News, 'All New Police Officers in England and Wales to Have Degrees', 15 December 2016.

46 Ibid.

47 College of Policing, *Policing Education Qualifications Framework Consultation* (College of Policing Limited, 2016), p. 8.

48 Mayhew and Holmes, 'Alternative Pathways', p. 26.

49 Martin Evans, 'Police Force Goes to Court Over Plans to Make All New Officers Graduates', *Telegraph*, 11 July 2019.

50 Conor D'Arcy and David Finch, *Finding Your Routes: Non-Graduate Pathways in the UK's Labour Market* (Resolution Foundation, 2016).

51 Ibid., p. 50.

52 Ibid.

53 Amanda Goodall, 'Why Technical Experts Make Great Leaders', *Harvard Business Review*, 24 April 2018.

54 Henseke et al., *Skills Trends at Work in Britain*.

55 Alison Wolf, *The XX Factor: How Working Women Are Creating a New Society* (Profile Books, 2013).

56 Jenny Chanfreau, Sally McManus et al., *Predicting Wellbeing* (NatCen, 2008), p. 10.

57 Noam Gidron and Peter A. Hall, 'The Politics of Social Status: Economic and Cultural Roots of the Populist Right', *British Journal of Sociology*, 68/51 (2017), p. 1.

CHAPTER 6: THE DIPLOMA DEMOCRACY

1 See Jonathan Sumption, *Shifting the Foundations*, BBC Reith Lectures (2019), available at https://www.bbc.co.uk/programmes/b00729d9/episodes/player.

2 Ibid.

3 Mark Bovens and Anchrit Wille, *Diploma Democracy: The Rise of Political Meritocracy* (Oxford University Press, 2017), p. 1.

4 Jennifer E. Manning, *Membership of the 113th Congress: A Profile*, Congressional Research Service Report, 24 November 2014, p. 5.

5 Much of the data on the educational background of politicians and other matters in this chapter is taken from Bovens and Wille, *Diploma Democracy*.

6 Ibid.

7 Bill Bishop, *The Big Sort: Why the Clustering of Like-Minded America Is Tearing Us Apart* (Houghton Mifflin Harcourt, 2008).

8   Martin Gilens, *Affluence and Influence: Economic Inequality and Political Power in America* (Princeton University Press, 2012); David C. Kimball et al., 'Who Cares about the Lobbying Agenda?', *Interest Groups and Advocacy* 1/1 (2012).

9   Will Dahlgreen, *50 Years On, Capital Punishment Still Favoured*, You-Gov blog, 13 August 2014, available at https://yougov.co.uk/topics/politics/articles-reports/2014/08/13/capital-punishment-50-years-favoured.

10 Anthony Wells, *Where the Public Stands on Immigration*, YouGov blog, 27 April 2018, available at https://yougov.co.uk/topics/politics/articles-reports/2018/04/27/where-public-stands-immigration.

11 NatCen Social Research, *What UK Thinks: EU*, available at https://whatukthinks.org/eu/future-of-britain/about-natcen-social-research/.

12 YouGov poll, January 2011.

13 YouGov poll, October 2016.

14 YouGov poll, 5/6 February, 2018.

15 Public Religion Research Institute, *2018 American Values Survey*, available at https://www.prri.org/research/partisan-polarization-dominates-trump-era-findings-from-the-2018-american-values-survey/.

16 John Baxter Oliphant, *Public Support for the Death Penalty Ticks Up*, Pew Research Center, 11 June 2018.

17 CBS News-Refinery29 survey conducted by YouGov, 13 August, 2018, available at https://www.cbsnews.com/news/young-women-whats-on-their-minds-as-midterm-elections-approach/.

18 Daniel Cox, Rachel Lienesch and Robert P. Jones, *Beyond Economics: Fears of Cultural Displacement Pushed the White Working Class to Trump*, PRRI/The Atlantic Report, 5 September, 2017.

19 Public Religion Research Institute, *2018 American Values Survey*.

20 Tony Blair, 'British Prime Minister Tony Blair's Speech to the Polish Stock Exchange in Warsaw 6 October 2000', available at https://euobserver.com/news/2450.

21 Alison Wolf, 'Have Middle-class Women Captured Family Policy?', *Society Central*, 2015, available at https://societycentral.ac.uk/2015/01/14/middle-class-women-captured-family-policy/.

22 Geoff Dench, 'Putting Social Contribution Back into Merit', in *The Rise and Rise of Meritocracy* (Blackwell Publishing, 2006).

23 David Runciman, *How Democracy Ends* (Profile Books, 2019), p. 179.

24 Matthew Parris, 'Tories Should Turn Their Backs on Clacton', *The Times*, 6 September 2014.

25 Nicolas Mars, 'Vince Cable Says Some Brexit Voters Nostalgic for Era When "Faces Were White"', *Politics Home*, 11 March 2018.

26 John Gray, 'The Dangers of a Higher Education', *A Point of View*, BBC Radio 4, 23/25 February 2018.

27 Fareed Zakaria, *The Future of Freedom* (W. W. Norton and Company, 2003).

28 Alan S. Blinder, 'Is Government too Political?', *Foreign Affairs*, November/December 1997.

29 Peter Mair, *Ruling the Void: The Hollowing of Western Democracy* (Verso, 2013).

30 Ibid.

31 Will Hutton and Andrew Adonis, *Saving Britain: How We Must Change to Prosper in Europe* (Abacus, 2016).

32 Talk given at Cumberland Lodge, 29 April 2017.

33 Robert Putnam, *Bowling Alone: The Collapse and Revival of American Community* (Simon & Schuster, 2000).

34 Bovens and Wille, *Diploma Democracy*.

35 US General Social Survey.

36 Paul Johnson, 'My Son Taught Me a Lesson about University: Trying to Find an Apprenticeship for My Teenager Exposed How Biased We Are Against Training', *The Times*, 5 January 2018.

37 Cited in Bovens and Wille, *Diploma Democracy*.

38 Matthew Smith, *Are MPs Elected to Exercise Their Own Judgement or Do Their Constituents' Bidding?*, YouGov blog, 13 August, 2019, available at https://yougov.co.uk/topics/politics/articles-reports/2019/08/13/are-mps-elected-exercise-their-own-judgement-or-do.

39 Cited in Bovens and Wille, *Diploma Democracy*.

40 Nicholas Carnes and Noam Lupu, 'What Good Is a College Degree? Education and Leader Quality Reconsidered', *Journal of Politics*, 78/1 (2016), pp. 35–49.

41 YouGov Profiles data, courtesy of YouGov.

42 Bovens and Wille, *Diploma Democracy*, p. 172.

43 Stephen Hawkins, Daniel Yudkin, Miriam Juan-Torres and Tim Dixon, *Hidden Tribes: A Study of America's Polarized Landscape*, a study by the social cohesion think tank More in Common, 2018, available at https://hiddentribes.us/pdf/hidden_tribes_report.pdf.

44 Charles Murray, *Coming Apart: The State of White America, 1960– 2010* (Random House, 2012).

45 George Orwell, *Politics and the English Language* (Penguin, 2013).

CHAPTER 7: WHATEVER HAPPENED TO HAND?

1   The connection is made by Kwame Anthony Appiah in *The Lies That Bind*, p. 168.

2   Michael Young and Peter Willmott, *Family and Kinship in East London* (Routledge, 2013), p. 14.

3   Mike Savage et al., 'A New Model of Social Class? Findings from the BBC's Great British Class Survey Experiment', *Sociology*, 47/2 (2013), pp. 219–50.

4   Michael Hout, 'Social and Economic Returns to College Education in the United States', *Annual Review of Sociology* 38 (2012), pp. 379–400.

5   Michael Hout, private correspondence.

6   Christoph Lakner and Branko Milanovic, 'Global Income Distribution: From the Fall of the Berlin Wall to the Great Recession', *World Bank Economic Review* 30/2 (2016), pp. 203–32.

7   David Bailey, Caroline Chapain and Alex de Ruyter, 'Employment Outcomes and Plant Closures in a Post-Industrial City: An Analysis of the Labour Market Status of MG Rover Workers Three Years On', *Urban Studies* 49/7 2011), pp. 1595–612.

8   Crawford, *The Case for Working with Your Hands*, p. 3.

9   Tara Tiger Brown, 'The Death of Shop Class and America's Skilled Workforce', *Forbes*, 30 May 2012.

10 Conversation with the author.

11 See, for example, Office for National Statistics, *Construction Statistics, Great Britain: 2017*, available at https://www.ons.gov.uk/business industryandtrade/constructionindustry/articles/constructionstatistics/number192018edition.

12 Office for National Statistics, *Self-employment Jobs by Industry*, 17 December 2019, available at https://www.ons.gov.uk/employmentand labourmarket/peopleinwork/employmentandemployeetypes/datasets/selfemploymentjobsbyindustryjobs04.

13 Alan Tovey, 'Crisis in Construction Apprenticeships to Be Investigated', *Telegraph*, 1 July 2014, available at https://www.telegraph.co.uk/finance/jobs/10936940/Crisis-in-construction-apprenticeships-to-be-investigated.html.

14 Office for National Statistics, *Migrant Labour Force Within the Construction Industry*, June 2018, available at https://www.ons.gov.uk/peoplepopulationandcommunity/populationandmigration/international migration/articles/migrantlabourforcewithintheconstructionindustry/2018-06-19.

15 Mark Winterbotham et al., *Employer Skills Survey 2017: UK Findings*, Department of Education,16 August 2018, available at https://www.gov.uk/government/publications/employer-skills-survey-2017-uk-report.

16 Ibid.

17 Ibid.

18 CBI/ Pearson, *Educating for the Modern World*, 5 November 2018, pp. 16–17, available at https://www.cbi.org.uk/articles/educating-for-the-modern-world/.

19 Alexia Fernández Campbell, 'The US Is Experiencing a Widespread Worker Shortage. Here's Why', *Vox*, 18 March 2019.

20 For the US see: Daniel Zhao, 'Local Pay Reports: Pay Growth Steady At 2.3 Percent in January', *Glassdoor Economic Research Blog*, 29 January 2019, available at https://www.glassdoor.com/research/january-2019-local-pay-reports/. For the UK, see David Vivian et al., *UK Employer Skills Survey 2015: UK Results*, Department of Education, May 2016, available at https://assets.publishing.service.gov.uk/government/uploads/system/uploads/attachment_data/file/704104/Employer_Skills_Survey_2015_UK_Results-Amended-2018.pdf.

21 Harriet Agnew, 'France Faces Growing Threat of Skills Shortages', *Financial Times*, 18 October 2018.

22 Paul Vickers, *International Immigration and the Labour Market, UK: 2016*, Office for National Statistics, 12 April 2017, available at https://www.ons.gov.uk/peoplepopulationandcommunity/populationandmigration/internationalmigration/articles/migrationandthelabourmarketuk/2016.

23 Gidron and Hall, 'The Politics of Social Status', p. 10.

24 Michele Lamont, *The Dignity of Working Men: Morality and the Boundaries of Race, Class and Immigration* (Harvard University Press and the Russell Sage Foundation, 2000).

25 Justin Gest, *The New Minority: Working Class Politics in an Age of Immigration and Inequality* (Oxford University Press, 2016).

26 Arlie Russell Hochschild, *Strangers in Their Own Land: Anger and Mourning on the American Right* (The New Press, 2016).

27 Office for National Statistics, 17 December 2019 *Dataset A01: Summary of Labour Market Statistics*, available at https://www.ons.gov.uk/employmentandlabourmarket/peopleinwork/employmentandemployeetypes/datasets/summaryoflabourmarketstatistics/current.

28 CIPD, *Megatrends: Is Work in the UK Really Becoming Less Secure?*, CIPD report, 2019, p. 8, available at https://www.cipd.co.uk/knowledge/work/trends/megatrends/labour-market-insecurity.

29 Office for National Statistics, *Dataset EMP17: People in Employment on Zero Hours Contracts*, 12 August 2019, available at https://cy.ons. gov.uk/employmentandlabourmarket/peopleinwork/employmentan demployeetypes/datasets/emp17peopleinemploymentonzerohours contracts/current.

30 U.S. Bureau of Labor Statistics, *Contingent Work and Alternative Employment Arrangements – May 2017*, press release, 7 June 2018.

31 See Employment Rate, Labour Market Statistics, OECD, available at https://data.oecd.org/emp/employment-rate.htm.

32 Nye Cominetti, Kathleen Henehan and Stephen Clarke, *Low Pay Britain 2019*, Resolution Foundation Report, May 2019, p. 4, available at https://www.resolutionfoundation.org/app/uploads/2019/05/Low-Pay-Britain-2019-report.pdf.

33 Francis Green, 'Assessing Job Quality in the Affluent Economy', in *Demanding Work: The Paradox of Job Quality in the Affluent Economy* (Princeton University Press, 2007).

34 CIPD, *Megatrends*, p. 9.

35 Clarke and Cominetti, *Setting the Record Straight*.

36 International Labour Organization, *Employment by Sex and Occupation*, ILO modelled estimates, November 2018, available at https://www.ilo.org/shinyapps/bulkexplorer39/?lang=en&segment=indicator &id=EMP_2EMP_SEX_OCU_NB_A.

37 Mckay and Simpson, *British Social Attitudes 33: Work*, p. 1.

38 Pew Research Center, *The State of American Jobs*, 6 October, 2016, p. 13, available at https://www.pewsocialtrends.org/2016/10/06/the-state-of-american-jobs/.

39 McKay and Simpson, *British Social Attitudes 33: Work*, p. 14.

40 Ibid, p. 17.

41 Christian Welzel, 'Change in Materialist/Post-Materialist Priorities in 5 EU Countries Including UK, 1970 and 2000' from Chapter 10 in Russell J. Dalton and Hans-Dieter Klingemann: *The Oxford Handbook of Political Behaviour* (Oxford University Press, 2007).

42 McKay and Simpson, *British Social Attitudes 33: Work*, p. 7.

43 Pew Research Center, *The State of American Jobs*, p. 56.

44 Ibid, p. 57.

45 Ibid.

46 YouGov, '37% of British Workers Think Their Jobs Are Meaningless', 12 August, 2015, available at https://yougov.co.uk/topics/lifestyle/articles-reports/2015/08/12/british-jobs-meaningless.

47 See Gidron and Hall, 'The Politics of Social Status', p. 74.

48 Private analysis of ISSP data.

49 Gidron and Hall, 'The Politics of Social Status', p. 75.

50 Tak Wing Chan, *Understanding the Social and Cultural Bases of Brexit* (UCL Institute of Education, 2017).

CHAPTER 8: WHATEVER HAPPENED TO HEART?

1   Office for National Statistics, *New Earnings Survey and Annual Survey of Hours and Earnings*; United States Census Bureau, *Statistical Abstract of the United States 1976*; US Bureau of Labor Statistics, *May 2017 National Occupational Employment and Wage Estimates United States*.

2   Yuval Noah Harari, *Homo Deus: A Brief History of Tomorrow* (Harvill Secker, 2016), p. 199.

3   Ibid., p. 1.

4   Daniel Cox and Robert P. Jones, *America's Changing Religious Identity: Findings from the 2016 American Values Atlas*, Public Religion Research Institute, 6 September 2017.

5   Conrad Hackett, *U.S. Public Becoming Less Religious*, Pew Global Research Center, 3 November 2015, available at https://www.pewforum. org/2015/11/03/u-s-public-becoming-less-religious/.

6   Pew Global Research Center, *When Americans Say They Believe in God, What Do They Mean?*, 25 April 2018, available at https://www. pewforum.org/2018/04/25/when-americans-say-they-believe-in-god-what-do-they-mean/?utm_source=adaptivemailer&utm_ medium=email&utm_campaign=18–04-25%20beliefs%20about%20 god%20immediate&org=982&lvl=100&ite=2476&lea=559516&ctr=0 &par=1&trk=.

7   David Voas and Steve Bruce, *British Social Attitudes 36: Religion*, NatCen, 2019, available at https://www.bsa.natcen.ac.uk/media/39293/ 1_bsa36_religion.pdf.

8   Pew Global Research Center, *Being Christian in Western Europe*, 29 May 2018, available at https://www.pewforum.org/2018/05/29/being-christian-in-western-europe/.

9   Yuval Noah Harari, 'Why Technology Favors Tyranny', *The Atlantic*, October 2018.

10 Deaton, 'Why Is Democratic Capitalism Failing So Many?'

11 Richard Layard, *Happiness: Lessons from a New Science* (Penguin, 2005).

12 Brooks, 'The Nuclear Family Was a Mistake'.

13 Deaton, 'Why Is Democratic Capitalism Failing So Many?'

14 Harry Benson, *Family Stability Improves as Divorce Rates Fall*, Marriage Foundation, January 2019, available at https://marriagefoundation. org.uk/research/family-stability-improves-as-divorce-rates-fall/.

15 The Centre for Social Justice, *Why Family Matters*, March 2019, p. 5, available at https://www.centreforsocialjustice.org.uk/library/why-family-matters-comprehensive-analysis-of-the-consequences-of-family-break down.

16 ONS/NHS Digital, *Health Survey for England 2016 Well-being and Mental Health*, 13 December 2017, available at http://healthsurvey. hscic.gov.uk/media/63763/HSE2016-Adult-wel-bei.pdf.

17 NHS Digital, *Antidepressants Were the Area with Largest Increase in Prescription Items in 2016*, 29 June 2017, available at https://digital. nhs.uk/news-and-events/news-archive/2017-news-archive/ antidepressants-were-the-area-with-largest-increase-in-prescription-items-in-2016.

18 NHS Digital, *Mental Health Bulletin 2017–18 Annual Report*, available at https://digital.nhs.uk/data-and-information/publications/statistical/ mental-health-bulletin/2017–18-annual-report.

19 Nat Cen, University of Leicester, Department of Health, *Adult Psychiatric Morbidity Survey 2014: Survey of Mental Health and Wellbeing in England*, NHS Digital, 29 September 2016, available at https://digital. nhs.uk/data-and-information/publications/statistical/adult-psychiatric-morbidity-survey/adult-psychiatric-morbidity-survey-survey-of-mental-health-and-wellbeing-england-2014.

20 Edmund S. Higgins, 'Is Mental Health Declining in the U.S.?', *Scientific American*, 1 January 2017.

21 Mental Health America, *The State of Mental Health in America 2019*, available at https://www.mhanational.org/sites/default/files/2019–09/ 2019%20MH%20in%20America%20Final.pdf.

22 Stephen Ilardi, *Depression Is a Disease of Civilisation*, Ted Talk, May 2013, available at https://www.youtube.com/watch?v=drv3BPoFdi8.

23 'An Epidemic of Loneliness', *The Week*, 6 January 2019.

24 Louise C. Hawkley et al., *Loneliness in Older Adults in the USA and Germany: Measurement Invariance and Validation*, NORC Working Paper Series WP-2015–004, 2016.

25 Kantar Public, *Trapped in a Bubble: An Investigation into Triggers for Loneliness in the UK*, British Red Cross/ Co-op, December 2016, available at https://www.befriending.co.uk/resources/24731-trapped-in-a-bubble-an-investigation-into-triggers-for-loneliness-in-the-uk.

26 Centre for Social Justice, *The Forgotten Role of Families*, 2017, available at https://www.centreforsocialjustice.org.uk/core/wp-content/uploads/2017/11/The-forgotten-role-of-families-why-its-time-to-find-our-voice-on-families-1.pdf.

27 Brooks, 'The Nuclear Family Was a Mistake'.

28 Harry Benson, *The Myth of 'Long-term Stable Relationships Outside Marriage'*, The Marriage Foundation, May 2013, available at https://marriagefoundation.org.uk/research/the-myth-of-long-term-stable-relationships-outside-of-marriage/.

29 Branko Milanovic, *Capitalism, Alone* (Harvard University Press, 2019).

30 Richard Florida, *The Rise of the Creative Class (Revisited)* (New York: Basic Books, 2012).

31 Madeleine Bunting, *Labours of Love: The Crisis of Care* (Granta, 2020).

32 Interview with the author.

33 Tom De Castell, 'Rise in Nurse Vacancy Rate in England Prompts Fresh Warnings', *Nursing Times*, 12 September 2018; Stephanie Jones-Berry, 'Why As Many As One in Four Nursing Students Could Be Dropping Out of Their Degrees', *Nursing Standard*, 3 September 2018; Office for National Statistics, *What Are the Vacancy Trends in the Public Sector?*, 6 August 2019, available at https://www.ons.gov.uk/economy/governmentpublicsectorandtaxes/publicspending/articles/whatarethevacancytrendsinthepublicsector/2019–08-06.

34 Office for National Statistics, *Is Staff Retention an Issue in the Public Sector?*, 17 June 2019, available at https://www.ons.gov.uk/economy/governmentpublicsectorandtaxes/publicspending/articles/isstaffretentionanissueinthepublicsector/2019–06-17.

35 See, for example, 'German Opposition Slams Government for 36,000 Vacant Jobs in Care Industry', *Deutsche Welle*, 25 April 2018.

36 Barra Roantree and Kartik Vira, *The Rise and Rise of Women's Employment in the UK*, IFS Briefing Note BN234, April 2018, available at https://www.ifs.org.uk/publications/12951.

37 Office for National Statistics, *Women Shoulder the Responsibility of 'Unpaid Work'*, 10 November 2016, available at https://www.ons.gov.uk/employmentandlabourmarket/peopleinwork/earningsandworkinghours/articles/womenshouldertheresponsibilityofunpaidwork/2016–11-10.

38 Interview with the author.

39 Wolf, *The XX Factor*.

40 Wolf, 'Middle-class Women'.

41 Virginia Held, *The Ethics of Care* (Oxford University Press, 2005), p. 64.

42 Fullfact, *The Number of Nurses and Midwives in the UK*, 23 January 2018, available at https://fullfact.org/health/number-nurses-midwives-uk/.

43 Amy Wax, *Caring Enough: Sex Roles, Work and Taxing Women* (VillaNova University, 1999).

44 Office for National Statistics, Northern Ireland Statistics and Research Agency, *Quarterly Labour Force Survey*, July–September, 2019, UK Data Service, SN: 8588: http://doi.org/10.5255/UKDA-SN-8588-1.

45 Linda H. Aiken et al., 'Nurse Staffing and Education and Hospital Mortality in Nine European Countries: A Retrospective Observational Study', *Lancet* 383/9931 (2014), pp. 1824–30.

46 Professor Charles Goodhart, *Dementia Plus Demography Equals Care Crisis*, unpublished paper.

47 Camilla Cavendish, *The Cavendish Review: An Independent Review into Healthcare Assistants and Support Workers in the NHS and Social Care Settings* (2013), p. 7, available at https://assets.publishing.service.gov.uk/government/uploads/system/uploads/attachment_data/file/236212/Cavendish_Review.pdf.

48 Warwick Lightfoot, Will Heaven and Jos Henson Gric, *21st Century Social Care*, Policy Exchange, May 2019.

49 Fabian Wallace-Stephens, *What New Jobs Will Emerge in the 2020s?*, Royal Society of Arts, 8 January 2020.

50 Bureau of Labor Statistics, *Occupational Employment Projections to 2024*, December 2015, available at https://www.bls.gov/opub/mlr/2015/article/occupational-employment-projections-to-2024.htm.

51 Jonathan Gershuny and Oriel Sullivan (eds), *What We Really Do All Day: Insights from the Centre for Time Use Research* (Pelican, 2019), p. 113.

52 See, for example, Ministry of Justice, Department for Children, Schools and Families, *Reducing Re-offending: Supporting Families, Creating Better Futures: A Framework for Improving the Local Delivery of Support for the Families of Offenders*, 2009, available at https://dera.ioe.ac.uk/207/7/reducing-reoffending-supporting-families_Redacted.pdf.

53 Anchor, Care England survey, 21 June 2018.

54 Daniel Susskind, *A World Without Work: Technology, Automation and How We Should Respond* (Allen Lane, 2020), p. 105.

55 Skills for Care, *The State of the Adult Social Care Sector and Workforce in England*, September 2017, available at https://www.skillsforcare.org.uk/adult-social-care-workforce-data/Workforce-intelligence/publications/

national-information/The-state-of-the-adult-social-care-sector-and-work force-in-England.aspx.

56 Gershuny and Sullivan, *What We Really Do All Day*, p. 143.

57 Office for National Statistics, *Women Shoulder the Responsibility of 'Unpaid Work'*.

58 Ibid., p. 135.

59 Office for National Statistics, *Billion Pound Loss in Volunteering Effort*, March 2017, available at https://www.ons.gov.uk/employment andlabourmarket/peopleinwork/earningsandworkinghours/articles/ billionpoundlossinvolunteeringeffort/2017–03-16.

60 Marilyn French, *The Women's Room* (Virago, 1977).

61 Gretchen Livingston, *Adult Caregiving Often Seen as Very Meaningful by Those Who Do It*, Pew Research Center, 8 November, 2018, available at https://www.pewresearch.org/fact-tank/2018/11/08/adult-care giving-often-seen-as-very-meaningful-by-those-who-do-it/.

62 Mary Harrington, 'How Motherhood Put an End to My Liberalism', *UnHerd*, 9 October 2019, available at https://unherd.com/2019/12/ how-motherhood-put-an-end-to-my-liberalism-2/.

63 Catherine Hakim, 'A New Approach to Explaining Fertility Patterns: Preference Theory', *Population and Development Review* 29/3 (2003), pp. 349–74.

64 ICPSR, *British Social Attitudes Survey 1989*, available at https://www. icpsr.umich.edu/icpsrweb/ICPSR/studies/3092.

65 Bronnie Ware, *The Top Five Regrets of the Dying* (Hay House, 2019).

CHAPTER 9: THE FALL OF THE KNOWLEDGE WORKER

1 Krugman, 'White Collars Turn Blue'.

2 Baldwin, *The Globotics Upheaval*, pp.12–13.

3 Brown et al., *The Global Auction*.

4 Ibid.

5 Ibid.

6 Ibid.

7 Richard and Daniel Susskind, *The Future of the Professions: How Technology Will Transform the Work of Human Experts* (Oxford University Press, 2017), p. 1.

8 Ibid., p. 2.

9 Ibid., p. xi.

10 OECD, 'How Does the Earnings Advantage of Tertiary-educated Workers Evolve Across Generations?', *Education Indicators in Focus* 62 (2018).

11 Vignoles et al., *The Impact of Undergraduate Degrees*.

12 House of Lords, *Treating Students Fairly: The Economics of Post-School Education*, Economic Affairs Committee, 2nd Report of Session 2017–19, June 2018, p. 25.

13 Vignoles et al., *The Impact of Undergraduate Degrees*, pp. 50–51.

14 Chris Belfield et al., *The Relative Labour Market Returns to Different Degrees* (IFS, 2018).

15 Vignoles et al., *The Impact of Undergraduate Degrees*, p. 6.

16 Ibid, pp. 61–2.

17 Belfield et al., *The Relative Labour Market Returns*, pp. 6, 61.

18 Vignoles et al., *The Impact of Undergraduate Degrees*, p. 19.

19 Bellfield et al., *The Relative Labour Market Returns*, p. 34.

20 Ken Mayhew, 'Human Capital, Growth and Inequality', *Welsh Economic Review*, 2016.

21 Jared Ashworth and Tyler Ransom, *Has the College Wage Premium Continued to Rise? Evidence From Multiple US Surveys*, IZA Institute of Labor Economics, July 2018.

22 Stefan Speckesser and Héctor Espinoza, 'A Comparison of Earnings Related to Higher Level Vocational/Technical and Academic Education', Research Discussion Paper 019, CVER, April 2019, available at http://cver.lse.ac.uk/textonly/cver/pubs/cverdp019.pdf.

23 OECD, *Skills Matter: Additional Results from the Survey of Adult Skills*, OECD Skills Studies, 2019, available at https://www.oecd-ilibrary.org/sites/1f029d8f-en/1/2/1/index.html?itemId=/content/publication/1f029d8f-en&_csp_=9ca26e268264865d390e376cd0e17bb9&itemIGO=oecd&itemContentType=book.

24 Richard Clegg, *Graduates in the UK Labour Market: 2017*, Office for National Statistics, November 2017, available at https://www.ons.gov.uk/employmentandlabourmarket/peopleinwork/employmentandemployeetypes/articles/graduatesintheuklabourmarket/2017.

25 Peter Elias et al., 'Reassessing the Employment Outcomes of Higher Education', in Jennifer M. Case and Jeroen Huisman (eds.), *Researching Higher Education: International Perspectives on Theory, Policy and Practice* (Routledge Press, 2015), pp. 114–31.

26 Maja Savic, *Overeducation and Hourly Wages in the UK Labour Market, 2006 to 2017*, Office for National Statistics, April 2019, available at https://www.ons.gov.uk/economy/nationalaccounts/uksectoraccounts/

compendium/economicreview/april2019/overeducationandhourlywages
intheuklabourmarket2006to2017.

27 Henseke et al., *Skills Trends at Work in Britain*.

28 Mayhew and Holmes, 'Alternative Pathways'.

29 Ibid., and Mayhew and Holmes, 'Over-qualification and skills'.

30 Geoff Mason. 'Graduate Utilisation in British Industry: The Initial
    Impact of Mass Higher Education', *National Institute Economic
    Review* 156 (May 1996), pp. 93–103.

31 Gerbrand Tholen, 'The Role of Higher Education within the Labour
    Market: Evidence from Four Skilled Occupations', paper presented at
    SKOPE/ESRC Festival of Science, St Anne's College, Oxford (2014),
    available at http://www.skope.ox.ac.uk/wp-content/uploads/2014/09/
    Tholen-Presentation-2.pdf. Susan James, Chris Warhurst, Gerbrand
    Tholen and Johanna Commander, 'Graduate Skills or the Skills of
    Graduates, What Matters Most? An Analysis from a Graduatising
    Occupation', paper presented at the 30th International Labour Process
    Conference, Stockholm University, Stockholm (2012), available at
    http://www.researchcatalogue.esrc.ac.uk/grants/RES-557–28-5003/
    outputs/read/17ddaf35-9dc3-498e-b9e3-2a04624cf43f.

32 Chris Belfield, Jack Britton, Lorraine Dearden and Laura van der Erve,
    *Higher Education Funding in England: Past, Present and Options for
    the Future*, IFS Briefing Note BN211, 5 July 2017, available at https://
    www.ifs.org.uk/publications/9334.

33 Mayhew and Holmes, 'Alternative Pathways', pp. 4, 50.

34 Francis Green and Golo Henseke, 'Should Governments of OECD
    Countries Worry About Graduate Underemployment?', *Oxford Review
    of Economic Policy*, 32/4 (2016), pp. 514–37.

35 Susskind, *A World Without Work*, p. 103.

36 Bukodi and Goldthorpe, *Social Mobility*.

37 John Boys, CIPD, private correspondence using *ONS Dataset EMP04:
    Employment by Occupation*.

38 Jacques Bughin, Eric Hazan, Susan Lund, Peter Dahlström, Anna Wies-
    inger and Amresh Subramaniam, *Skills Shift: Automation and the
    Future of the Workforce*, McKinsey Global Institute (MGI) discussion
    paper, May 2018.

39 Ibid.

40 'EY Transforms Its Recruitment Selection Process for Graduates,
    Undergraduates and School Leavers', press release from Ernst and
    Young (3 August 2015).

41 'EY: How to Excel in a Strengths-Based Graduate Interview', available at https://targetjobs.co.uk/employers/ey/ey-how-to-excel-in-a-strengths-based-graduate-interview-323859.

42 See UK High Pay Centre, http://highpaycentre.org/files/FINAL_PAY_RATIOS_ESSAY_COLLECTION.pdf.

43 Adair Turner, 'Capitalism in the Age of Robots: Work, Income and Wealth in the 21st Century', lecture at School of Advanced International Studies, Johns Hopkins University, Washington, D.C., 10 April 2018, p. 29, available at https://www.ineteconomics.org/uploads/papers/Paper-Turner-Capitalism-in-the-Age-of-Robots.pdf.

44 Tyler Cowen, *Average Is Over: Powering America Beyond the Age of the Great Stagnation* (E. P. Dutton, 2013).

45 Ibid.

CHAPTER 10: COGNITIVE DIVERSITY AND THE FUTURE OF EVERYTHING

1 David Brooks, 'The Road to Character', Intelligence Squared lecture, Royal Geographical Society, London, 26 May 2015, available at https://www.youtube.com/watch?v=_iGewxH3dgY.

2 Iain McGilchrist, *The Master and His Emissary: The Divided Brain and the Making of the Western World* (Yale University Press, 2009).

3 Jonathan Rowson and Iain McGilchrist, *Divided Brain, Divided World: Why the Best Part of Us Struggles to be Heard*, RSA, February 2013, pp. 4–5, available at https://www.thersa.org/globalassets/pdfs/blogs/rsa-divided-brain-divided-world.pdf.

4 Richard Layard, *Can We Be Happier?* (Pelican, 2020).

5 Matthew Syed, *Rebel Ideas: The Power of Diverse Thinking* (John Murray Press, 2019).

6 Carnegie Mellon, 'Different Kinds of Thinking Make Teams Smarter', *Futurity*, 2 July 2019, available at https://www.futurity.org/collective-intelligence-teams-2097152/.

7 Musa al-Gharbi, 'On the Relationship between Ideological and Demographic Diversity', available at https://musaalgharbi.com/2019/04/29/relationship-between-ideological-demographic-diversity/.

8 Dag Detter and Stefan Folster, *Out of the Box Economics: Inventive and Little Known Ways of Tackling the World of Tomorrow Today* (Forthcoming, 2021).

9 Turner, 'Capitalism in the Age of Robots', p. 30.

10 Mariana Mazzucato, *The Value of Everything: Making and Taking in the Global Economy* (Penguin, 2019).

11 Lemann, *The Big Test*, p. 347.

12 The formulation of French geographer Christophe Guilluy. See Christophe Guilluy, *Twilight of the Elites: Prosperity, the Periphery and the Future of France* (Yale University Press, 2019).

13 Nicholas Boys Smith, 'How Communities Lost Their Soul', *UnHerd*, 4 October 2019, available at https://unherd.com/2019/10/how-communities-lost-their-soul/.

14 Sue Halpern, 'The One Traffic-light Town with some of the Fastest Internet in the US', *New Yorker*, 3 December 2019.

15 Turner, 'Capitalism in the Age of Robots', p. 31.

16 Wendell Steavenson, *Back to the Rind* (FT Books, 2019).

17 Bee Wilson, *The Way We Eat Now: Strategies for Eating in a World of Change* (Fourth Estate, 2019).

18 Joseph E. Aoun, *Robot Proof: Higher Education in the Age of Artificial Intelligence* (The MIT Press, 2017).

19 Andy Haldane, 'Ideas and Institutions – A Growth Story', speech to the Guild Society, University of Oxford, 23 May 2018, available at https://www.bankofengland.co.uk/speech/2018/andy-haldane-speech-given-at-the-oxford-guild-society.

20 John Maynard Keynes, *Essays in Persuasion* (Classic House Books, 2009).

21 Tom Holland, *Dominion: The Making of the Western Mind* (Little, Brown, 2019).

22 Jonathan Rauch, *The Happiness Curve: Why Life Gets Better After Midlife* (Bloomsbury, 2018).

Select Bibliography

Appiah, Kwame Anthony, *The Lies that Bind: Rethinking Identity* (London: Profile Books, 2018).

Arum, Richard, and Josipa Roksam, *Academically Adrift: Limited Learning on College Campuses* (Chicago: University of Chicago Press, 2011).

Augar Review, *Post-18 Review of Education and Funding: Independent Panel Report*, UK government report, 30 May 2019, available at https://assets.publishing.service.gov.uk/government/uploads/system/uploads/attachment_data/file/805127/Review_of_post_18_education_and_funding.pdf.

Autor, David, 'Work of the Past, Work of the Future', Richard T. Ely Lecture to the annual meeting of the American Economic Association (2019).

Baldwin, Richard, *The Globotics Upheaval: Globalization, Robotics and the Future of Work* (London: Weidenfeld and Nicolson, 2019).

Bell, Daniel, *The Coming of Post-Industrial Society: A Venture in Social Forecasting* (London: Penguin, 1976).

Bishop, Bill, *The Big Sort: Why the Clustering of Like-Minded America Is Tearing Us Apart* (New York: Houghton Mifflin Harcourt, 2008).

Blanden, Jo, Paul Gregg and Stephen Machin, *Intergenerational Mobility in Europe and North America: A Report Supported by the Sutton Trust*, Centre for Economic Performance, London School of Economics/Sutton Trust, 2005.

Bloodworth, James, *The Myth of Meritocracy* (London: Biteback Publishing, 2016).

— *Hired: Undercover in Low-Wage Britain* (London: Atlantic, 2019).

Bovens, Mark, and Anchrit Wille, *Diploma Democracy: The Rise of Political Meritocracy* (Oxford: Oxford University Press, 2017).

Brown, Richard, Hugh Lauder and David Ashton, *The Global Auction: The Broken Promises of Education, Jobs and Incomes* (Oxford: Oxford University Press, 2011).

Bukodi, Erzsébet and John H. Goldthorpe, *Social Mobility and Education in Britain: Research, Politics and Policy* (Cambridge: Cambridge University Press, 2019).

Bunting, Madeleine, *Labours of Love: The Crisis of Care* (London: Granta, 2020).

Burton, John, *Leading Good Care* (London: Jessica Kingsley, 2015).

Caplan, Bryan, *The Case Against Education: Why the Education System Is a Waste of Time and Money* (Princeton: Princeton University Press, 2018).

Case, Anne and Angus Deaton, *Deaths of Despair and the Future of Capitalism* (Princeton: Princeton University Press, 2020).

Cavendish, Camilla, *Extra Time: 10 Lessons for an Ageing World* (London: HarperCollins, 2019).

Christodoulou, Daisy, *Seven Myths About Education* (London: Routledge, 2014).

Collier, Paul, *The Future of Capitalism: Facing the New Anxieties* (London: Allen Lane, 2018).

Cowen, Tyler, *Average Is Over: Powering America Beyond the Age of the Great Stagnation* (New York: Dutton, 2013).

Crawford, Matthew, *The Case for Working with Your Hands* (London: Penguin, 2011).

Deaton, Angus, 'Why Is Democratic Capitalism Failing So Many? And What Should We Do About It?', keynote address, Tri-Nuffield Conference (16 May 2019), available at https://www.youtube.com/watch?v=ref8y99ewHQ.

Dench, Geoff (ed.), *The Rise and Rise of Meritocracy* (Oxford: Blackwell, 2006).

— *What Women Want: Evidence from British Social Attitudes* (London: Hera Trust, 2010).

Florida, Richard, *The Rise of the Creative Class Revisited* (New York: Basic Books, 2014).

Flynn, James, *Are We Getting Smarter? Rising IQ in the Twenty-First Century* (Cambridge: Cambridge University Press, 2012).

Gardner, Howard, *Frames of Mind: The Theory of Multiple Intelligences* (New York: Basic Books, 1983).

Gershuny, Jonathan and Oriel Sullivan (eds.), *What We Really Do All Day: Insights from the Centre for Time Use Research* (London: Pelican, 2019).

Gest, Justin, *The New Minority: White Working Class Politics in an Age of Immigration and Inequality* (New York: Oxford University Press, 2016).

Gidron, Noam and Peter Hall, 'The Politics of Social Status: Economic and Cultural Roots of the Populist Right', *British Journal of Sociology* 68/51 (2017).

Goldin, Claudia and Lawrence Katz, *The Race Between Education and Technology* (Cambridge, Mass.: Harvard University Press, 2009).

Goleman, Daniel, *Emotional Intelligence: Why It Can Matter More Than IQ* (London: Bantam, 2006).

Goodhart, Charles, 'Dementia Plus Demography Equals Care Crisis', unpublished paper.

Guyatt, Richard, 'Head, Hand and Heart', inaugural lecture, Royal College of Art (1951), in *Two Lectures* (London: Royal College of Art, 1977).

Haidt, Jonathan, *The Righteous Mind: Why Good People Are Divided by Politics and Religion* (London: Penguin, 2013).

Haldane, Andy, 'Ideas and Institutions – A Growth Story', speech to the Guild Society, University of Oxford, 23 May 2018, available at https://www.bankofengland.co.uk/speech/2018/andy-haldane-speech-given-at-the-oxford-guild-society.

Harari, Yuval Noah, *Homo Deus: A Brief History of Tomorrow* (London: Harvill Secker, 2016).

— *21 Lessons for the 21st Century* (London: Jonathan Cape, 2018).

Held, Virginia, *The Ethics of Care: Personal, Political and Global* (New York: Oxford University Press, 2006).

Hochschild, Arlie Russell, *Strangers in Their Own Land: Anger and Mourning on the American Right* (New York: The New Press, 2016).

— *The Managed Heart: Commercialization of Human Feeling* (Berkeley: University of California Press, 2012).

Holland, Tom, *Dominion: The Making of the Western Mind* (London: Little, Brown, 2020).

Kahneman, Daniel, *Thinking, Fast and Slow* (London: Penguin, 2012).

Keynes, John Maynard, *Essays in Persuasion* (London: Rupert Hart-Davis, 1951).

Labaree, David F., *A Perfect Mess: The Unlikely Ascendancy of American Higher Education* (Chicago: The University of Chicago Press, 2017).

Lamont, Michele, *The Dignity of Working Men: Morality and the Boundaries of Race, Class and Immigration* (Cambridge, Mass.: Harvard University Press, 2000).

Lasch, Christopher, *The Revolt of the Elites: And the Betrayal of Democracy* (New York: W. W. Norton, 1995).

Layard, Richard, *Can We Be Happier? Evidence and Ethics* (London: Penguin, 2020).

Leadbeater, Charles, *Living on Thin Air* (London: Penguin, 2010).

Lemann, Nicholas, *The Big Test: The Secret History of the American Meritocracy* (New York: Farrar, Straus and Giroux, 2000).

Lenon, Barnaby, *Other People's Children* (London: John Catt Educational, 2018).

Lind, Michael, *The New Class War: Saving Democracy from the Metropolitan Elite* (London: Atlantic, 2020).

Mair, Peter, *Ruling the Void: The Hollowing of Western Democracy* (London: Verso, 2013).

Markovits, Daniel, *The Meritocracy Trap* (London: Allen Lane, 2019).

Marmot, Michael, *Status Syndrome: How Your Social Standing Directly Affects Your Health* (London: Bloomsbury, 2005).

Mayhew, Ken and Craig Holmes, *Over-qualification in the Graduate Labour Market*, CIPD report, 18 August 2015, available at https://www.cipd.co.uk/knowledge/work/skills/graduate-labour-market-report.

Mazzucato, Mariana, *The Value of Everything: Making and Taking in the Global Economy* (London: Penguin, 2019).

McGilchrist, Iain, *The Master and His Emissary: The Divided Brain and the Making of the Western World* (London: Yale University Press, 2012).

Milanovic, Branko, *Global Inequality: A New Approach for the Age of Globalization* (Cambridge, Mass.: Harvard University Press, 2016).

Mumford, James, *Vexed: Ethics Beyond Political Tribes* (London: Bloomsbury, 2020).

Murray, Charles, *Coming Apart: The State of White America, 1960–2010* (New York: Crown Forum, 2013).

McKinsey Global Institute, 'Skill Shift: Automation and the Future of the Workforce', discussion paper, May 2018, available at https://www.mckinsey.com/~/media/mckinsey/featured%20insights/future%20of%20organizations/skill%20shift%20automation%20and%20the%20future%20of%20the%20workforce/mgi-skill-shift-automation-and-future-of-the-workforce-may-2018.ashx.

Orwell, George, *Politics and the English Language* (London: Penguin, 2013).

Perry, Grayson, *The Descent of Man* (London: Penguin, 2017).

Plomin, Robert, *Blueprint: How DNA Makes Us Who We Are* (London: Allen Lane, 2018).

Putnam, Robert D., *Bowling Alone: The Collapse and Revival of American Community* (New York: Simon and Schuster, 2000).

Rauch, Jonathan, *The Happiness Curve: Why Life Gets Better After Midlife* (New York: Green Tree, 2018).

Reeves, Richard, *Dream Hoarders: How the American Upper Middle Class Is Leaving Everyone Else in the Dust, Why That Is a Problem, and What to Do About It* (Washington: The Brookings Institution, 2018).

Reich, Robert, *The Work of Nations* (London: Simon & Schuster, 1991).

Robson, David, *The Intelligence Trap: Why Smart People Do Stupid Things and How to Make Wiser Decisions* (London: Hodder and Stoughton, 2019).

Runciman, David, *How Democracy Ends* (London: Profile Books, 2019).

Saunders, Peter, *Social Mobility Myths* (London: Civitas, 2010).

Savage, Michael, *Social Class in the 21st Century* (London: Pelican, 2015).

Seldon, Anthony, *The Fourth Education Revolution: Will Artificial Intelligence Liberate or Infantilise Humanity?* (Buckingham: The University of Buckingham Press, 2018).

Shattock, Michael, *Making Policy in British Higher Education* (Maidenhead: Open University Press, 2012).

Slaughter, Anne-Marie, *Unfinished Business: Women Men Work Family* (New York: Penguinrandomhouse, 2015).

Soskice, David and Torben Iversen, *Democracy and Prosperity: Reinventing Capitalism Through a Turbulent Century* (Princeton: Princeton University Press, 2019).

Sumption, Jonathan, *Shifting the Foundations*, BBC Reith Lectures (2019), available at https://www.bbc.co.uk/programmes/b00729d9/episodes/player.

Susskind Daniel, *A World Without Work: Technology, Automation and How We Should Respond* (London: Allen Lane, 2020).

Susskind, Daniel and Richard Susskind, *The Future of the Professions: How Technology Will Transform the Work of Human Experts* (Oxford: Oxford University Press, 2017).

Syed, Matthew, *Rebel Ideas: The Power of Diverse Thinking* (London: John Murray, 2019).

Taleb, Nassim Nicholas, *Skin in the Game: Hidden Asymmetries in Daily Life* (London: Penguin, 2019).

Tamir, Yuli, 'Staying in Control: What do We really Want Public Opinion to achieve?'. *Educational Theory* 61/14 (August 2011).

Turner, Adair, 'Capitalism in the Age of Robots: Work, Income and Wealth in the 21st Century', lecture at the School of Advanced International Studies, Johns Hopkins University, Washington, D.C., 10 April 2018, available at https://www.ineteconomics.org/uploads/papers/Paper-Turner-Capitalism-in-the-Age-of-Robots.pdf.

Vance, J. D., *Hillbilly Elegy: A Memoir of a Family and Culture in Crisis* (London: HarperCollins, 2016).

Whyte, William, *Somewhere to Live: Why British Students Study Away from Home and Why It Matters*, Higher Education Policy Institute report, 14 November 2019, available at https://www.hepi.ac.uk/wp-content/uploads/2019/11/HEPI_Somewhere-to-live_Report-121-FINAL.pdf.

Willetts, David, *A University Education* (Oxford: Oxford University Press, 2017).

— *The Pinch: How the Baby Boomers Took Their Children's Future – And Why They Should Give it Back* (London: Atlantic, 2019).

Williams, Joan C, *White Working Class: Overcoming Class Cluelessness in America* (Boston: Harvard Business Review Press, 2017).

Wolf, Alison, *Does Education Matter?* (London: Penguin, 2002).

— *The XX Factor: How Working Women Are Creating a New Society* (London: Profile Books, 2013).

Young, Michael, *The Rise of the Meritocracy, 1870–2033* (London: Penguin, 1973).

Young, Toby, 'The Fall of the Meritocracy', *Quadrant*, 7 September 2015, available at https://quadrant.org.au/magazine/2015/09/fall-meritocracy/.

Acknowledgements

My last book, *The Road to Somewhere*, covered themes I had been thinking about for some years, so I was able to write it quickly and without much help. This book has been different. It covers many subjects, such as human intelligence and the care economy, about which I had little prior knowledge and on which I can only write as an interested generalist. This time, however, I have had invaluable research assistance from Richard Norrie and Tom Hamilton-Shaw. I have also had special support and engagement from a couple of institutions and several individuals. Above all I want to thank Dean Godson and other colleagues at the Policy Exchange think tank in London, where I work part-time, for allowing me both the time to work on the book and to explore some of its themes in my Policy Exchange work. I hope I can repay the organization's generosity over the coming years. I was also invited to spend a month at the Institut für die Wissenschaften vom Menschen (IWM) a wonderful institute in Vienna where I was able to get the book underway in March 2019 and discuss some of its ideas with many lively minds from across Europe; special thanks to Ivan Krastev and Dessy Gavrilova for making my time there so enjoyable. I want to say a special thanks to a further dozen people: to David Lucas for having the original insight that launched the book; to Toby Mundy (my agent and friend) for picking it up and running with it; to Ken Charman, Alun Francis and Paul Morland for a constant flow of ideas and feedback; to Madeleine Bunting and Julie Goldie for insights into the world of care both domestic and institutional; to Eric Kaufmann, Matt Goodwin, Pamela Dow, Mary Harrington and Michael Lind for vital suggestions. Thanks are also due to my publishers: to my editor at Penguin Press, Maria Bedford, for her thoughtful interventions and oversight, and the same to Stuart Roberts at Simon & Schuster in the US—and thanks too to the teams at both publishers who have worked on the book.

Then there is a much larger group of people who have been helpful in some way, (apologies to anyone I have left out): Andrew Adonis, Claire Ainsley, Douglas Alexander, Jake Arnold-Forster, Ewa Atanassow, Toby Baxendale, Mark Bovens, Paul Broks, Belinda Brown, Phillip Brown, Noah Carl, Emily Carver, Camilla Cavendish, Peter Cheese, Daisy Christodoulou, Robert Colls, Ian Deary, Peter Dolton, Edward Fidoe, Catherine Fieschi, Beccy Goodhart, Charles Goodhart, Rose Goodhart, Helen Goulden, Christine Goronowicz, Alexander Gray, John Gray, Manuela Grayson, Andy Haldane, Jonathan Hanbury, Nick Hillman, Craig Holmes, Pamela Idelson, Paul Johnson, Allyson Kaye, Lucy Kellaway, Sam Kershaw, Mark Leach, Alison Leary, Simon Lebus, Charlotte Leslie, Oliver Letwin, Tim Leunig, Paul Lewis, Warwick Lightfoot, John Lloyd, Iain Mansfield, Jill Manthorpe, Elaine Maxwell, Ken Mayhew, Jasper McMahon, Rosie Meek, Munira Mirza, James Mumford, Joanna Newman, Orna NiChionna, Ian Norman, Tim Oates, Paul Ormerod, Edward Peck, Louise Perry, Nina Power, Jonathan Rauch, David Robson, Juliet Rodgers, Jonathan Rutherford, Freddie Sayers, Isabel Scholes, Tom Simpson, Swaran Singh, Richard Sloggett, David Soskice, Rebecca Stott, Yuli Tamir, Nick Timothy, Adair Turner, Bobby Vedral, Anna Vignoles, Robin Wales, Adele Waters, Amy Wax, Simon Wessely, Joanna Williams, Mark Williams, Christopher Winch, Alison Wolf, Jon Yates, Toby Young.

Finally, I want to mention some of the podcasts I listened to regularly while writing the book and sometimes found useful ideas that informed the book: LSE Public Lectures & Events; Unherd Confessions with Giles Fraser; Talking Politics; Exponential View; Rebel Wisdom; Real Talk with Zuby; Conversations with Tyler; The Psychology Podcast with Dr Scott Barry Kaufman; Making Sense, Sam Harris.

Index